CONTEMPORARY PHILOSOPHICAL LITERATURE

Books LLC®, Wiki Series, Memphis, USA, 2011. ISBN: 9781157184201. www.booksllc.net
Copyright: http://creativecommons.org/licenses/by-sa/3.0/deed.en

Table of Contents

Books by Daniel Dennett
Brainstorms 2
Breaking the Spell: Religion as a Natural Phenomenon 2
Consciousness Explained 2
Darwin's Dangerous Idea 3
Elbow Room (book) 6
Freedom Evolves 8
Sweet Dreams: Philosophical Obstacles to a Science of Consciousness 9
The Mind's I 9

Books by Martin Heidegger
Being and Time 11
Contributions to Philosophy (From Enowning) 14
Heidegger Gesamtausgabe 14
Hölderlin's Hymn "The Ister" 19
The Origin of the Work of Art 23
The Question Concerning Technology 25

Contemporary philosophical literature
Between Past and Future 27
Croatian Journal of Philosophy 28
Essays and Aphorisms on the Higher Man 28
Ethica thomistica 28
Inquiry: An Interdisciplinary Journal of Philosophy 36
Jürgen Habermas bibliography 36
Laughter (Bergson) 37
Liberty and Nature: An Aristotelian Defense of Liberal Order 39
Norms of Liberty: A Perfectionist Basis for Non-Perfectionist Politics 39
Organon F 39
Philosophy and Theology 39
Re.press 39
Social Epistemology (journal) 40
Studies in Logic, Grammar and Rhetoric 40
The Moral Landscape 40
The Philosophic Thought of Ayn Rand 45
The Post Card: From Socrates to Freud and Beyond 46
The Sublime Object of Ideology 46
Think: A Compelling Introduction to Philosophy 47
Truth and Method 47
Word and Object 47
Xueren 47

Existentialist works
Ai City 48
Blade Runner 50
Come Find Yourself 59
Cowboy Bebop 59
Donnie Darko 62
Godkiller (series) 65
Les Temps modernes 66
Madlax 67
Neon Genesis Evangelion 71
Neon Genesis Evangelion (anime) 74
Taxi Driver 80
Themes in Blade Runner 84
Welcome to the N.H.K. 87
Wolf's Rain 91

Works by Jacques Derrida
Acts of Literature 95
Archive Fever 95
Echographies of Television 95
Ethics, Institutions, and the Right to Philosophy 98
Glas (book) 99
Limited Inc 100
Of Grammatology 101
Points...: Interviews, 1974-1994 101
Positions 101
Right to Philosophy 102
Specters of Marx 102
Speech and Phenomena 103
The Rhetoric of Drugs 103
Writing and Difference 104

Introduction

Purchase of this book entitles you to a free trial membership in the publisher's book club at www.booksllc.net. (Time limited offer.) Simply enter the barcode number from the back cover onto the membership form. The book club entitles you to select from hundreds of thousands of books at no additional charge. You can also download a digital copy of this and related books to read on the go. Simply enter the title or subject onto the search form to find them.

Each chapter in this book ends with a URL to a hyperlinked online version. Type the URL exactly as it appears. If you change the URL's capitalization it won't work. Use the online version to access related pages, websites, footnotes, tables, color photos, updates. Click the version history tab to see the chapter's contributors. Click the edit link to suggest changes.

A large and diverse editor base collaboratively wrote the book, not a single author. After a long process of discussion and debate, the chapters gradually took on a neutral point of view reached through consensus. Additional editors expanded and contributed to chapters striving to achieve balance and comprehensive coverage. This reduced the regional or cultural bias found in many other books and provided access and breadth on subject matter otherwise little documented.

Brainstorms

For the Atlanta public access show, see Brainstorms (show)
Brainstorms: Philosophical Essays on Mind and Psychology (MIT Press 1981) is a book by the American philosopher Daniel Dennett. In these essays, he reflects on the early achievements of Artificial Intelligence to develop his ideas on consciousness.

Source (edited): "http://en.wikipedia.org/wiki/Brainstorms"

Breaking the Spell: Religion as a Natural Phenomenon

Breaking the Spell: Religion as a Natural Phenomenon is a 2006 book by the American philosopher and cognitive scientist, Daniel Dennett, which argues for a scientific analysis of religion in order to predict the future of this phenomenon. Dennett implies that the spell he hopes to break is not religious belief itself, but the conviction that religion is off-limits to scientific inquiry.

The book is divided into three parts. Part I discusses the motivation and justification for the entire project: *Can* science study religion? *Should* science study religion? After answering in the affirmative, Part II proceeds to use the tools of evolutionary biology and memetics to suggest possible theories regarding the origin of religion and subsequent evolution of modern religions from ancient folk beliefs. Part III analyzes religion and its effects in today's world: Does religion make us moral? Is religion what gives meaning to life? What should we teach the children? Dennett bases much of his analysis on empirical evidence, though he often points out that much more research in this field is needed.

Definition

Dennett's working definition of religions is, "social systems whose participants avow belief in a supernatural agent or agents whose approval is to be sought." He notes that this definition is "a place to start, not something carved in stone."

Structure

- Part I: Opening Pandora's Box
  1. Breaking which spell?
  2. Some questions about science
  3. Why good things happen
- Part II: The Evolution of Religion
  4. The roots of religion
  5. Religion, the early days
  6. The evolution of stewardship
  7. The invention of team spirit
  8. Belief in belief
- Part III: Religion Today
  9. Toward a buyer's guide to religions
  10. Morality and religion
  11. Now what do we do?
- Appendix A: The new replicators
- Appendix B: Some more questions about science
- Appendix C: The bellboy and the lady named Tuck
- Appendix D: Kim Philby as a real case of indeterminacy of radical interpretation

Translations

Breaking the Spell has been translated into several other languages, including

- German - translation by Frank Born as *Den Bann brechen. Religion als natürliches Phänomen*, Frankfurt a. M.: Verlag der Weltreligionen im Insel Verlag 2008. ISBN 9783458710110
- Greek - translation by Dimitris Xygalatas and Nikolas Roubekas as *Απομυθοποίηση*, Thessaloniki: Vanias 2007. ISBN 9789602881989
- Italian - translation by S. Levi as *Rompere l'incantesimo. La religione come fenomeno naturale*, Milano: Cortina Raffaello 2007. ISBN 9788860300973
- Polish - translation by Barbara Stanosz as *Odczarowanie. Religia jako zjawisko naturalne*, Warsaw: Państwowy Instytut Wydawniczy 2008. ISBN 9788306031386
- Portuguese - translation by Helena Londres as *Quebrando O Encanto. A Religião Como Fenômeno Natural*, Rio de Janeiro: Globo 2006. ISBN 9788525042880
- Spanish - translation by Felipe de Brigard as *Romper el hechizo: la religión como un fenómeno natural*, Madrid: Katz 2007. ISBN 9788496859005

Source (edited): "http://en.wikipedia.org/wiki/Breaking_the_Spell:_Religion_as_a_Natural_Phenomenon"

Consciousness Explained

Consciousness Explained is a 1991 book by the American philosopher Daniel Dennett which offers an account of how consciousness arises from interaction of physical and cognitive processes in the brain.

Synopsis

The book puts forward a "multiple drafts" model of consciousness, suggesting that there is no single central place (a "Cartesian Theater") where conscious experience occurs; instead there are "various events of content-fixation occurring in various places at various times in the brain". The brain consists of a "bundle of semi-independent agencies"; when "content-fixation" takes place in one of these, its effects may propagate so that it leads to the utterance of one of the sentences that make up the story in which the central character is one's "self". Dennett's view of consciousness is that it is the apparently serial account for the brain's underlying *parallelism*.

One of the book's more controversial claims is that qualia do not (and cannot) exist. Dennett's main argument is that the various properties attributed to qualia by philosophers—qualia are supposed to be incorrigible, ineffable, private, directly accessible and so on—are incompatible, so the notion of qualia is incoherent. The non-existence of qualia would mean that there is no hard problem of consciousness, and "philosophical zombies", which are supposed to act human in every way while somehow lacking qualia, cannot exist. So, as Dennett wryly notes, he is committed to the belief that we are all zombies—adding that his remark is very much open to misinterpretation.

Dennett claims that our brains hold only a few salient details about the world, and that this is the only reason we are able to function at all. Thus, we don't store elaborate pictures in short-term memory, as this is not necessary and would consume valuable computing power. Rather, we log what has changed and assume the rest has stayed the same, with the result that we miss some details, as demonstrated in various experiments and illusions, some of which Dennett outlines. Research subsequent to Dennett's book indicates that some of his postulations were more conservative than expected. A year after *Consciousness Explained* was published, Dennett noted "I wish in retrospect that I'd been more daring, since the effects are stronger than I claimed". And since then examples continue to accumulate of the illusory nature of our visual world.

A key philosophical method is heterophenomenology, in which the verbal or written reports of subjects are treated as akin to a theorist's fiction—the subject's report is not questioned, but it is not assumed to be an incorrigible report about that subject's inner state. This approach allows the reports of the subject to be a datum in psychological research, thus circumventing the limits of classical behaviorism.

Also Dennett says that only a theory that explained conscious events in terms of unconscious events could explain consciousness at all: «To explain is to explain *away*».

Reactions

Critics of Dennett's approach, such as David Chalmers and Thomas Nagel, argue that Dennett's argument misses the point of the inquiry by merely re-defining consciousness as an external property and ignoring the subjective aspect completely. This has led detractors to nickname the book *Consciousness Ignored* and *Consciousness Explained Away*. Dennett and his supporters, however, respond that the aforementioned "subjective aspect" as commonly used is non-existent and unscientific, and that his "re-definition" is the only coherent description of consciousness.

However, John Searle argues that Dennett, who insists that discussing subjectivity is nonsense because it is unscientific and science presupposes objectivity, is making a category error. Searle argues that the goal of science is to establish and validate statements which are epistemically objective, (i.e., whose truth can be discovered and evaluated by any interested party), but are not necessarily ontologically objective. Searle calls any value judgment epistemically subjective. Thus, "McKinley is prettier than Everest" is epistemically subjective, whereas "McKinley is higher than Everest" is epistemically objective. In other words, the latter statement is evaluable (in fact, falsifiable) by an understood ('background') criterion for mountain height, like 'the summit is so many meters above sea level'. No such criteria exist for prettiness. Searle says that on Dennett's view, there is no consciousness in addition to the computational features, because that is all that consciousness amounts to for him: meme effects of a von Neumann(esque) virtual machine implemented in a parallel architecture and therefore implies that conscious states are illusory, but Searle points out: "where consciousness is concerned, the existence of the appearance is the reality."

Source (edited): "http://en.wikipedia.org/wiki/Consciousness_Explained"

Darwin's Dangerous Idea

Darwin's Dangerous Idea: Evolution and the Meanings of Life (1995) is a book by Daniel Dennett which argues that Darwinian processes are the central organizing force that gives rise to complexity. Dennett asserts that natural selection is a blind and algorithmic process which is sufficiently powerful to account for the evolution of life including the complexities of human minds and societies. These assertions have generated a great deal of debate and discussion in the general public. The book was a finalist for the 1995 National Book Award in non-fiction.

Background

Dennett's previous book was *Consciousness Explained* (1991). Dennett noted discomfort with Darwinism among not only lay people but even academics, and decided it was time to write a book dealing with the subject. *Darwin's Dangerous Idea* is not meant to be a work of science, but an interdisciplinary book; Dennett admits that he doesn't understand all of the scientific details himself. He goes into a moderate level of detail, but leaves it for the reader to go into greater depth if desired, providing plenty of references to this end.

In writing the book, Dennett wanted to "get thinkers in other disciplines to take evolutionary theory seriously, to show them how they have been underestimating it, and to show them why they have been listening to the wrong sirens." To do this he tells a story; one that is mainly original but which includes some material from his previous work.

Dennett taught an undergraduate seminar at Tufts University on Darwin and philosophy, which included most of the ideas in the book. He also had the help of fellow staff and other academics, some of whom read drafts of the book. It is dedicated to W. V. O. Quine, "teacher and friend".

Synopsis

Part I: Starting in the Middle

"Starting in the Middle", Part I of *Darwin's Dangerous Idea*, gets its name from a quote by Willard Van Orman Quine: "Analyze theory-building how we will, we all must start in the middle. Our conceptual firsts are middle-sized, middle-distance objects, and our introduction to them and to everything comes midway in the cultural evolution of the race."

The first chapter "Tell Me Why" is named after a song.
Tell me why the stars do shine,
Tell me why the ivy twines,
Tell me why the sky's so blue.
Then I will tell you just why I love you.
Because God made the stars to shine,
Because God made the ivy twine,
Because God made the sky so blue.
Because God made you, that's why I love you.
Before Charles Darwin, God was seen as the ultimate cause of all design, or the ultimate answer to 'why?' questions. John Locke argued for the primacy of mind before matter, and David Hume, while exposing problems with Locke's view, could not see any alternative.

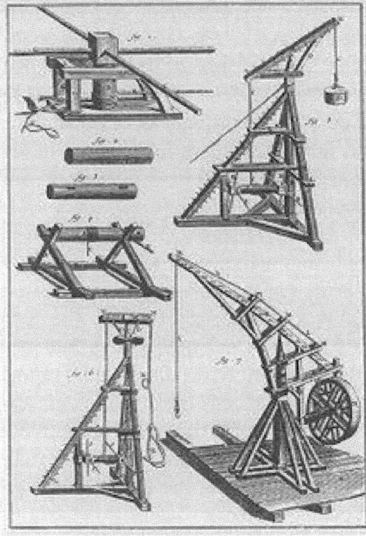

Darwin's Dangerous Idea makes extensive use of cranes as an analogy.

Darwin provided just such an alternative: evolution. Besides providing evidence of common descent, he introduced a mechanism to explain it: natural selection. According to Dennett, natural selection is a mindless, mechanical and algorithmic process—Darwin's dangerous idea. The third chapter introduces the concept of "skyhooks" and "cranes" (see below). He suggests that resistance to Darwinism is based on a desire for skyhooks, which do not really exist. According to Dennett, good reductionists explain apparent design without skyhooks; greedy reductionists try to explain it without cranes.

Chapter 4 looks at the tree of life, such as how it can be visualized and some crucial events in life's history. The next chapter concerns the possible and the actual, using the 'Library of Mendel' (the space of all logically possible genomes) as a conceptual aid.

In the last chapter of part I, Dennett treats human artifacts and culture as a branch of a unified Design Space. Descent or homology can be detected by shared design features that would be unlikely to appear independently. However, there are also "Forced Moves" or "Good Tricks" that will be discovered repeatedly, either by natural selection (see convergent evolution) or human in-

vestigation.

Part II: Darwinian Thinking in Biology

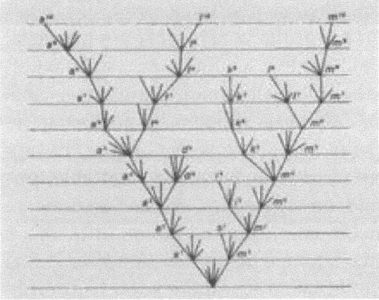

Tree diagram in *Origin*

The first chapter of part II, "Darwinian Thinking in Biology", asserts that life originated without any skyhooks, and the orderly world we know is the result of a blind and undirected shuffle through chaos.

The eighth chapter's message is conveyed by its title, "Biology is Engineering"; biology is the study of design, function, construction and operation. However, there are some important differences between biology and engineering. Related to the engineering concept of optimization, the next chapter deals with adaptationism, which Dennett endorses, calling Gould and Lewontin's "refutation" of it an illusion. Dennett thinks adaptationism is, in fact, the best way of uncovering constraints.

The tenth chapter, entitled "Bully for Brontosaurus", is an extended critique of Stephen Jay Gould, who Dennett feels has created a distorted view of evolution with his popular writings; his "self-styled revolutions" against adaptationism, gradualism and other orthodox Darwinism all being false alarms. The final chapter of part II dismisses directed mutation, the inheritance of acquired traits and Teilhard's "Omega Point", and insists that other controversies and hypotheses (like the unit of selection and Panspermia) have no dire consequences for orthodox Darwinism.

Part III: Mind, Meaning, Mathematics and Morality

The frontispiece to Thomas Hobbes' *Leviathan*, which appears at the beginning of chapter 16 "On the Origin of Morality".

"Mind, Meaning, Mathematics and Morality" is the name of Part III, which begins with a quote from Nietzsche. Chapter 12, "The Cranes of Culture", discusses cultural evolution. It asserts that the meme has a role to play in our understanding of culture, and that it allows humans, alone among animals, to "transcend" our selfish genes. "Losing Our Minds to Darwin" follows, a chapter about the evolution of brains, minds and language. Dennett criticizes Noam Chomsky's perceived resistance to the evolution of language, its modeling by artificial intelligence, and reverse engineering.

The evolution of meaning is then discussed, and Dennett uses a series of thought experiments to persuade the reader that meaning is the product of meaningless, algorithmic processes.

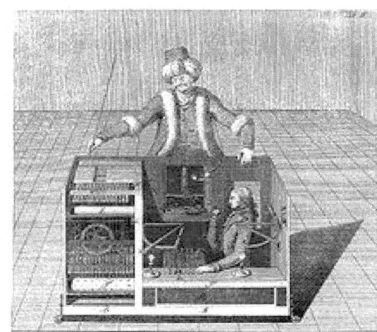

Von Kempelen's chess automaton, discussed in chapter 15.

Chapter 15 asserts that Gödel's Theorem does not make certain sorts of artificial intelligence impossible. Dennett extends his criticism to Roger Penrose. The subject then moves on to the origin and evolution of morality, beginning with Thomas Hobbes (who Dennett calls "the first sociobiologist") and Friedrich Nietzsche. He concludes that only an evolutionary analysis of ethics makes sense, though he cautions against some varieties of 'greedy ethical reductionism'. Before moving to the next chapter, he discusses some sociobiology controversies.

The penultimate chapter, entitled "Redesigning Morality", begins by asking if ethics can be 'naturalized'. Dennett does not believe there is much hope of discovering an algorithm for doing the right thing, but expresses optimism in our ability to design and redesign our approach to moral problems. In "The Future of an Idea", the book's last chapter, Dennett praises biodiversity, including cultural diversity. In closing, he uses *Beauty and the Beast* as an analogy; although Darwin's idea may seem dangerous, it is actually quite beautiful.

Central concepts

Design Space

Dennett believes there is little or no principled difference between on one hand the naturally generated products of evolution, and on the other the manmade artifacts of human creativity and culture. For this reason he indicates deliberately that the complex fruits of the tree of life are in a very meaningful sense "designed"—even though he does not believe evolution was guided by a higher intelligence.

Dennett supports using the notion of memes to better understand cultural evolution. He also believes even human creativity might operate by the Darwinian mechanism. This leads him to propose that the "space" describing biological "design" is connected with the space describing human culture and technology.

A precise mathematical definition of Design Space is not given in *Darwin's Dangerous Idea*. Dennett acknowledges this and admits he is offering a philosophical idea rather than a scientific formulation.

Natural selection as an algorithm

Dennett describes natural selection as a substrate-neutral, mindless algorithm for moving through Design Space.

Universal acid

Dennett writes about the fantasy of a "universal acid" as a liquid that is so corrosive that it would eat through anything that it came into contact with, even a potential container. Such a powerful substance would transform everything it was applied to; leaving something very different in its wake. This is where Dennett draws parallels from the "universal acid" to Darwin's idea:
"it eats through just about every traditional concept, and leaves in its wake a revolutionized world-view, with most of the old landmarks still recognizable, but transformed in fundamental ways." While there are people who would like to see Darwin's idea contained within the field of biology, Dennett asserts that this dangerous idea inevitably "leaks" out to transform other fields as well.

Skyhooks and cranes

Dennett uses the term "skyhook" to describe a source of design complexity that does not build on lower, simpler layers—in simple terms, a miracle.

In philosophical arguments concerning the reducibility (or otherwise) of the human mind, Dennett's concept pokes fun at the idea of intelligent design emanating from on high, either originating from God, or providing its own grounds in an absurd, Münchhausen-like bootstrapping manner.

Dennett also accuses various competing neo-Darwinian ideas of making use of such supposedly unscientific skyhooks in explaining evolution, coming down particularly hard on the ideas of Stephen Jay Gould.

Dennett contrasts theories of complexity that require such miracles with those based on "cranes", structures which permit the construction of entities of greater complexity but which are themselves founded solidly "on the ground" of physical science.

Reception

In the New York Review of Books, John Maynard Smith gave praise for *Darwin's Dangerous Idea*:

"It is therefore a pleasure to meet a philosopher who understands what Darwinism is about, and approves of it. Dennett goes well beyond biology. He sees Darwinism as a corrosive acid, capable of dissolving our earlier belief and forcing a reconsideration of much of sociology and philosophy. Although modestly written, this is not a modest book. Dennett argues that, if we understand *Darwin's dangerous idea*, we are forced to reject or modify much of our current intellectual baggage…"

In the New York Review of Books, Stephen Jay Gould criticised *Darwin's Dangerous Idea* for being an "influential but misguided ultra-Darwinian manifesto".

"Daniel Dennett devotes the longest chapter in *Darwin's Dangerous Idea* to an excoriating caricature of my ideas, all in order to bolster his defense of Darwinian fundamentalism. If an argued case can be discerned at all amid the slurs and sneers, it would have to be described as an effort to claim that I have, thanks to some literary skill, tried to raise a few piddling, insignificant, and basically conventional ideas to "revolutionary" status, challenging what he takes to be the true Darwinian scripture. Since Dennett shows so little understanding of evolutionary theory beyond natural selection, his critique of my work amounts to little more than sniping at false targets of his own construction. He never deals with my ideas as such, but proceeds by hint, innuendo, false attribution, and error."

Gould was also a harsh critic of Dennett's idea of the "universal acid" of natural selection and of his subscription to the idea of memetics; Dennett responded, and the exchange between Dennett, Gould, and Robert Wright was printed in the New York Review of Books.

Biologist H. Allen Orr wrote a scathing review emphasizing similar points in the Boston Review,
Source (edited): "http://en.wikipedia.org/wiki/Darwin%27s_Dangerous_Idea"

Elbow Room (book)

Elbow Room: The Varieties of Free Will Worth Wanting (1984) is a book by the American philosopher Daniel Dennett, which discusses the philosophical issues of free will and determinism.

In 1983, Dennett delivered the John Locke Lectures at Oxford on the topic of free will. In 1984, these ideas were published in the book *Elbow Room: The Varieties of Free Will Worth Wanting*. In this book Daniel Dennett explored what it means for people to have free will. The title, *Elbow Room*, is a reference to the question: are we deterministic machines with no real freedom of action or do we in fact have some elbow room, some real choice in our behavior?

Synopsis

Determinism doesn't make humans equivalent to animals

A major task taken on by Dennett in *Elbow Room* is to clearly describe just what people are as biological entities and why they find the issue of free will to be of importance. In discussing what people are and why free will matters to us, Dennett makes use of an evolutionary perspective. Dennett describes the mechanical behavior of the digger wasp *Sphex*. This insect follows a series of genetically programmed steps in preparing for egg laying. If an experimenter interrupts one of these steps the wasp will repeat that step again. For an animal like a wasp, this process of repeating the same behavior can go on indefinitely, the wasp never seeming to notice what is going on. This is the type of mindless, pre-determined behavior that humans can avoid. Given the chance to repeat some futile behavior endlessly, people can notice the futility of it, and by an act of free will do something else. We can take this as an operational definition of what people mean by free will. Dennett points out the fact that as long as people see themselves as able to avoid futility, most people have seen enough of the free will issue. Dennett then invites all who are satisfied with this level of analysis to get on with living while he proceeds into the deeper hair-splitting aspects of the free will issue.

From a biological perspective, what is the difference between the wasp and a person? The person can, through interaction with his/her environment, construct an internal mental model of the situation and figure out a successful behavioral strategy. The wasp, with a much smaller brain and different genetic program, does not learn from its environment and instead is trapped in an endless and futile behavioral loop that is strictly determined by its genetic program. It is in this sense of people as animals with complex brains that can model reality and appear to choose among several possible behaviors that Dennett says we have free will.

Both determinism and indeterminism seem to rule out free will

The deeper philosophical issue of free will can be framed as a paradox. On one hand, we all feel like we have free will, a multitude of behavioral choices to select among. On the other hand, modern biology generally investigates humans as though the processes at work in them follow the same biological principles as those in wasps. How do we reconcile our feeling of free will with the idea that we might be mechanical components of a mechanical universe?

What about determinism? When we say that a person chooses among several possible behaviors is there really a choice or does it just seem like there is a choice? Do people just (through the action of their more complex brains) simply have better behaviors than wasps, while still being totally mechanical in executing those behaviors? Dennett gives his definition of determinism on page one: *All physical events are caused or determined by the sum total of all previous events*. This definition dodges a question that many people feel should not be dodged: if we repeatedly replayed the universe from the same point in time would it always reach the same future? Since we have no way of performing this experiment, this question is a long-term classic in philosophy and physicists have tried to interpret the results of other experiments in various ways in order to figure out the answer to this question. Modern day physics-oriented philosophers have sometimes tried to answer the question of free will using the many-worlds interpretation according to which every time there is quantum indeterminacy each possibility occurs and new universes branch off. Since the 1920s, physicists have been trying to convince themselves that quantum indeterminacy can in some way explain free will. Dennett suggests that this idea is silly. How, he asks, can random resolutions of quantum-level events provide people with any control over their behavior?

Indeterminism is not a solution to the free will problem

Since Dennett wrote *Elbow Room* (1984) there has been an on-going attempt by some scientists to answer this question by suggesting that the brain is a device for controlling quantum indeterminacy so as to construct behavioral choice. Dennett argues that such efforts to salvage free will by finding a way out of the prison of determinism are wasted.

Control is the kind of freedom "worth wanting"

Dennett discusses many types of free will (1984). Many philosophers have claimed that determinism and free will are incompatible. What the physicists seem to be trying to construct is a type of free will that involves a way for brains to make use of quantum indeterminacy so as to make choices that alter the universe in our favor, or if there are multiple universes, to choose among the possible universes. Dennett suggests that we can have another kind of free will, a type of free will which we can be perfectly happy with even if it does not give us the power to act in more than one way at any given time. Dennett is able to accept determinism and free will at the same time. How so?

We have free will

The type of free will that Dennett thinks we have is finally stated clearly in the last chapter of the book: the power to be active agents, biological devices that respond to our environment with rational, desirable courses of action. Dennett has slowly, through the course of the book, stripped the idea of behavioral choice from his idea of free will. How can we have free will if we do not have indeterministic choice? Dennett emphasizes control over libertarian choice. If our hypothetically mechanical brains are in control of our behavior and our brains produce good behaviors for us, then do we really need such choice? Is an illusion of behavioral choices just as good as actual choices? Is our sensation of having the freedom to execute more than one behavior at a given time really just an illusion? Dennett argues that choice exists in a general sense: that because we base our decisions on context, we limit our options as the situation becomes more specific. In the most specific circumstance (actual events), he suggests there is only one option left to us.

Determinism does not rule out moral responsibility

If people are determined to act as they do, then what about personal responsibility? How can we hold people responsible and punish them for their behaviors if they have no choice in how they behave? Dennett gives a two part answer to this question. First, we hold people responsible for their actions because we know from historical experience that this is an effective means to make people behave in a socially acceptable way. Second, holding people responsible only works when combined with the fact that people can be informed of the fact that they are being held responsible and respond to this state of affairs by controlling their behavior so as to avoid punishment. People who break the rules set by society and get punished may be behaving in the only way they can, but if we did not hold them accountable for their actions, people would behave even worse than they do with the threat of punishment. This is a totally utilitarian approach to the issue of responsibility: there is no need for moral indignation when people break the rules of proper behavior. Is it, then, moral to punish people who are unable to do other than break a rule? Yes, people have the right to come together and improve their condition by creating rules and enforcing them. We would be worse off if we did not do so. Again, an argument for utility.

Fatalism is destructive

One final issue: if people do not have real behavioral choices, why not collapse into fatalism? Again, Dennett's argument is that we may not have behavioral choice, but we do have control of our behavior. Dennett asks us to look around at the universe and ask, can I even conceive of beings whose will is freer than our own? For Dennett, the answer to this question is, no, not really. In *Elbow Room*, he tries to explain why all the attempts that people have tried to make to prove that people have libertarian choice have failed and are, in the final analysis, not really important anyhow. As humans, we are as much in control of our behavior as anything in the universe. As humans, we have the best chance to produce good behavior. We should be satisfied with what we have and not fret over our lack of libertarian free will.

Some complaints about *Elbow Room* relate to our intuitions about free will. Some say that Dennett's theory does not satisfactorily deal with the issue of why we feel so strongly that we do have behavioral choice. One answer to this question is that our sensation of having behavioral choice has been carefully selected by evolution. The well developed human sensation of having free will and being able to select among possible behaviors has strong survival value. People who lose the feeling that they can plan alternative behaviors and execute their choice of possible behaviors tend to become fatalistic and stop struggling for survival. According to Dennett, belief in free will is a necessary condition for having free will. When we are planning for the future and thinking about possible actions to take in the future, we are utilizing considerable amounts of biologically expensive resources (brain power). Evolution has designed us to feel strongly that all of our effort of planning pays off, that we control what we do. If this connection between our brains' efforts to model reality and predict the future and so make possible good outcomes is disconnected from our sense of self and our will, then fatalism and self-destructive behaviors are close at hand.

Source (edited): "http://en.wikipedia.org/wiki/Elbow_Room_(book)"

Freedom Evolves

Freedom Evolves is a 2003 popular science and philosophy book by Daniel C. Dennett. Dennett describes the book as an installment of a life-long philosophical project, earlier parts of which were *The Intentional Stance*, *Consciousness Explained* and *Elbow Room*. It attempts to give an account of free will and moral responsibility which is complementary to Dennett's other views on consciousness and personhood.

Synopsis

As in *Consciousness Explained*, Dennett advertises the controversial nature of his views extensively in advance. He expects hostility from those who fear that a skeptical analysis of freedom will undermine people's belief in the reality of moral considerations; he likens himself to an interfering crow who insists on telling Dumbo he doesn't really need the feather he believes is allowing him to fly.

Free will and altruism

Dennett's stance on free will is compatibilism with an evolutionary twist – the view that, although in the strict physical sense our actions might be pre-determined, we can still be free in all the ways that matter, because of the abilities we evolved. Free will, seen this way, is about freedom to make decisions without duress, as opposed to an impossible and unnecessary freedom from causality itself. To clarify this distinction, he coins the term 'evitability' as the opposite of 'inevitability', defining it as the ability of an agent to anticipate likely consequences and act to avoid undesirable ones. Evitability is entirely compatible with, and actually requires, human action being deterministic. Dennett moves on to altruism, denying that it requires acting to the benefit of others without gaining any benefit yourself. He argues that it should be understood in terms of helping yourself by helping others, expanding the self to be more inclusive as opposed to being selfless. To show this blend, he calls such actions 'benselfish', and finds the roots of our capacity for this in the evolutionary pressures that produced kin selection. In his treatment of both free will and altruism, he starts by showing why we should not accept the traditional definitions of either term. This strategy comes down to dissolving problems, instead of solving them. Rather than try to answer certain flawed questions, he questions the assumptions of the questions themselves and undermines them.

Beneficial mutual arrangements

Dennett also suggests that adherence to high ethical standards might pay off for the individual, because if others know your behaviour is restricted in these ways, the scope for certain beneficial mutual arrangements is enhanced. This is related to game theoretical considerations: in the famous Prisoner's Dilemma, 'moral' agents who cooperate will be more successful than 'non-moral' agents who do not cooperate. Cooperation wouldn't seem to naturally arise since agents are tempted to 'defect' and restore a Nash equilibrium, which is often not the best possible solution for all involved. Dennett concludes by contemplating the possibility that people might be able to opt in or out of moral responsibility: surely, he suggests, given the benefits, they would choose to opt in, especially given that opting out includes such things as being imprisoned or institutionalized.

Libet's experiments

Daniel Dennett also argues that no clear conclusion about volition can be derived from Benjamin Libet's experiments supposedly demonstrating the non-existence of conscious volition. According to Dennett, ambiguities in the timings of the different events involved. Libet tells when the readiness potential occurs objectively, using electrodes, but relies on the subject reporting the position of the hand of a clock to determine when the conscious decision was made. As Dennett points out, this is only a report of where it *seems* to the subject that various things come together, not of the objective time at which they actually occur.

Suppose Libet knows that your readiness potential peaked at millisecond 6,810 of the experimental trial, and the clock dot was straight down (which is what you reported you saw) at millisecond 7,005. How many milliseconds should he have to add to this number to get the time you were conscious of it? The light gets from your clock face to your eyeball almost instantaneously, but the path of the signals from retina through lateral geniculate nucleus to striate cortex takes 5 to 10 milliseconds — a paltry fraction of the 300 milliseconds offset, but how much longer does it take them to get to *you*. (Or are you located in the striate cortex?) The visual signals have to be processed before they arrive at wherever they need to arrive for you to make a conscious decision of simultaneity. Libet's method presupposes, in short, that we can locate the *intersection* of two trajectories: • the rising-to-consciousness of signals representing the decision to flick • the rising to consciousness of signals representing successive clock-face orientations so that these events occur side-by-side as it were in place where their simultaneity can be noted.

Robert Kane

Dennett spends a chapter criticising Robert Kane's theory of libertarian free will. Kane believes freedom is based on certain rare and exceptional events, which he calls self-forming actions or SFA's. Dennett notes that there is no guarantee such an event will occur in an individual's life. If it does not, the individual does not in fact have free will at all, according to Kane. Yet they will seem the same as anyone else. Dennett finds an essentially *indetectable* notion of free will to be incredible.

Source (edited): "http://en.wikipedia.org/wiki/Freedom_Evolves"

Sweet Dreams: Philosophical Obstacles to a Science of Consciousness

Sweet Dreams: Philosophical Obstacles to a Science of Consciousness is a book by the American philosopher Daniel Dennett based on the text of the Jean Nicod lectures he gave in 2001.

Zombies

Dennett extends his well noted attack on the philosophical notion of qualia by using the metaphor of zombies as well as addressing many popular thought experiments. Dennett's conclusion is that there is no qualia and that the mind, and consciousness, can be understood and explained from the Naturalist school of thought.

Fame in the Brain

In Sweet Dreams, Dennett reposes the question of consciousness addressed in his 1991 book Consciousness Explained. In Consciousness Explained, Dennett established what he called the "Multiple Drafts Model" of consciousness, which suggested that there was no singular space in the conscious mind. In other words, there is no special location in the brain that can be seen as the "consciousness module." Instead, he states that consciousness is smeared throughout the brain. He extends the model by creating a similar figure that he calls "Fame in the Brain" and suggests that the mind acts, to some degree, as an echo chamber, as well as the "bundle of semi-independent agencies" that he suggested in Consciousness Explained.

The main tenet of "Fame in the Brain" is that consciousness, much like fame, is not the cause, but the aftermath or certain brain processes. Dennett asks us to imagine an author whose book has yet to be released, but will result in unimagineable fame when it does. On Tuesday, when the book is to come out, he is scheduled to go on Oprah, be interviewed on the BBC, and likely be nominated for several awards. However, on Monday, an earthquake destroys the entire city of San Francisco. Naturally, all the media hype that would have revolved around this author is drowned in the focus on San Francisco. Dennett asks, can this man be considered "famous"? He says that the man is in fact not famous even though the book that would have made him famous remains unchanged. This is because fame, according to Dennett, is not about the cause of the fame, but about the aftermath: the interviews, the magazine covers, the paparazzi, etc. Consciousness is the same way. In order for something to be considered "conscious," there must be enough correlating neural events that go with it (e.g. memory formation).

Source (edited): "http://en.wikipedia.org/wiki/Sweet_Dreams:_Philosophical_Obstacles_to_a_Science_of_Consciousness"

The Mind's I

This page is about the book; for the album by Dark Tranquillity, see The Mind's I (album). *For the* Star Wars *novel, see* Splinter of the Mind's Eye.
The Mind's I: Fantasies and reflections on self and soul (ISBN 0-553-34584-2) is a 1981 book composed and arranged by Douglas R. Hofstadter and Daniel C. Dennett. It is a collection of essays and creations about the nature of the mind and the self, tied together with commentary by the editors.

This book is an exploration of the human mind and soul, ranging from early philosophical and fictional musings on a subject that could seemingly only be examined in the realm of thought, to works from the 20th century where the nature of the self became a viable topic for scientific study.

Contents

The book's 27 chapters are each made up of a previously published work by authors such as Jorge Luis Borges, Alan Turing, Richard Dawkins, Raymond Smullyan, John Searle, Stanisław Lem, Thomas Nagel (as well as Hofstadter and Dennett themselves), each followed up by a commentary by Hofstadter and/

or Dennett. Dennett and Hofstadter both support the idea that we can learn much about human minds and souls by exploring human mentality in terms of information processing. Dennett and Hofstadter are both proponents of the idea that the wonders of human mentality can be accounted for by mechanical brain processes — which leaves nothing theoretical to prevent us from building human-like mental processes into our mechanical devices. A few views that run counter to this notion, such as John Searle's widely-known presentation of the Chinese room argument, are included in this book mainly as targets for refutation.

The book is divided into six sections, each focusing on a particular aspect of the problem of self.

Part I

Part I, "A Sense of Self", begins with two works of fiction that challenge the notions of self and identity (including the Argentine writer Jorge Luis Borges's "Borges and I"), provoking the reader to think more closely about just what is meant by "self". It closes with an essay by Harold Morowitz on the reductionist view of the mind.

Part II

Part II, entitled "Soul Searching", takes on the idea of soul — that spark which separates thinking beings from unthinking machines. Included here is Alan Turing's famous article from 1950, in which he proposes an operational test — popularly known as the "Turing test" — for machine intelligence, judged successful if a machine can use human language well enough to pass as human. No machine has yet come close to passing the Turing test, and certainly not at the time of the book's publication. (It is argued that merely behaving as if you have human-like intelligence in no way shows that you have human-like intelligence: see Turing test for history and criticisms.) As it happens, the two main efforts of artificial intelligence research towards machine learning since *The Mind's I* was published (trainable neural nets and expert systems) failed to bring us any closer to true intelligence, so the elusive nature of machine intelligence presented still stands. A dialogue of Hofstadter's own picks up the idea of the Turing test and spins a thought-provoking scenario from it. Two fictional pieces by Terrel Miedaner on finding intelligence in places we wouldn't expect end the section.

Part III

The formation of mind from elements individually incapable of thought is the central theme of Part III, "From Hardware to Software". The evolution of the mind toward its current state is addressed in the first two reprinted works. Following that is a reprint of "Prelude... Ant Fugue" from Hofstadter's Pulitzer-winning book, *Gödel, Escher, Bach,* in which he builds up the metaphor of the mind as anthill: each individual part with only rudimentary function, coming together to be more than the sum of its parts.

Part IV

Part IV explores its titular issue, "Mind as Program". What is the self: the mind, or the body? Can they be separated? Can the location of the consciousness be separate from one's physical location. In that case, where are you, really? Dennett's fantastical account of being separated from his brain and David Sanford's response tackle these issues. In this section the mind is considered as software: as patterns of thought and action, as separate from the physical body housing it as a piece of software is from the machine it runs on.

Part V

Part V, "Created Selves and Free Will", includes John Searle's notorious "Minds, Brains and Programs" (originally an article published in *The Behavioral and Brain Sciences*, 1980), which states: "...mental processes are computational processes over formally defined elements." Searle has objections to the idea that computer programs might ever produce mind, but the idea that mentality involves computation can be traced through the history of Western philosophy where it has long been explored in the context of trying to explain human reason in terms of formal logical systems. A dramatic and famous rejection of the formal systems idea was that of Ludwig Wittgenstein, a philosopher who Dennett respects. After first embracing the idea of reducing everything to logical atoms (*Tractatus Logico-Philosophicus*), Wittgenstein later rejected the idea that human language games should be formulated as formal systems (*Philosophical Investigations*). However, many philosophers and artificial intelligence researchers remain captivated by the formal systems approach. For example, Dennett has tried to help the MIT Cog project develop formal computer programming methods towards the goal of producing human-like intelligence. In his book "Contemporary Philosophy of Mind", Georges Rey provides an example of continuing attempts to express human intelligence in machines through computational processes over formally defined elements. An alternative but minority approach has grown out of the work of people like Gerald Edelman and his student Olaf Sporns through which it is suggested that machine intelligence can most efficiently be achieved by creating autonomous robotic systems that can learn the way human children learn through interacting with their environment.

Part VI

The book closes with "The Inner Eye", a collection of short pieces on the subjective nature of experience. How can one describe what it is like to be a particular entity, without actually being it yourself? Thomas Nagel, Raymond Smullyan, Douglas Hofstadter, and Robert Nozick tackle the problem of translating the experiences of one being into terms another can understand. But can we ever know what it is like to be another self? For that matter, what can we know about what it is like to be ourselves? Hofstadter and Dennett's commentary suggest that self-knowledge is elusive, to say nothing of the experience of other minds.

Essays

- "Borges and I", Jorge Luis Borges

- "On Having No Head", D. E. Harding
- "Rediscovering the Mind", Harold Morowitz
- "Computing Machinery and Intelligence", Alan Turing
- "The Turing Test: A Coffeehouse Conversation", Douglas Hofstadter
- "The Princess Ineffabelle", Stanisław Lem
- "The Soul of Martha, A Beast", Terrel Miedaner
- "The Soul of the Mark III Beast", Terrel Miedaner
- "Spirit", Allen Wheelis
- "Selfish Genes and Selfish Memes", Richard Dawkins
- "Prelude... Ant Fugue", Douglas Hofstadter
- "The Story of a Brain", Arnold Zuboff
- "Where Am I?", Daniel Dennett
- "Where Was I?", David Hawley Sanford
- "Beyond Rejection", Justin Leiber
- "Software", Rudy Rucker
- "The Riddle of the Universe and Its Solution", Christopher Cherniak
- "The Seventh Sally or How Trurl's Own Perfection Led to No Good", Stanisław Lem
- "Non Serviam", Stanisław Lem
- "Is God a Taoist?", Raymond Smullyan
- "The Circular Ruins", Jorge Luis Borges
- "Minds, Brains, and Programs", John Searle
- "An Unfortunate Dualist", Raymond Smullyan
- "What Is It Like to Be a Bat?", Thomas Nagel
- "An Epistemological Nightmare", Raymond Smullyan
- "A Conversation With Einstein's Brain", Douglas Hofstadter
- "Fiction", Robert Nozick

Source (edited): "http://en.wikipedia.org/wiki/The_Mind%27s_I"

Being and Time

Being and Time (German: *Sein und Zeit*, 1927) is a book by the German philosopher Martin Heidegger. Although written quickly, and despite the fact that Heidegger never completed the project outlined in the introduction, it remains his most important work and has profoundly influenced 20th-century philosophy, particularly existentialism, hermeneutics and deconstruction.

Heidegger's original project

Being and Time was originally intended to consist of two major parts, each part consisting of three divisions. Heidegger was forced to prepare the book for publication when he had completed only the first two divisions of part one. The remaining divisions planned for *Being and Time* (particularly the divisions on time and being, Kant, and Aristotle) were never published, although in many respects they are addressed in one form or another in Heidegger's other works. In terms of structure, *Being and Time* remains as it was when it first appeared in print; it consists of the lengthy two-part introduction, followed by Division One, the "Preparatory Fundamental Analysis of Dasein," and Division Two, "Dasein and Temporality."

Introductory summary

Being

On the first page of *Being and Time*, Heidegger describes the project in the following way: "our aim in the following treatise is to work out the question of the sense of *being* and to do so concretely." Heidegger claims that traditional ontology has prejudicially overlooked this question, dismissing it as overly general, undefinable, or obvious.

Instead Heidegger proposes to understand being itself, as distinguished from any specific entities (beings). "'Being' is not something like a being." Being, Heidegger claims, is "what determines beings as beings, that in terms of which beings are already understood." Heidegger is seeking to identify the criteria or conditions by which any specific entity can show up at all (see world disclosure).

If we grasp Being, we will clarify the meaning of being, or "sense" of being ("Sinn des Seins"), where by "sense" Heidegger means that "in terms of which something becomes intelligible as something." According to Heidegger, as this sense of being precedes any notions of how or in what manner any particular being or beings exist, it is pre-conceptual, non-propositional, and hence pre-scientific. Thus, in Heidegger's view, *fundamental* ontology would be an explanation of the understanding preceding any other way of knowing, such as the use of logic, theory, specific ontology or act of reflective thought. At the same time, there is no access to being other than via beings themselves—hence pursuing the question of being inevitably means asking about *a* being with regard to its being. Heidegger argues that a true understanding of being (*Seinsverständnis*) can only proceed by referring to particular beings, and that the best method of pursuing being must inevitably, he says, involve a kind of hermeneutic circle, that is (as he explains in his critique of prior work in the field of hermeneutics), it must rely upon repetitive yet progressive acts of interpretation. "The methodological sense of phenomenological description is *interpretation*."

Dasein

Thus the question Heidegger asks in the introduction to *Being and Time* is: what is the being that will give access to the question of the meaning of Being? Heidegger's answer is that it can only be that being for whom the question of Being is important, the being for whom Being matters. As this answer already indicates, the being for whom Being is a question is not a *what*, but a *who*. Heidegger calls this being *Dasein* (an ordinary German word meaning, roughly, "(human) existence" or, more literally, "being-there"), and the method pursued in *Being and Time* consists in the attempt to delimit the characteristics of *Dasein*, in order thereby to approach the meaning of Being itself through an interpretation of the temporality of *Dasein*. *Dasein* is not "man," but is nothing other than "man"—it is this distinction that enables Heidegger to claim that *Being and Time* is something other than philosophical anthropology.

Heidegger's account of *Dasein* passes through a dissection of the experiences of *Angst* and mortality, and then through an analysis of the structure of "care" as such. From there he raises the problem of "authenticity," that is, the potentiality or otherwise for mortal *Dasein* to exist *fully* enough that it might actually understand being. Heidegger is clear throughout the book that nothing makes certain that *Dasein is* capable of this understanding.

Time

Finally, this question of the authenticity of individual *Dasein* cannot be separated from the "historicality" of *Dasein*. On the one hand, *Dasein*, as mortal, is "stretched along" between birth and death, and thrown into its world, that is, thrown into its *possibilities*, possibilities which *Dasein* is charged with the task of assuming. On the other hand, *Dasein's* access to this world and these possibilities is always via a history and a tradition—this is the question of "world historicality," and among its consequences is Heidegger's argument that *Dasein's* potential for authenticity lies in the possibility of choosing a "hero."

Thus, more generally, the outcome of the progression of Heidegger's argument is the thought that the being of *Dasein* is time. Nevertheless, Heidegger concludes his work with a set of enigmatic questions foreshadowing the necessity of a destruction (that is, a transformation) of the history of philosophy in relation to temporality—these were the questions to be taken up in the never completed continuation of his project: The existential and ontological constitution of the totality of Dasein is grounded in temporality. Accordingly, a primordial mode of temporalizing of ecstatic temporality itself must make the ecstatic project of being in general possible. How is this mode of temporalizing of temporality to be interpreted? Is there a way leading from primordial *time* to the meaning of *being*? Does *time* itself reveal itself as the horizon of *being*?

Phenomenology in Heidegger and Husserl

Although Heidegger describes his method in *Being and Time* as phenomenological, the question of its relation to the phenomenology of Edmund Husserl is complex. The fact that Heidegger believes that ontology includes an irreducible hermeneutic (interpretative) aspect, for example, might be thought to run counter to Husserl's claim that phenomenological description is capable of a form of scientific positivity. On the other hand, however, several aspects of the approach and method of *Being and Time* seem to relate more directly to Husserl's work.

The central Husserlian concept of the directedness of all thought—intentionality—for example, while scarcely mentioned in *Being and Time*, has been identified by some with Heidegger's central notion of "*Sorge*" (Cura, care or concern). But for Heidegger, *theoretical* knowledge represents only one kind of intentional behaviour, and he asserts that it is grounded in more fundamental modes of behaviour and forms of practical engagement with the surrounding world. Whereas a theoretical understanding of things grasps them according to "presence," for example, this may conceal that our first experience of a being may be in terms of its being "ready-to-hand." Thus, for instance, when someone reaches for a tool such as a hammer, their understanding of what a hammer *is* is not determined by a theoretical understanding of its presence, but by the fact that it is something we need at the moment we wish to do hammering. Only a *later* understanding might come to contemplate a hammer *as* an object.

Hermeneutics

The total understanding of being results from an explication of the implicit knowledge of being that inheres in *Dasein*. Philosophy thus becomes a form of interpretation. But, since there is no external reference point outside being from which to begin this interpretation, the question becomes to know in which way to proceed with this interpretation. This is the problem of the "hermeneutic circle," and the necessity for the interpretation of the meaning of being to proceed in stages: this is why Heidegger's technique in *Being and Time* is sometimes referred to as hermeneutical phenomenology.

This interpretative aspect of Heidegger's project had a profound influence on the hermeneutic approach of his student Hans-Georg Gadamer.

Destruction of metaphysics

As part of his ontological project, Heidegger undertakes a reinterpretation of previous Western philosophy. He wants to explain why and how theoretical knowledge came to seem like the most fundamental relation to being. This explanation takes the form of a destructuring (*Destruktion*) of the philosophical tradition, an interpretative strategy that reveals the fundamental experience of being at the base of previous philosophies that had become entrenched and hidden within the theoretical attitude of the metaphysics of presence. This *Destruktion* is not simply a negative operation but rather a positive transformation, or recovery.

In *Being and Time* Heidegger briefly undertakes a destructuring of the philosophy of Descartes, but the second volume, which was intended to be a *Destruktion* of Western philosophy in all its stages, was never written. In later works Heidegger uses this approach to interpret the philosophies of Aristotle, Kant, Hegel, and Plato, among others.

This aspect of Heidegger's work exerted a profound influence on Jacques Derrida, although there are also important differences between Heidegger's *Destruktion* and Derrida's deconstruction.

Translations

So far, there are complete translations of Sein und Zeit in 21 languages: in Bulgarian, Chinese, Czech, Dutch, English, Finnish, French, Greek, Georgian, Hungarian, Italian, Japanese, Korean, Polish, Portuguese, Romanian, Russian, Croatian, Slovenian, Spanish and Swedish. There is a recent partial translation in Persian, and there are in preparation translations in Arabic, Norwegian and Turkish. Geographically, within these 25 languages, the European languages seem to dominate in comparison to the Extra-European languages (18 versus 7). Regarding the family languages in which translations of Sein und Zeit were made, the best represented are the Slavic languages, 6 languages having the privilege of possessing a translation of this work: Bulgarian, Czech, Polish, Russian, Croatian and Slovenian. Then, there are 5 Romanic languages in which this translation have been made: in French, Italian, Portuguese, Romanian and Spanish. Only three Germanic languages have a translation of Being and Time: Dutch, English, and Swedish (however, as the forth one, the Norwegian translation is under preparation). Also, there are translations in two Finno-Ugric languages (in Finnish and Hungarian) and in one basic Indo-European language (Greek). The extra-European spread of Sein und Zeit through extra-European languages is illustrated in several translations: a translation in one Caucasian language (Georgian), in one Semitic language (Arabic), in one Turkic language (Turkish), in one Indo-Iranian language (Persian), in one Sino-Tibetan language (Chinese) and in other two Altaic languages (Japanese and Korean).

The Eurocentric dominance is however equilibrated by the fact that the most numerous translations are in an Asiatic language: Sein und Zeit has been translated 6 times in Japanese. The next place is occupied also by an Asian language, the Korean, who has 3 complete translations accomplished of Heidegger's magum opus. Then, two translations can be found in English, French, Italian and Spanish (French has a third but partial translation). Only one complete translation is to be found in Bulgarian, Chinese, Czech, Dutch, Finnish, Greek, Georgian, Hungarian, Polish, Portuguese, Romanian (where another partial translation can be found), in Russian, Croatian, Slovenian, and Swedish. Finally, only a partial translation is to be found in Persian. Statistically, there are three women translators of Sein und Zeit: Marcia Sá Cavalcante Schuback in Portuguese, Joan Stambaugh in English and Andrina Tonkli-Komel in Slovenian. To the "quantitative" record of the Japanese culture, with its 6 complete translations (some of them reworked and re-edited), one can add another one: the Japanese has also the merit of having made, chronologically, the first translation of Sein und Zeit in 1939-40. This first Japanese translation was followed only in 1951 by the Spanish translation, in 1953 by the Italian one, in 1962 by the English one. In 1964, when the first partial French version was being made, the Japanese translators have already finished the fourth complete translation of Sein und Zeit.

Related work

Being and Time is the towering achievement of Heidegger's early career, but there are other important works from this period:

- The publication in 1992 of the early lecture course, *Platon: Sophistes* (*Plato's Sophist*, 1924), made clear the way in which Heidegger's reading of Aristotle's *Nicomachean Ethics* was crucial to the formulation of the thought expressed in *Being and Time*.
- The lecture course, *Prolegomena zur Geschichte des Zeitbegriffs* (*History of the Concept of Time: Prolegomena*, 1925), was something like an early version of *Being and Time*.
- The lecture courses immediately following the publication of *Being and Time*, such as *Die Grundprobleme der Phänomenologie* (*The Basic Problems of Phenomenology*, 1927), and *Kant und das Problem der Metaphysik* (*Kant and the Problem of Metaphysics*, 1929), elaborated some elements of the destruction of metaphysics which Heidegger intended to pursue in the unwritten second part of *Being and Time*.

Although Heidegger never completed the project outlined in *Being and Time*, later works explicitly addressed the themes and concepts of *Being and Time*. Most important among the works which do so are the following:

- Heidegger's inaugural lecture upon his return to Freiburg, "*Was ist Metaphysik?*" ("What Is Metaphysics?", 1929), was an important and influential clarification of what Heidegger meant by being, non-being, and nothingness.
- *Einführung in die Metaphysik* (*An Introduction to Metaphysics*), a lecture course delivered in 1935, is identified by Heidegger, in his preface to the seventh German edition of *Being and Time*, as relevant to the concerns which the second half of the book would have addressed.
- *Beiträge zur Philosophie (Vom Ereignis)* (*Contributions to Philosophy [From Enowning]*, composed 1936–38, published 1989), perhaps Heidegger's most sustained attempt at reckoning with the legacy of *Being and Time*.
- "Zeit und Sein" ("Time and Being"), a lecture delivered at the University of Freiburg on January 31, 1962. This was Heidegger's most direct confrontation with *Being and Time*. It was followed by a seminar on the lecture, which took place at Todtnauberg on September 11–13, 1962, a summary of which was written by Alfred Guzzoni. Both the lecture and the summary of the seminar are included in *Zur Sache des Denkens* (1969; translated as *On Time and Being* [New York: Harper & Row, 1972]).

Influence

Being and Time influenced many philosophers and writers, among them Hannah Arendt, Leo Strauss, Alexandre

Kojeve, Hans-Georg Gadamer, Giorgio Agamben, Jean-Paul Sartre, Emmanuel Lévinas, Maurice Merleau-Ponty, Alain Badiou, Herbert Marcuse, Jacques Derrida, Michel Foucault and Bernard Stiegler. More specifically, several important philosophical works were directly influenced by *Being and Time*, although in very different ways in each case. Most notable among the works influenced by *Being and Time* are the following:

- *Being and Nothingness* (1943), by Jean-Paul Sartre
- *Truth and Method* (1960), by Hans-Georg Gadamer
- *Totality and Infinity* (1961), by Emmanuel Levinas
- *Being and Event* (1988), by Alain Badiou
- *Technics and Time, 1* (1994), by Bernard Stiegler

Source (edited): "http://en.wikipedia.org/wiki/Being_and_Time"

Contributions to Philosophy (From Enowning)

Contributions to Philosophy (From Enowning) is the title of the English translation of German philosopher Martin Heidegger's *Beitrage Zur Philosophie (Vom Ereignis)* (Trans. Parvis Emad and Kenneth Maly. Indiana University Press, 1989). Composed privately between 1936 and 1938, the work is thought to reflect "the turn" (die Kehre) in Heidegger's thought post-*Being and Time* (1927).

In his *Contributions*, Heidegger builds on the notions of earth and world, which he had previously introduced in "The Origin of the Work of Art," and introduces the concept of "the last god." The result is a move away from the centrality of the phenomenological analyses of Dasein, toward the grounding of Da-sein as a historical decision of human beings. Earth can be understood as the condition of possibilities for world; neither earth nor world can exist without the other, and are thus engaged in a constant and productive struggle or strife. This struggle exists in the crossing from the "first beginning" of Western thought, which began with the ancient Greeks and determined the entire history of metaphysics, to the "other beginning," which will move beyond metaphysics by properly and originarily posing the question of the truth of be-ing (*Seyn*). In a parallel fashion, human beings counter god(s), and a space between these four points is opened up for the moment of "enowning," which grounds the "essential sway" of be-ing.

The "Preview" to the *Contributions* lays out provisionally the unfolding of the work and the methodology, here centered on grounding "the essential swaying of be-ing" rather than on the existential analytic of Dasein put forward in *Being and Time*. The work is organized into six "joinings," which reflect the crossing to the new or other beginning, and are each equally originary in the shift from man as *animal rationale* to man as da-sein, and from the shift from thinking as representation to inceptual, or be-ing-historical, thinking:

1. Echo: the constant interplay between be-ing and be-ing as not granting, or self-sheltering. In this chapter, Heidegger discusses the necessary ills of machination, the gigantic, and calculation, which out of the history of metaphysics reduce the question of be-ing to the belief that all beings - the focus of metaphysics - are created, reproducible, and entirely explainable. This is "necessary" because it is always already a part of the history of the first beginning, and the only thing distressing enough to potentially lead to a more originary distress, which leads to the creative question of be-ing.
2. Playing-Forth refers to the hermeneutical relationship between the first beginning and the other beginning, bringing to mind *Being and Time's* destruction of the history of ontology. Metaphysics is not to be defeated, but rather to be truly understood for the first time, an understanding that will ground this thinking in its history, and allow for the true question of philosophy to be raised.
3. Leap: the posing of the question of be-ing is the leap. The leap does not know what it is leaping into or towards, but in leaping opens up the space for more originary thinking. Since da-sein *is* projecting-opening, the leap opens a site in which the essential swaying of be-ing may be grounded in thinking-saying. The leap may simply be an originary phenomenological reduction: the leap into a genuine shift in thinking, and a new beginning in the history of philosophy.
4. Grounding
5. The Ones to Come
6. The Last God

Source (edited): "http://en.wikipedia.org/wiki/Contributions_to_Philosophy_(From_Enowning)"

Heidegger Gesamtausgabe

Heidegger Gesamtausgabe is the term for the collected works of German philosopher Martin Heidegger, published by Vittorio Klostermann.

The *Gesamtausgabe* was begun during Heidegger's lifetime. He defined the order of publication and controversially dictated that the principle of editing should be "ways not works." Publication has not yet been completed.

A contents list with details of all English translations (including those currently in preparation) is available here.

The *Gesamtausgabe* is divided into four series:
I. Published writings, 1910–1976
II. Lecture courses, 1919–1944
- Marburg lecture courses, 1923–1928

- Freiburg lecture courses, 1928–1944
- Early Freiburg lecture courses, 1919–1923

III. Unpublished material, lectures, and notes

IV. Notes and recordings

I. Abteilung: Veröffentlichte Schriften 1910–1976

1. Frühe Schriften (1912–1916), ed. F.-W. von Herrmann, 1978, XII, 454p.

2. Sein und Zeit (1927), ed. F.-W. von Herrmann, 1977, XIV, 586p.

3. Kant und das Problem der Metaphysik (1929), ed. F.-W. von Herrmann, 1991, XVIII, 318p.

4. Erläuterungen zu Hölderlins Dichtung (1936–1968), ed. F.W. von Herrmann, 1981, 2nd edn. 1996, 208p.

5. Holzwege (1935–1946), ed. F.-W. von Herrmann, 1977, 2nd edn. 2003, VI, 382p.
- Der Ursprung des Kunstwerkes (1935/36)
- Die Zeit des Weltbildes (1938)
- Hegels Begriff der Erfahrung (1942/43)
- Nietzsches Wort »Gott ist tot« (1943)
- Wozu Dichter? (1946)
- Der Spruch des Anaximander (1946)

6.1. Nietzsche 1 (1936–1939), ed. B. Schillbach, 1996, XIV, 596p.

6.2. Nietzsche 11 (1939–1946), ed. B. Schillbach, 1997, VIII, 454p.

7. Vorträge und Aufsätze (1936–1953), ed. F.-W. von Herrmann, 2000, XVIII, 298p.
- Die Frage nach der Technik (1953)
- Wissenschaft und Besinnung (1953)
- Überwindung der Metaphysik (1936–1946)
- Wer ist Nietzsches Zarathustra? (1953)
- Was heißt Denken? (1952)
- Bauen Wohnen Denken (1951)
- Das Ding (1950)
- »...dichterisch wohnet der Mensch...« (1951)
- Logos (Heraklit, Fragment 50) (1951)
- Moira (Parmenides, Fragment VIII, 34–41) (1952)
- Aletheia (Heraklit, Fragment 16) (1954)

8. Was heisst Denken? (1951–1952), ed. P.-L. Coriando, 2002, VIII, 268p.

9. Wegmarken (1919–1961), ed. F.-W. von Herrmann, 1976, 2nd edn. 1996, 3rd edn. 2004, X, 488p.
- Anmerkungen zu Karl Jaspers »Psychologie der Weltanschauungen« (1919/21)
- Phänomenologie und Theologie (1927)
- Aus der letzten Marburger Vorlesung (1927)
- Was ist Metaphysik? (1929)
- Vom Wesen des Grundes (1929)
- Vom Wesen der Wahrheit (1930)
- Platons Lehre von der Wahrheit (1931/32, 1940)
- Vom Wesen und Begriff der Φύσις. Aristoteles, Physik B, 1 (1939)
- Nachwort zu »Was ist Metaphysik?« (1943)
- Brief über den Humanismus (1946)
- Einleitung zu »Was ist Metaphysik?« (1943)
- Zur Seinsfrage (1955)
- Hegel und die Griechen (1958)
- Kants These über das Sein (1961)

10. Der Satz vom Grund (1955–1956), ed. P. Jaeger, 1997, VIII, 192p.

11. Identität und Differenz (1955–1957)
- Was ist das - die Philosophie? (1955)
- Identität und Differenz (1957) D
- Der Satz der Identität (1957)
- Die ontotheologische Verfassung der Metaphysik (1957)
- Die Kehre (1949)
- Grundsätze des Denkens (1957)
- Ein Vorwort. Brief an Pater William J. Richardson (1962)
- Brief an Takehiko Kojima (1963)

12 Unterwegs zur Sprache (1950–1959), ed. F.-W. von Herrmann, 1985, 262p.
- Die Sprache (1950)
- Die Sprache im Gedicht. Eine Erörterung von Georg Trakls Gedicht (1952)
- Aus einem Gespräch von der Sprache. (1953/54) Zwischen einem Japaner und einem Fragenden
- Das Wesen der Sprache (1957/58)
- Das Wort (1958)
- Der Weg zur Sprache (1959)

13 Aus der Erfahrung des Denkens (1910–1976), ed. H. Heidegger, 1983, 2nd edn. 2002, VIII, 254p.
- Abraham a Sankta Clara (1910)
- Frühe Gedichte (1910–1916)
- Schöpferische Landschaft: Warum bleiben wir in der Provinz? (1953)
- Wege zur Aussprache (1957); Winke (1941)
- Chorlied aus der Antigone des Sophokles (1943)
- Zur Erörterung der Gelassenheit. Aus einem Feldweggespräch über das Denken (1944/45)
- Aus der Erfahrung des Denkens (1947)
- Der Feldweg (1949)
- Holzwege ("Dem künftigen Menschen…") (1949)
- Zu einem Vers von Mörike. Ein Briefwechsel mit Martin Heidegger von Emil Staiger (1951)
- Was heisst Lesen? (1954)
- Vom Geheimnis des Glockenturmes (1954)
- Für das Langenharder Hebelbuch (1954)
- Über die Sixtina (1955)
- Die Sprache Johann Peter Hebels (1955)
- Begegnungen mit Ortega y Gasset (1955)
- Was ist die Zeit? (1956)
- Hebel der Hausfreund (1957)
- Aufzeichnungen aus der Werkstatt (1959)
- Sprache und Heimat (1960)
- Über Igor Strawinsky (1962)
- Für René Char (1963)
- Adalbert Stifters "Eisgeschichte" (1964)
- Wink in das Gewesen (1966)
- Die Kunst und der Raum (1969)
- Zeichen (1969)
- Das Wohnen des Menschen (1970)
- Gedachtes (1970)
- Rimbaud vivant (1972)
- Sprache (1972)
- Der Fehl heiliger Namen (1974)
- Fridolin Wiplingers letzter Besuch (1974)
- Erhart Kästner zum Gedächtnis (1975)
- Grusswort für Bernhard Welte (1976)

14 Zur Sache des Denkens (1962–1964)
15 Seminare (1951–1973), ed. C. Ochwadt, 1986, 2nd edn. 2005, 448p.
- Martin Heidegger - Eugen Fink: HERAKLIT
- VIER SEMINARE: Seminar in Le Thor 1966, 1968, 1969, Seminar in Zähringen 1973

16 Reden und andere Zeugnisse eines Lebensweges (1910–1976), ed. H. Heidegger, 2000, XXII, 842p.

II. Abteilung: Vorlesungen 1919–1944

Marburger Vorlesungen 1923–1928

17. Einführung in die phänomenologische Forschung (Winter semester 1923/24), ed. F.-W. von Herrmann, 1994, 2nd edn. 2006, XIV, 332p.

18. Grundbegriffe der aristotelischen Philosophie (Summer semester 1924), ed. M. Michalski, 2002, XIV, 418p.

19. Platon: Sophistes (Winter semester 1924/25), ed. I. Schüssler, 1992, XXXII, 668p.

20. Prolegomena zur Geschichte des Zeitbegriffs (Summer semester 1925), ed. P. Jaeger, 1979, 2nd edn. 1988, 3rd edn. 1994, XII, 448p.

21. Logik. Die Frage nach der Wahrheit (Winter semester 1925/26), ed. W. Biemel, 1976, 2nd edn. 1995, VIII, 418p.

22. Grundbegriffe der antiken Philosophie (Summer semester 1926) ed. F.-K. Blust, 1993, 2nd edn. 2004, XIV, 344p.

23. Geschichte der Philosophie von Thomas von Aquin bis Kant (Winter semester 1926/27), ed. H. Vetter, 2006. XII, 248p.

24. Die Grundprobleme der Phänomenologie (Summer semester 1927), ed. F.-W. von Herrmann, 1975, 2nd edn. 1989, 3rd edn. 1997, X, 474p.

25. Phänomenologische Interpretation von Kants Kritik der reinen Vernunft (Winter semester 1927/28), ed. I. Görland, 1977, 2nd edn. 1987, 3rd edn. 1995, XII, 436p.

26. Metaphysische Anfangsgründe der Logik im Ausgang von Leibniz (Summer semester 1928), ed. K.Held, 1978, 2nd edn 1990, VI, 292p.

Freiburger Vorlesungen 1928–1944

27. Einleitung in die Philosophie (Winter semester 1928/29), ed. O. Saame et I. Saame-Speidel, 1996, 2nd edn. 2001, XII, 404p.

28. Der deutsche Idealismus (Fichte, Schelling, Hegel) und die philosophische Problemlage der Gegenwart (Summer semester 1929)/ Im Anhang: Nachschrift "Einführung in das akademische Studium" (Summer semester 1929), ed. C. Strube, 1997, XII, 368p.

29/30. Die Grundbegriffe der Metaphysik. Welt - Endlichkeit - Einsamkeit (Winter semester 1929/30), ed. F.-W. von Herrmann, 1983, 2nd edn. 1992, 3rd edn. 2004, XX, 542p.

31. Vom Wesen der menschlichen Freiheit. Einleitung in die Philosophie (Summer semester 1930), ed. H. Tietjen, 1982, 2nd edn. 1994, XII, 308p.

32. Hegels Phänomenologie des Geistes (Winter semester 1930/31), ed. I. Görland, 1980, 2nd edn. 1988, 3rd edn. 1997, VIII, 224p.

33. Aristoteles, Metaphysik J 1-3. Von Wesen und Wirklichkeit der Kraft (Summer semester 1931), ed. H. Hüni, 1981, 2nd edn. 1990, 3rd edn. 2006, VIII, 228p.

34. Vom Wesen der Wahrheit. Zu Platons Höhlengleichnis und Theätet (Winter semester 1931/32), ed. H. Mörchen, 1988, 2nd edn. 1997, X, 338p.

35. Der Anfang der abendländischen Philosophie (Anaximander und Parmenides) (Summer semester 1932), ed. H. Hüni.

36/37. Sein und Wahrheit / 1. Die Grundfrage der Philosophie (Summer semester 1933), 2. Vom Wesen der Wahrheit (Winter semester 1933/34), ed. H. Tietjen, 2001, XVI, 308p.

38. Logik als die Frage nach dem Wesen der Sprache (Summer semester 1934), ed. G.Seubold, 1998, VIII, 176p.

39. Hölderlins Hymnen "Germanien" und "Der Rhein" (Winter semester 1934/35, ed. S.Ziegler, 1980, 2nd edn. 1989, 3rd edn. 1999, XII, 296p.

40. Einführung in die Metaphysik (Summer semester 1935), ed. P. Jaeger, 1983, X, 234p.

41. Die Frage nach dem Ding. Zu Kants Lehre von den transzendentalen Grundsätzen (Winter semester 1935/36), ed. P. Jaeger, 1984, VIII, 254p.

42. Schelling: Vom Wesen der menschlichen Freiheit (1809) (Summer semester 1936), ed. I. Schüssler, 1988, X, 290p.

43. Nietzsche: Der Wille zur Macht als Kunst (Winter semester 1936/37), ed. B. Heimbüchel, 1985, XII, 298p.

44. Nietzsches metaphysische Grundstellung im abendländischen Denken: Die ewige Wiederkehr des Gleichen (Summer semester 1937), ed. M. Heinz, 1986, VIII, 254p.

45. Grundfragen der Philosophie. Ausgewählte "Probleme" der "Logik" (Winter semester 1937/38), ed. F.-W. von Herrmann, 1984, 2nd edn. 1992, XIV, 234p.

46. Nietzsches II. Unzeitgemässe Betrachtung (Winter semester 1938/39), ed. H.-J. Friedrich

47. Nietzsches Lehre vom Willen zur Macht als Erkenntnis (Summer semester 1939), ed. E. Hanser, 1989, XVI, 330p.

48. Nietzsche: Der europäische Nihilismus (2nd trimester 1940), ed. P. Jaeger, 1986, XVI, 340p.

49. Die Metaphysik des deutschen Idealismus. Zur erneuten Auslegung von Schelling: Philosophische Untersuchungen über das Wesen der menschlichen Freiheit und die damit zusammenhängenden Gegenstände (1809), ed. G. Seubold, 1991, 2nd edn. 2006, X, 210p.

50. Nietzsches Metaphysik (announced for the winter semester 1941/42)/ **Einleitung in die Philosophie - Denken und Dichten** (Winter semester 1944/45), ed. P. Jaeger, 1990, VIII, 162p.

51. Grundbegriffe (Summer semester 1941), ed. P. Jaeger, 1981, 2nd edn. 1991, X, 128p.

52. Hölderlins Hymne "Andenken" (Winter semester 1941/42), ed. C. Ochwaldt, 1982, 2nd edn. 1992, X, 204p.

53. Hölderlins Hymne "Der Ister"

(Summer semester 1942), ed. W. Biemel, 1984, 2nd edn. 1993, VIII, 210p.

54. Parmenides (Winter semester 1942/43), ed. M. S. Frings, 1982, 2nd edn. 1992, XII, 252p.

55. Heraklit. 1. Der Anfang des abendländischen Denkens (Summer semester 1943) / **2. Logik. Heraklits Lehre vom Logos** (Summer semester 1944), ed. M. S. Frings, 1979, 2nd edn. 1987, 3rd edn. 1994, XII, 406p.

Frühe Freiburger Vorlesungen 1919–1923

56/57. Zur Bestimmung der Philosophie. 1. Die Idee der Philosophie und das Weltanschauungsproblem (Kriegsnotsemester 1919) / **2. Phänomenologie und transzendentale Wertphilosophie** (Summer semester 1919) / **3. Anhang: Über das Wesen der Universität und des akademischen Studiums** (Summer semester 1919), ed. B. Heimbüchel, 1987, 2nd edn. 1999, X, 226p.

58. Grundprobleme der Phänomenologie (Winter semester 1919/20), ed. H.-H. Gander, 1992, X, 274p.

59. Phänomenologie der Anschauung und des Ausdrucks. Theorie der philosophischen Begriffsbildung (Summer semester 1920), ed. C. Strube, 1993, VIII, 202p.

60. Phänomenologie des religiösen Lebens. 1. Einleitung in die Phänomenologie der Religion (Semestre d'hiver 1920/21), ed. M. Jung et T. Regehly / **2. Augustinus und der Neuplatonismus** (Summer semester 1921) / **3. Die philosophischen Grundlagen der mittelalterlichen Mystik** (Prepared notes and introduction to an undelivered course 1918/19), ed. C. Strube, 1995, XIV, 352p.

61. Phänomenologische Interpretationen zu Aristoteles. Einführung in die phänomenologische Forschung (Winter semester 1921/22), ed. W. Bröcker et K. Bröcker-Oltmanns, 1985, 2nd edn. 1994, XIV, 204p.

62. Phänomenologische Interpretation ausgewählter Abhandlungen des Aristoteles zu Ontologie und Logik (Summer semester 1922), ed. G. Neumann, 2005, XXIV, 452p.

63. Ontologie. Hermeneutik der Faktizität (Summer semester 1923), ed. K. Bröcker-Oltmanns, 1988, 2nd edn. 1995, XII, 116p.

III. Abteilung: Unveröffentliche Abhandlungen / Vorträge - Gedachtes

64. Der Begriff der Zeit (1924), ed. F.-W. von Herrmann, 2004, VI, 134p.
- I. Die Fragestellung Diltheys und Yorcks Grundtendenz
- II. Die ursprünglichen Seinscharaktere des Daseins
- III. Dasein und Zeitlichkeit
- IV. Zeitlichkeit und Geschichtlichkeit
- Anhang: Der Begriff der Zeit. Vortrag vor der Marburger Theologenschaft Juli 1924

65. Beiträge zur Philosophie (Vom Ereignis) (1936–1938), ed. F.-W. von Herrmann, 1989, 2nd edn. 1994, XVI, 522p.
- I. Vorblick
- II. Der Anklang
- III. Das Zuspiel
- IV. Der Sprung
- V. Die Gründung, a) Da-Sein und Seinsentwurf, b) Das Da-sein, c) Das Wesen der Wahrheit, d) Der Zeit-Raum als der Ab-grund, e) Die Wesung der Wahrheit als Bergung
- VI. Die Zu-künftigen
- VII. Der letzte Gott
- VIII. Das Seyn

66. Besinnung (1938/39), ed. F.-W. von Herrmann, 1997, XIV, 438p.
- I. Einleitung
- II. Der Vorsprung in die Einzigkeit des Seyns
- III. Die Philosophie
- IV. Zum Entwurf des Seyns
- V. Wahrheit und Wissen
- VI. Das Seyn
- VII. Das Seyn und der Mensch
- VIII. Das Seyn und der Mensch
- IX. Der Anthropomorphismus
- X. Geschichte
- XI. Die Technik
- XII. Historie und Technik
- XIII. Seyn und Macht
- XIV. Das Seyn und das Sein
- XV. Das Denken des Seyns
- XVI. Die Seynsvergessenheit
- XVII. Die Seynsgeschichte
- XVIII. Götter
- XIX. Die Irre
- XX. Zur Geschichte der Metaphysik
- XXI. Die metaphysische Warumfrage
- XXII. Seyn und "Werden"
- XXIII. Das Sein als Wirklichkeit
- XXIV. Das Seyn und die "Negativität"
- XXV. Sein und Denken. Sein und Zeit
- XXVI. Eine Sammlung des Besinnens
- XXVII. Das seynsgeschichtliche Denken und die Seinsfrage
- XXVIII. Der seynsgeschichtliche Begriff der Metaphysik / Anhang: Mein bisheriger Weg (1937/38)

67. Metaphysik und Nihilismus, ed. H.-J. Friedrich, 1999, XII, 274p.
- 1. Die Überwindung der Metaphysik (1938/39)
- 2. Das Wesen des Nihilismus (1946–1948)

68. Hegel, ed. I. Schüssler, 1993, X, 154p.
- 1. Die Negativität (1938/39)
- 2. Erläuterung der "Einleitung" zu Hegels Phänomenologie des Geistes (1942)

69. Die Geschichte des Seyns, ed. P. Trawny, 1998, XII, 230p.
- 1. Die Geschichte des Seyns (1938/40)
- 2. Koinon. Aus der Geschichte des Seyns (1939)

70. Über den Anfang (1941), ed. F.-W. von Herrmann, 2005, XII, 200p.
- I. Die Anfängnis des Anfangs
- II. Anfang und das anfängliche Denken
- III. Ereignis und Da-sein
- IV. Bemerkungen über das Auslegen
- V. Die Seynsgeschichte
- VI. Sein und Zeit und das anfängliche Denken als Geschichte des Seyns

71. Das Ereignis (1941/42), ed. F.-W. von Herrmann
- Vorworte
- Der erste Anfang
- Der Anklang
- Der Unterschied
- Die Verwindung

- Das Ereignis. Der Wortschatz seines Wesens
- Das Ereignis
- Das Ereignis und das Menschenwesen
- Das Daseyn
- Der andere Anfang
- Weisungen in das Ereignis
- Das seynsgeschichtliche Denken (Dichten und Denken)

72. Die Stege des Anfangs (1944), ed. F.-W. von Herrmann
73. Zum Ereignis-Denken
74. Zum Wesen der Sprache, ed. T. Regehly
75. Zu Hölderlin / Griechenlandreisen, ed. C. Ochwadt, 2000, VI, 380p.
76. Zur Metaphysik / Neuzeitlichen Wissenschaft / Technik, ed. C. Strube
77. Feldweg-Gespräche (1944/45), ed. I. Ingrid Schüssler, 1995, VI, 250p.
- 1. Agcibasih. Ein Gespräch selbdritt auf einem Feldweg zwischen einem Forscher, einem Gelehrten und einem Weisen
- 2. Der Lehrer trifft den Türmer an der Tür zum Turmaufgang
- 3. Abendgespräch in einem Kriegsgefangenenlager in Russland zwischen einem Jüngeren und einem Älteren

78. Der Spruch des Anaximander (1946)
79. Bremer und Freiburger Vorträge, ed. P. Jaeger, 1994, 2nd edn. 2005, VI, 182p.
- 1. Einblick in das was ist. Bremer Vorträge 1949: Das Ding / Das Gestell / Die Gefahr / Die Kehre
- 2. Grundsätze des Denkens. Freiburger Vorträge 1957

80. Vorträge
- Frage und Urteil (Vortrag im Rickert Seminar 10. Juli 1915)
- Wahrsein und Dasein. Aristoteles, Ethica Nicomachea Z (Vortrag in der Kant-Gesellschaft Köln WS 1923/24)
- Kasseler Vorträge (1925)
- Begriff und Entwicklung der phänomenologischen Forschung (Vortrag im Marburger kulturwissenschaftlichen Kränzchen 4. Dezember 1926)
- Phänomenologie und Theologie. 1. Teil: Die nichtphilosophischen als positive Wissenschaften und die Philosophie als transzendentale Wissenschaft (Vortrag vor der evangelischen Theologenschaft in Tübingen 8. Juli 1927)
- Die heutige Problemlage der Philosophie (Vortrag in der Kantgesellschaft Karlsruhe 4. Dezember 1929 und vor der wissenschaftlichen Vereinigung zu Amsterdam 21. März 1930)
- Philosophische Anthropologie und Metaphysik des Daseins (Vortrag in der Kantgesellschaft Frankfurt 24. Januar 1929)
- Hegel und das Problem der Metaphysik (Vortrag in der wissenschaftlichen Vereinigung zu Arnsterdam 22. März 1930)
- Augustinus: Quid est tempus? Confessiones lib. XI (Vortrag in Beuron 26. Oktober 1930)
- to yeudoV (Vortrag im Freiburger Kränzchen 22. Juli 1952)
- Der Satz vom Widerspruch (Vortrag im Freiburger Kränzchen 16. Dezember 1932)
- Das Dasein und der Einzelne (Vortrag Zürich 18. Januar 1936)
- Europa und die deutsche Philosophie (Vortrag im Kaiser Wilhelm-Institut Bibliotheca Hertziana Rom 8. April 1936)
- Von der Grundbestimmung des Wissens (Vortrag im Freiburger Kränzchen 9. Juni 1959)
- Der Spruch des Parmenides (Vortrag im Freiburger Kränzchen Juni 1940)
- Zur Geschichte des Existenzbegriffs (Vortrag im Freiburger Kränzchen 7. Juni 1941)
- Über die Be-stimmung der Künste im gegenwärtigen Weltalter (Vortrag in Baden-Baden Haus Schweizer 7. und 8. Mai 1959)
- Max Kommerell (Vortrag in der Gedächtnisfeier von Max Kommerell 27. Februar 1962)
- Überlieferte Sprache und technische Sprache (Vortrag auf dem Lehrgang für Gewerbeschullehrer auf der Comburg 18. Juli 1962)
- Bemerkungen zu Kunst - Plastik - Raum (Vortrag St. Gallen 3. Oktober 1964)
- Die Herkunft der Kunst und die Bestimmung des Denkens (Vortrag in der Akademie der Wissenschaften und Künste in Athen 4. April 1967)
- Die Bestimmung der Sache des Denkens (Vortrag 19. Juli 1967 in Kiel zu W. Bröckers 65. Geburtstag)

81. Gedachtes, ed. P.-L. Coriando
- I. Frühe unveröffentlichte Gedichte. Ich mied der Gottesnähe heldenschaffende Kraft / Fernes Land / Hast die Sonne du verloren
- II. Aus der Erfahrung des Denkens. Auf dem Heimweg / Der Ring des Seyns / Wende / Dann sind wir bedacht / Amo: volo ut sis / Sonata sonans / Ankunft / Winke / An-fang und Beginn im Ereignis "der" Freyheit / Aus der Werkstatt / Hütte am Abend / Pindari Isthmia V, 1-16 / Herákleitos ho skyteinós. Dem Freunde zu Weihnachten 1946 / Furchen
- III. Gedachtes für das Vermächtnis eines Denkens. Lerchensporn / Wage den Schritt /…durchrasend die Irrnis / Seynsfuge / Tod / Nichtendes Nichts / Gegnet noch Gegend / Die Nähe des letzten Gottes / Der Schritt zurück /Vermächtnis der Seynsfrage

IV. Abteilung: Hinweise und Aufzeichnungen

82. Zu eigenen Veröffentlichungen
83. Seminare: Platon - Aristoteles - Augustinus, ed. M. Michalski
84. Seminare: Leibniz - Kant, ed. H.-H. Gander
85. Seminar: Vom Wesen der Sprache. Die Metaphysik der Sprache und die Wesung des Wortes. Zu Herders Abhandlung "Über den Ursprung der Sprache", ed. I. Schüssler, 1999, XII, 220p.
86. Seminare: Hegel - Schelling
87. Seminare: Nietzsche: Seminare 1937 und 1944, ed. P. von Ruckteschell, 2004, XX, 324p.
88. Seminare: 1. Die metaphysischen Grundstellungen des abendländischen Denkens 2. Einübung in das philosophische Denken, ed. A. Denker
89. Zollikoner Seminare

90. Zu Ernst Jünger "Der Arbeiter", ed. P. Trawny, 2004, XVI, 460p.
91. Ergänzungen und Denksplitter
92. Ausgewählte Briefe I
93. Ausgewählte Briefe II
94. Überlegungen A
95. Überlegungen B
96. Überlegungen C
97. Anmerkungen A
98. Anmerkungen B
99. Vier Hefte I: Der Feldweg / Vier Hefte II: Durch Ereignis zu Ding und Welt
100. Vigiliae I, II/ Notturno
101. Winke I, II
102. Vorläufiges I-IV

Criticism of the *Gesamtausgabe*

- Theodore Kisiel, "Heidegger's *Gesamtausgabe*: An International Scandal of Scholarship", *Philosophy Today* 39 (1995), pp. 3–15.

Source (edited): "http://en.wikipedia.org/wiki/Heidegger_Gesamtausgabe"

Hölderlin's Hymn "The Ister"

Hölderlin's Hymn "The Ister" (German: *Hölderlins Hymne »Der Ister«*) is the title given to a lecture course delivered by German philosopher Martin Heidegger at the University of Freiburg in 1942. It was first published in 1984 as volume 53 of Heidegger's *Gesamtausgabe*. The translation by William McNeill and Julia Davis was published in 1996 by Indiana University Press. *Der Ister* is a poem by Friedrich Hölderlin, the title of which refers to an ancient name for a part of the Danube River.

Overview

In 1942, in the darkest depths of World War II and the National Socialist period, Heidegger chose to deliver a lecture course on a single poem by Friedrich Hölderlin: "*Der Ister*," about the river Danube. The course explored the meaning of poetry, the nature of technology, the relationship between ancient Greece and modern Germany, the essence of politics, and human dwelling. The central third of the lecture course is a reading of Sophocles' *Antigone*. Heidegger undertakes this reading of *Antigone* ostensibly because of the importance of this text for grasping the meaning of Hölderlin's poetry, but in doing so he repeats and extends a reading he had conducted in a different context in 1935. In terms of Heidegger's *oeuvre*, the 1942 lecture course is significant in that it is Heidegger's most sustained discussion of the essence of politics. Heidegger was only able to deliver two-thirds of the written text of the lecture course.

The lecture course is divided into three parts.

- **Part one** introduces the way in which Heidegger believes it is necessary to approach Hölderlin's poetry, arguing against the "metaphysical interpretation of art." He further argues that Hölderlin's poetry must be understood in terms of its essential kinship with the work of Sophocles.
- **Part two** retraces the interpretation of Sophocles' *Antigone* which Heidegger conducted in the 1935 lecture course, *An Introduction to Metaphysics*. He extends this reading, modifying it in subtle ways.
- **Part three**, which was in fact never delivered, returns to Hölderlin's poetry, arguing that the figure of the river in the poem is in fact the poet, and vice versa.

Part one: Poetising the essence of the rivers

The Ister hymn

The lecture course opens with a reflection on the Greek origin of the word "hymn," meaning song of praise, specifically in praise of the gods, the heroes, or contest victors, in preparation of the festival. Heidegger cites a line from Sophocles' *Antigone* connecting the noun and verb forms of the word, and then indicates that the sense in which Hölderlin's works are hymns must initially remain an open question.

Heidegger turns his attention to the first line of "*Der Ister*"—"Now come, fire!" What could this mean, if "fire" here indicates the sun or the dawn? What could it mean to call, or to have the vocation for such a calling, given that the dawn will come whether it is called or not? And what is meant by "Now," by naming the time of such a calling? From these questions Heidegger is drawn to ask what it means to "poetise," answering that poetising is always inaugurating something, that genuine poetising is always poetising "anew." Thus the "Now" of the first line speaks not only of the present, but toward the future.

Heidegger next focuses on the fact that it is clear that "the rivers come to language" in Hölderlin's poetry. On the one hand, the rivers are detached from human being, having their own "spirit"; on the other hand, the rivers are a locale at which human beings find their dwelling place. The question is thus that of the poetic essence of the river.

The metaphysical interpretation of art

Rather than delving immediately into this question, Heidegger makes a detour, elaborating the "metaphysical interpretation of art." He argues that metaphysical interpretations are incapable of comprehending Hölderlin's poetry.

According to the metaphysical interpretation, art presents objects in nature such as rivers, but this presentation is at the service of something else, of their "meaning" in the artwork. Heidegger speaks in this regard of the etymology of the words "allegory" and "metaphor." The metaphysical interpretation of art relies on the distinction between the sensuous and the non-sensuous, the aesthetic and the noetic, the sensible and the intelligible. And according to this interpretation the artwork exists not for itself, not *as* a sensuous object, but *for* the nonsensuous and suprasensuous, which is also named "spirit." In this way the superior and the true come to be identified with the spiritual.

Against the metaphysical interpretation of art, Heidegger asserts that the rivers in Hölderlin's poetry are in no way symbolic images of a higher or deeper content. He draws attention to the final lines of the poem—"Yet what that one does, that river, / No one knows"—in order to indicate that, whatever the rivers are, or whatever the river does, remains an enigma. Even the poet knows only that the river flows, but not what is *decided* in that flowing.

Locality and journeying
Heidegger then turns to a consideration of the river as the dwelling place of human beings. As such, the river is what brings human beings into their own and maintains them there. Yet what is their own often remains foreign to human beings for a long time, and can be abandoned by them because it threatens to overwhelm them. It is not something that produces itself, but must come to be appropriate, and needs to be appropriated. The river is of assistance in the becoming-homely of human beings, but this "assistance" is not an occasional support but a steadfast standing by.

To understand what this means, Heidegger considers some lines from another Hölderlin poem, "Voice of the People," in which the rivers are referred to as "vanishing" and as "full of intimation." That the rivers are vanishing means that they abandon the human landscape, without thereby being unfaithful toward that landscape. Yet as full of intimation, the rivers proceed into what is coming. Thus Heidegger sees Hölderlin as concerned with the temporality of the river in relation to the human, yet also with its spatiality—thus "the river is the journeying." The river is, he says, the journeying of becoming homely or, rather, the very locality attained in and through the journeying. His claim is that the river is the locality of the dwelling of human beings as historical upon the earth.

Rätsel
The river is an enigma (*Rätsel*). But Heidegger relates this to *Raten*, giving counsel, and to *Rat*, counsel, but also "care." To give counsel means to take into care. That the river is an enigma does not mean it is a puzzle we should wish to "solve." Rather, it means it is something we should bring closer to us *as* an enigma. We must understand this poetry, therefore, in something other than a calculative, technical way.

Space and time
Locality and journeying: this sounds like "space and time." Succession takes its course in time, as a sequence of moments, as a "flowing." But this is in fact only an understanding of space and time as an ordered, calculable, relationality. Whatever is subject to order must be posited in advance in such a way that it becomes accessible for order and control. Hence, for example, the reduction to co-ordinates. Yet for calculative observation, something is what it is only through what it performs. All modern thinking thinks in terms of order and performance. Human activity is thought as labour, equated with mechanical energy, and assessed according to the performative principle. Through such thinking space and time come to be considered so obvious as not to require any further thought.

Modern technology
Such modern thinking about space and time is essentially technological. Modern technology is different from every tool. Whereas the tool is a means, what is distinctive about modern technology is that this is no longer the case, and that it is instead unfolding a domination of its own. It demands its own kind of discipline and conquest. Thus, for example, the staged accomplishment of factories built for the purpose of fabricating machine tools for other factories. Modern machine technology is a specific kind of "truth." We may believe that technology, as the control of space and time, is never undertaken without purpose, and is therefore no end in itself. This, however, is a misunderstanding grounded in a failure to grasp the essence of modern technology. And this results from failing to question that which underpins it—the order and unity of "space and time."

Heidegger then deconstructs the concepts of space and time, arguing firstly that these cannot be merely "objects," as though they were some gigantic containers in which everything is accommodated. Yet neither can we conclude that they are merely subjective. Is space, over which wars erupt, merely imaginary? And is time, which tears us along and tears us away, merely subjective? Such metaphysical interpretations of space and time will be of no help in understanding the locality and journeying at the heart of Hölderlin's non-metaphysical poetising. Space and time comprise the framework for our calculative domination and ordering of the "world" through technology. But it remains undecided whether this process is turning human beings into mere planetary adventurers, or whether it is the beginning of another tendency, toward new forms of settlement and resettlement.

Dialogue
According to Heidegger, that poetry of Hölderlin's taking the form of the "hymn" has taken into its care this becoming homely in one's own. He asserts that "one's own" is in this case the German fatherland, but immediately adds that "coming to be at home is thus a passage through the foreign." This is why this poetry necessarily takes the form of a dialogue with foreign poets, specifically, Pindar and Sophocles. What must be carefully listened to in the hymnal poetry of Hölderlin is this "resonance" of Greek poetry, on which basis Heidegger turns to the interpretation of *Antigone*.

Part two: The Greek interpretation of human beings in Sophocles' *Antigone*

The choral ode
The choral ode from the *Antigone* of Sophocles is according to Heidegger the singular work radiating throughout the poetry of Hölderlin. Heidegger had previously interpreted this ode in his 1935 lecture course, *An Introduction to Metaphysics*, and in 1942 he both recapitulates and extends this interpretation.

Like "*Der Ister*," the ode begins with a call to the dawning sun, yet it is clear the ode is equally concerned with darkness. Although the ode is concerned with the light and darkness of human being, this should not be interpreted to mean that the two main figures, Creon and Antigone, form an opposition. Each of these figures proceed from out of the unity of essence and nonessence, but differently in each case.

Deinon

The decisive word, according to Heidegger, occurs at the beginning of the ode: *deinon*. Heidegger translates this as *das Unheimliche*, the uncanny. Heidegger emphasises what he calls the "counterturning" character of the term. *Deinon*, he says, means the fearful, the powerful, and the inhabitual. But none of these definitional elements is one-dimensional. As the fearful, the *deinon* is also that which, as worthy of honour, can awaken awe. As the powerful, it may be that which looms over us, or that which is merely violent. As the inhabitual, the extraordinary, the extraordinariness of skill, it exceeds the ordinary, but it can do so as that which governs the ordinary and the habitual. As *das Unheimliche*, *deinon* names the unity of all these meanings.

The ode names the human being as *deinon* in manifold ways, indeed as the *most* uncanny being, *das Unheimlichste*. Heidegger ties this to his prior argument that human beings as poetised by Hölderlin are "unhomely" ("*unheimisch*"), that is, on the way toward becoming homely. The extraordinariness of human being is this being unhomely that is also a becoming homely. Heidegger makes clear that this being unhomely does not mean simply homelessness, wandering around, adventurousness, or lack of rootedness. Rather, it means that the sea and the land are those realms that human beings transform through skillfulness and use. The homely is that which is striven for in the violent activity of passing through the inhabitual. Yet even so, the homely is not attained in this activity: as the ode says, man "comes to nothing."

Poros

Human being is thus the being which finds passage through everything, yet always comes up short, expressed in the couple *pantoporos aporos*, where *poros* means that irruption of power that finds its way through. Infinitely skillful and artful, human beings nevertheless can never circumvent death. This is something known by human beings, but mostly in the form of evading this knowledge. Human beings are in fact those beings which comport themselves to beings as such, and because they understand being, human beings alone can also forget being. The uncanniness of human beings is that they alone are capable of "catastrophe," in the sense of a reversal turning them away from their own essence.

Polis

Heidegger next turns to the couple *hypsipolis apolis*, "towering high above the site," and "forfeiting the site." This couple is based in the word *polis*, and Heidegger notes that, if this is the *origin* of the word "political," then it is a mistake to understand the former on the basis of the latter—the *polis* is precisely not a political concept. The "political" is conventionally understood in terms of consciousness, in a "technical" manner, as the way in which history is accomplished. It is thus marked by a failure to question itself.

Heidegger asks whether the *polis* might not be the name of that realm which constantly becomes questionable anew and remains worthy of question. Perhaps the *polis* is that around which everything question-worthy and uncanny turns in an exceptional way. Heidegger uses the word *Wirbel*, swirl, in this context, and speaks of the *polis* as essentially "polar." The pre-political essence of the *polis*, that which makes possible everything which we call political, is the open site from out of which all human relations toward beings are determined.

Human being

It is thus the essence of human being to both ascend within their site and to be without site. Human being bears within it this potential for reversal, a potential essentially grounded in the possibility of being mistaken, of taking nonbeings for beings and beings for nonbeings. Thus human beings are creatures of risk. They seek to become homely within a site, place everything at stake in this, and encounter the fact that the homely refuses itself to them.

This is the uncanniness of human being, and this is why *deinon* does not mean simply power and violence. Human beings do not themselves make themselves the most uncanny thing; it is not a matter of self-consciousness here. Only because human beings can say "it is," Heidegger says, can they say "I am." And only because they have a relation to being can they "say" at all, that is, can they be Aristotle's *zoon logon echon*. It is the distinction of human beings, in other words, to "see" the open.

Antigone

The closing words of the ode speak of the expulsion of the most uncanny from the hearth. If we were to interpret this as a rejection of Creon, according to Heidegger, then the choral ode would not be a "high song of culture" so much as a song in praise of mediocrity, of hatred toward the exception. To interpret otherwise than this means asking where Antigone herself stands in relation to the *deinon*.

In the introductory dialogue between Antigone and Ismene, Ismene tries to dissuade her sister from her resolution to bury their brother. Antigone's "pursuit" is, she says, concerned with that against which nothing can avail. Antigone, in other words, takes the impossible as her point of departure. She says herself that she wishes to suffer or bear the uncanny. In this she is removed from all human possibilities, and is the supreme uncanny.

The hearth

What, then, of the hearth? The chorus speaks not only of expulsion, but of "not sharing their delusion with my knowing." All knowledge of the *deinon* is sustained and guided by that knowing which knows the hearth. The content of this knowing is not stated directly, but it is, however, referred to as a *phronein*, a meditating from the heart. If this knowledge takes the form of intimation, it is not mere opinion.

If mythology is not simply an "immature" invention, then thinking stands in an essential relation to poetising. Thinking is not the sediment left after the de-mythologising of myth. Such reflections are intended by Heidegger to assist in the following gesture: the assertion that the hearth, named by the chorus, is being. "Being is the hearth." He then cites Plato on Hestia, the goddess named for the hearth. The expulsion referred to in the closing words of the choral ode is not a rejection of the unhomely, as much as an impulsion to be attentive to the homely, to risk belonging to it. Being unhomely is a not yet awakened, not yet decided, potential for being homely. This is Antigone's supreme action.

The purest poem

In Heidegger's translation, what determines this action is stated by Antigone as being beyond both the upper and lower gods, beyond Zeus and Dike, but neither can it be any human ordinance. Hence at stake in her action is the most uncanny risk. The closing words of the ode call in the direction of a knowledge of the proper essence of the unhomely one. In this most enigmatic part of his interpretation, Heidegger speaks of "the risk of distinguishing and deciding between that being unhomely proper to human beings and a being unhomely that is inappropriate." To be this risk is Antigone's essence.

Thus Heidegger concludes that to understand the truth of *Antigone*, it is necessary to think beyond the cult of the dead or the cult of blood-relatedness, which seem at first glance to be the motors of the tragedy. Antigone, he says, is herself the purest poem. Poetising is neither finding nor inventing, but a telling finding of being, revealing that which is always already revealed, the nearest of all that is near. The human potential for being, and the unhomely being homely of human beings upon the earth, is poetic. What is spoken in the choral ode remains indeterminate, but neither vague nor arbitrary. The indeterminate is, on the contrary, that which is undecided yet first to be decided. If this is the case, then the tragedy poetises that which is in the highest sense worthy of poetising. And this may be why this ode came to speak ever anew to the poet Hölderlin.

Part three: Hölderlin's poetising of the essence of the poet as demigod

One's own and the foreign

Sophocles' ode and Hölderlin's river hymns poetise the Same, yet they are not identical. To understand this, Heidegger turns to Hölderlin's famous letter to Casimir Böhlendorff, which thematises the relations between Germany and Greece. According to Heidegger's reading, what for the Greeks is their own is what is foreign to the Germans, and what is foreign to the Germans is what is proper to the Greeks. Hölderlin is the first to experience poetically that becoming homely means being unhomely, thus to understand the need of being unhomely, which he does by venturing into an encounter with the (Greek) foreign.

Spirit

Heidegger then cites Hölderlin: "namely at home is spirit / not at the commencement, not at the source." He asks: who is "spirit"? Despite the influence of German metaphysics, Heidegger argues that Hölderlin's use of this word was singular, as that which is alongside itself in thinking itself, and always as "communal" spirit. What spirit thinks is that which is fittingly destined for human beings, yet this is always that which is futural, never something that has been decided; it is something "non-actual" that is already "acting." Poetising is the telling of the thoughts of spirit.

Spirit is never "at home" in the beginning. At the beginning of the history of a people, their destiny is assigned, but what has been assigned is in coming; it is still veiled and equivocal. In the beginning, the ability to fit oneself to one's destiny is as yet disordered, unpracticed. Thus in spirit there prevails the longing for its own essence. But "spirit loves colony," that is, in the foreign it wills the mother who is difficult to attain. And it loves "bold forgetting," where forgetting means the readiness to learn from the foreign for the sake of what is one's own, so as to defer what is one's own until it is time. It is in this way that the law of being unhomely is the law of becoming homely.

Greeks and Germans

The Greeks, too, had to pass through the foreign. What was proper to the Greeks was "the fire from the heavens"; what was foreign was the "clarity of presentation." Through what was foreign to them they were able to build at the essential ground of the *polis*. For the Germans, on the other hand, the clarity of presentation is natural—the formation of projects, frameworks, etc. What is foreign is the fire from heaven, and thus they must learn to be struck by this fire, and thereby impelled to the correct appropriation of their gift for presentation. Otherwise they shall be exposed to the weakness of suppressing every fire, of pursuing delimitation and institution only for the sake of it. Hölderlin is the one who has been struck by this fire, yet why must this be said poetically?

Poem, river, demigod

Heidegger cites Hölderlin in order to seek an answer to this question. "Full of merit, yet poetically / Humans dwell upon the earth." "Full of merit" refers, according to Heidegger, to all that humans achieve through the arts, through *tekhne*, but all that is achieved this way amounts merely to culture. It can be achieved only on the basis of a "dwelling" which can be seized upon through making or achieving within the realm of the actual. Dwelling, the becoming homely of a being unhomely, is grounded in the poetic.

But what is poetry? There must be a poet who poetises in advance the essence of poetry. This will be the poet who ventures into the foreign, to let the fire come toward him. This is what occurs in Hölderlin's hymnal poetry. This river poetry never forgets the source, in its issuing and flowing from the source. What it says is the holy, which, *beyond* the gods, determines the gods. The poet stands between human beings and gods. The poet, and the river, are demigods.

Heidegger speaks of the lines of the hymn concerning the invitation to Hercules. We can know nothing of the Ister or the hymn if we do not understand who this guest is. The appropriation of one's own *is* only as the encounter and guest-like dialogue with the foreign. The river must remain in the realm of its source in such a way that it flows toward it from out of the foreign, which is why it "appears, however, almost / To go backwards." Heidegger again uses the word *Wirbeln* to indicate this swirling near the source.

Historical, ahistorical, unhistorical

This relation to the foreign is never an affirmation of the "natural" or the "organic." These are foreign to the law of history. This law places historical humankind on the difficult path toward its essence. If humankind abandons the law of history, it falls into the unhistorical. Nature is ahistorical, but being *un*historical, as a *rupture* with the historical, is a particular kind of catastrophe. Heidegger's example of the unhistorical is Americanism.

The Ister remains enigmatic but historical, in the strange way it flows but also remains close to the source. It is the river in which the foreign is already present as a guest at its source, the river in whose flowing there constantly speaks the dialogue between one's own and the foreign. The rivers are the poets who found the poetic, upon whose ground human beings dwell. Thus the poetic spirit of the river makes arable the land—it prepares the ground for the hearth of the house of history, opening the time-space within which a belonging to the hearth is possible.

A sign is needed

"A sign is needed": Hölderlin speaks of the sign as having a mind (*Gemüt*), where mind is the ground of all mindful courage (*Mut*). It is the poet who is named here as the sign. What is needed is the poet's word. Heidegger cites the poem "*Andenken*": "Yet what remains, the poets found." Heidegger relates the sign's showing to pain, to that knowing proper to being distinct. The sign, the demigod, the river, the poet: all these name poetically the singular ground of the becoming homely of human beings as historical, and the founding of this ground by the poet. At stake is a "partaking in feeling" with the gods, bearing the sun and moon, sharing the holy. This is for the benefit not only of human beings, but of the gods themselves, who are otherwise without feeling, without unity.

The stairs upon which the heavenly descend

Through the sign, through the rivers, the heavenly find their unity with one another, a unity which does not diminish their singularity. The rivers are their "joy." Hölderlin speaks of staircases on which the heavenly can descend. Where there are staircases, a dwelling place is also opened up poetically for humans. Poetising founding builds the stairs for this descent of the heavenly. The rivers are the children of the heavens, signs that bear sun and moon in mind, but at the same time the sons of the earth.

The hymn ends on an enigmatic note: "Yet what that one does, that river, / No one knows." What the vocation of the Ister is, it well knows, but the Rhine, which does not linger at its source but departs sideways, is altogether concealed. Yet the Ister hymn too breaks off—it shows, it makes manifest, yet it also conceals.

Is there a measure on earth?

Heidegger appends a concluding remark to his reading of the poem. His remarks on the hymn were intended to make us attentive to the poetising of the rivers. But because this is the poetising of the essence of poetry, concealed relations prevail. Such poetry cannot at all be referred to the poet's ego, or to "subjectivity." The poet is the river, and vice versa. The unity of locality and journeying here cannot be conceived in terms of "space" and "time," for these are themselves the offspring of the realm that lets their openness spring forth.

This poetry demands a transformation in our ways of thinking and experiencing, and we must think beyond representations, symbols, and images. But if we must find a new measure, it must be asked whether we are capable of it. Hölderlin asks about this measure, and concludes there is no such measure on earth. This sounds like despair. Yet what Hölderlin means is that we must dwell poetically upon this earth, bearing and suffering it rather than forcing and seizing it. If we are strong enough to think, it may be sufficient for us to ponder from afar the truth of this poetry and what it poetises, so that we may suddenly be struck by it. Heidegger ends with a quotation from yet another Hölderlin hymn, "The Journey":

A dream it becomes for him who would / Approach it by stealth, and punishes him / Who would equal it with force. / Often it surprises one / Who indeed has scarcely thought it.

Cinema

The lecture course formed the basis of the film *The Ister* (2004).
Source (edited): "http://en.wikipedia.org/wiki/H%C3%B6lderlin%27s_Hymn_%22The_Ister%22"

The Origin of the Work of Art

" [Art] gives things their look, and human beings their outlook. "
—*Heidegger*

The Origin of the Work of Art is the title of an article by German philosopher Martin Heidegger. Heidegger drafted the text between 1935 and 1937, reworking it for publication in 1950 and again in 1960. Heidegger based his article on a series of lectures he had previously delivered in Zurich and Frankfurt during the 1930s, first on the essence of the work of art and then on the question of the meaning of a "thing," marking the philosopher's first lectures on the notion of art.

Content

In his article, Heidegger explains the essence of art in terms of the concepts of being and truth. He argues that art is not only a way of expressing the element of truth in a culture, but the means of creating it and providing a springboard from which "that which is" can be revealed. Works of art are not merely representations of the way things are, but actually produce a community's shared understanding. Each time a new artwork is added to any culture, the meaning of what it is to exist is inherently changed.

Heidegger begins his essay with the question of what the source of a work of art is. The artwork and the artist, he explains, exist in a dynamic where each appears to be a provider of the other. "Neither is without the other. Nevertheless, neither is the sole support of the other." Art, a concept separate from both work and creator, thus exists as the source for them both. Rather than control lying with the artist, art becomes a force that uses the creator for art's own purposes. Likewise, the resulting work must be considered in the context of the world in which it exists, not that of its artist. In discovering the essence, however, the problem of the hermeneutic circle arises. In sum, the hermeneutic circle raises the paradox that, in any work, without understanding the whole, you can't fully comprehend the individual parts, but without understanding the parts, you cannot comprehend the whole. Applied to art and artwork, we find that without knowledge of the essence of art, we cannot grasp the essence of the artwork, but without knowledge of the artwork, we cannot find the essence of art. Heidegger concludes that to take hold of this circle you either have to define the essence of art or of the artwork, and, as the artwork is simpler, we should start there.

A Pair of Shoes (1885), by Vincent van Gogh.

Artworks, Heidegger contends, are things, a definition that raises the question of the meaning of a "thing," such that works have a thingly character. This is a broad concept, so Heidegger chooses to focus on three dominant interpretations of things:
1. Things as substances with properties , or as bearers of traits.
2. Things as the manifold of sense perceptions.
3. Things as formed matter.

The third interpretation is the most dominant (extended to all beings), but is derived from equipment: "This long familiar mode of thought preconceives all immediate experience of beings. The preconception shackles reflection on the Being of any given being." The reason Heidegger selects a pair of peasant shoes painted by Vincent Van Gogh is to establish a distinction between artwork and other "things," such as pieces of equipment, as well as to open up experience through phenomenological description. This was actually typical of Heidegger as he often chose to study shoes and shoe maker shops as an example for the analysis of a culture. Heidegger explains the viewer's responsibility to consider the variety of questions about the shoes, asking not only about form and matter—what are the shoes made of?—but bestowing the piece with life by asking of purpose—what are the shoes for? What world do they open up and belong to? . In this way we can get beyond correspondence theories of truth which posit truth as the correspondence of representations (form) to reality (matter).

Next, Heidegger writes of art's ability to set up an active struggle between "Earth" and "World." "World" represents meaning which is disclosed, not merely the sum of all that is ready-to-hand for one being but rather the web of significant relations in which Dasein, or human being(s), exist (a table, for example, as part of the web of signification, points to those who customarily sit at it, the conversations once had around it, the carpenter who made it, and so on - all of which point to further and further things). So a family unit could be a world, or a career path could be a world, or even a large community or nation. "Earth" means something like the background against which every meaningful "worlding" emerges. It is outside (unintelligible to) the ready-to-hand. Both are necessary components for an artwork to function, each serving unique purposes. The artwork is inherently an object of "world", as it creates a world of its own; it opens up for us other worlds and cultures, such as worlds from the past like the ancient Greek or medieval worlds, or different social worlds, like the world of the peasant, or of the aristocrat. However, the very nature of art itself appeals to "Earth", as a function of art is to highlight the natural materials used to create it, such as the colors of the paint, the density of the language, or the texture of the stone, as well as the fact that everywhere an implicit background is necessary for every significant explicit representation. In this way, "World" is revealing the unintelligibility of "Earth", and so admits its dependence on the natural "Earth". This reminds us that concealment (hiddenness) is the necessary precondition for unconcealment (aletheia), i.e, truth. The existence of truth is a product of this struggle—the process of art—taking place within the artwork.

Heidegger uses the example of a Greek temple to illustrate his conception of world and earth. Such works as the temple help in capturing this essence of art as they go through a transition from artworks to art objects depending on the status of their world. Once the culture has changed, the temple no longer is able to actively engage with its surroundings and becomes passive—an art object. He holds that a working artwork is crucial to a community and so must be able to be understood. Yet, as soon as meaning is pinned down and the work no longer offers resistance to rationalization, the engagement is over and it is no longer active. While the notion appears contradictory, Heidegger is the first to admit that he was confronting a riddle—one that he did not intend to answer as much as to describe in regard to the meaning of art.

Influence and criticism

A main influence on Heidegger's conception of art was Friedrich Nietzsche. In Nietzsche's Will to Power, Heidegger struggled with his notions about the dynamic of truth and art. Nietzsche contends that art is superior to truth, something Heidegger eventually disagrees with not because of the ordered relationship Nietzsche puts forth but because of the philosopher's definition of truth itself, one he claims is overly traditional. Heidegger, instead, questioned traditional artistic methods. His criticism of museums, for instance, has been widely noted. Critics of Heidegger claim that he employs circuitous arguments and often avoids logical reasoning under the ploy that this is better for finding truth. (In fact, Heidegger is employing a revised version of the phenomenological method; see the hermeneutic circle). Meyer Schapiro claims that the Van Gogh boots represented are not really peasant boots but those of Van Gogh himself, a detail that would negate Heidegger's reading of the importance of the shoes' purpose inferred from the visual. (Problems with both Heidegger and Schapiro's reading are discussed at length in Jacques Derrida's *Restitutions of the Truth in Pointing ['Pointure']* and in the writing of Babette Babich). Yet, his notions about art have made a relevant contribution to discussions on artistic truth. For example, Gadamer uses a lot of Heidegger's work in his book *Truth and Method*.

Source (edited): "http://en.wikipedia.org/wiki/The_Origin_of_the_Work_of_Art"

The Question Concerning Technology

For Martin Heidegger broadly, the question of being formed the essence of his philosophical inquiry. In **The Question Concerning Technology**, (*Die Frage nach der Technik*) Heidegger sustains this inquiry, but turns to the particular phenomenon of technology, seeking to derive the essence of technology and humanity's role of being with it. Heidegger originally published the text in 1954, in *Vorträge und Aufsätze*.

The Question Concerning Technology was originally named "The Framework" and first presented on December 1, 1949 in Bremen. It was at this time presented at a as the second out of four lectures, collectively called "Insight into what is." The other lectures were titled "The Thing", "The Danger" and "The Turning."

Discussion of Terminology

An opening to understanding his discussion is the somewhat mythical concept of "that which precedes all: the earliest" (327). For Heidegger, everything has an essence, yet that essence is concealed to humans. To access this essence, we must engage in "a painstaking effort to think through still more primally what was primally thought"; this is "not the absurd wish to revive what is past, but rather the sober readiness to be astounded before the coming of the dawn" (327). The ideal, then, is the "bringing-forth," in Greek poiesis: bringing-forth is to challenge the unconcealment of the essence, rather than to accept the concealed, what we see without or before poiesis. Heidegger writes:

"Bringing-forth brings out of concealment into unconcealment. Bringing-forth propriates only insofar as something concealed comes into unconcealment. This coming rests and moves freely within what we call revealing [das Entbergen]. The Greeks have the word aletheia for revealing. The Romans translate this with veritas. We say "truth" and usually understand it as correctness of representation. (317)"

The ideal here is the attainment of "truth," or "correctness of representation," because the forms we see are figures of concealed histories; the true forms are concealed, and only through "unconcealment," or the removal of that which is concealed, can we access the truth. [Heidegger - in *The Origin of the work of art* states that a 'world' and earth can be unconcealed to us through art using the examples of The Greek Temple and The Old Womans Shoes by Van Gough].

Heidegger turns to technology, the nominative subject of the essay, etymologically: the word stems from the Greek techne, which is "the name not only for the activities and skills of the craftsman but also for the arts of the mind and the fine arts" (318). For the Greeks, techne was intimately linked to poiesis, the poetic, and thus linked to the "bringing forth" so essential in the pursuit of aletheia/veritas/truth.

Technology, in its modern form, is thought more as manufacturing; in revealing the Greek origins of the modern term, Heidegger initiates his discussion of technology – "It is as revealing, and not as manufacturing, that techne is a bringing-forth ... Technology comes to presence in the realm where revealing and unconcealment take place, where aletheia, truth, happens" (319). In this initiation, he performs his argument, by bringing-forth the concealed roots of the word "technology." In doing so, he asserts that modern technology, as with techne, is a bringing-forth, a revealing. Focusing his terminology further, he writes, "the revealing that rules modern technology is a challenging" (320). Now, Heidegger aligns a slew of terms all of which are modes toward aletheia/veritas/truth – "bringing-forth [Her-vor-bringen]" (317), "unconcealment" (317-318), 'revealing [das Entbergen]"

(318) "challenging [Herausfordern]" (320).

Unconcealing his questioning concerning technology further, Heidegger aims centrally at defining the modern technology's essence, which he names "Gestell [enframing]" (324). Here, "Enframing means the gathering together of the setting-upon that sets upon man, i.e. challenges him forth, to reveal the actual, in the mode of ordering, as standing-reserve" (325). Put just as unlucidly, enframing refers to the calling out, impelling, or challenging-forth, of humans to reveal, or unconceal the "actual" (the aletheia/veritas/truth) as ever-present and "on call" (322) (the "standing-reserve"). Put differently, "Enframing, as a challenging-forth into ordering, sends into a way of revealing. Enframing is an ordaining of destining, as is every way of revealing. Bringing-forth, poiesis, is also a destining in this sense" (330). Enframing is "destining", from which "the essence of all history is determined" (329). Enframing is the essence of modern technology, for Heidegger, because he roots modern technology in techne: it is a means for sourcing true forms and ideas that exist before the figures we perceive.

Hydroelectric Power Plant v. The Windmill

Heidegger employs the hydroelectric power plant and the windmill as examples of how technology has fundamentally altered man's relationship not only to the earth, but also to Being itself. In effect, the distinction between these two man-made entities is elemental to the overall understanding of different epochs of Being. In one sense, the Windmill comes from an older or primordial period of Being whereby man merely sought to use the distinctive forces of nature in a more harmonious fashion when compared to the monstrosity that is the hydroelectric power plant. The construction and development of the hydroelectric power plant along the Rhine River brings about a series of revelations relating to the meaning of Being. Man has set about to challenge nature, and therefore, modern technology is the means and activity through which this challenge comes into existence. The following passage truly captures the heart of what Heidegger means by this challenge.

The hydroelectric plant is set into the current of the Rhine. It sets the Rhine to supplying its hydraulic pressure, which then sets the turbines turning. This turning sets those machines in motion whose thrust sets going the electric current for which the long-distance power station and its network of cables are set up to dispatch electricity. In the context of the interlocking processes pertaining to the orderly disposition of electrical energy, even the Rhine itself appears to be something at our command.

This passage essentially asserts that, although the meaning of Being appears to be more obscured as technology becomes increasingly complex, it is still there. One has to look a bit closer at the specific processes involved with modern machinery in order to capture a small piece of the essence of Being. So whenever a man switches on a light, he ought to recognize that the energy required to power the light is one distinct process with respect to the bringing-forth of Being. We, as human beings, have elementally, if not permanently, altered our relationship to Being through the advent of modern technological undertakings. And what's more is that there is nothing too technological about the true essence of technology, as Heidegger has shown that technology's ultimate essence resides in a rather poetic dwelling near the truth of Being.

The Role of Humans

Therein lies the crucial question of Heidegger's argument: what is the role of humans in enframing, in unconcealing and revealing the truth? Heidegger engages with this question for the remainder of the essay, for humanity's passive or active engagement with modern technology defines its "danger" or "saving power." "As the one who is challenged forth in this way, man stands with the essential realm of enframing" (329). Enframing is the putting-in-position of man to reveal the actual as original; if enframing is the essence of modern technology (328), then the essence of modern technology is this putting-in-position of man to reveal the actual as original and still present, if concealed.

Yet the role of humans is nevertheless limited. The truth exists outside of human work, and so he only "takes part in ordering as a way of revealing…the unconcealment itself, within which ordering unfolds, is never a human handiwork" (324). Put differently, "Does such revealing happen somewhere beyond all human doing? No. But neither does it happen exclusively in man, or definitively through man" (329). Enframing is "never human handiwork", does not happen "beyond all human doing", and yet does not happen "in man" or "through man" -- perhaps because of this ambiguity of human agency in enframing, Heidegger sees great potential for both danger and saving power in human engagement with modern technology. Indeed, it is so imperative because "man becomes truly free only insofar as he belongs to the realm of destining and so becomes one who listens, though not one who simply obeys (330). Humans are incarcerated because we do not know the origins; to find them, we must 'listen but not simply obey.' But freedom is only the means to the true aim, for "to occurrence of revealing, i.e. truth, freedom stands in the closest and most intimate kinship" (330).

Supreme Danger or Saving Power

Whether modern technology realizes its (or humans realize technology's) "supreme danger" or "saving power" seems to lie with humans ability to listen, reflect, and witness. The grave danger emerges from humans standing "so decisively in subservience to on [sic] the challenging-forth of enframing that he does not grasp enframing as a claim, that he fails to see himself as the one spoken to, and hence also fails in every way to hear in what respect he exists, in terms of his essence, in a realm where he is addressed, so that he can never encounter only himself" (332). For Heidegger, "enframing is a claim", as a declamation or a claim on land, and humans' inability or unwillingness to 'listen, but not obey' (330) to the challenging-forth of modern technology represents the greatest danger, for then the technology becomes determinant of its truth, rather than humans becoming cognizant of concealed truth.

Conversely, the key to realizing the "saving power" of modern technology lies in pondering, and witnessing, its "essential unfolding", the unfolding of its essence. Rather than becoming "transfixed in the will to master it [technology as instrument]" (337), "when … we ask how the instrumental unfolds essentially as a kind of causality, then we experience this essential unfolding as the destining of a revealing" (338). As Heidegger turns to the potential "saving power" of modern technology, his diction becomes admittedly "in a lofty sense ambiguous" – at the end of the essay, truth becomes a "constellation, the stellar course of the mystery" (338-339). Etymologically, in German konstellation finds kinship with the German for enframing, Gestell, suggesting their alignment. Imagistically, Heidegger conjures the night sky, innumerable points of light immeasurably distant from human perception; each point, if possible to challenge-forth, would lead towards "the growing light" (338) and the "shining forth" (339) of an individual star, immeasurably bright, with its own origin, Heidegger's "the earliest". Yet, we also know that many of the stars in the night sky of today have long since died, lost their source of light, suggesting that while pondering the essential unfolding of modern technology may escape danger, and may hold saving power, it may not lead us to ultimate truth.

Source (edited): "http://en.wikipedia.org/wiki/The_Question_Concerning_Technology"

Between Past and Future

Between Past and Future is book written by German philosopher Hannah Arendt. It was published for the first time in 1961 by The Viking Press in the United States and by Faber and Faber Ltd in Great Britain. The first edition consisted of six essays, and two more were added to a 1968 revision. The book is a collection of various essays written between 1954 and 1968. The final version of the book includes essays dealing with different philosophical subjects including freedom, education, authority, tradition, history and politics. The subtitle of the final version is *Eight exercises in political thought*.

All of the essays share a central idea" Humans are living between the past and the uncertain future. They must permanently think to exist, and each man is required to learn thinking. For a long time humans have resorted to tradition, but in modern times, this tradition has been abandoned, there is no more respect for tradition and culture. With her essays, Hannah Arendt tries to find solutions to help human think again today. According to her, there is no way to live again with tradition, and modern philosophy has not succeeded in helping humans to live correctly.

Preface

The title of the preface is *The Gap between Past and Future*. The first sentence of the preface is a citation of French poet and résistant René Char: "Notre héritage n'est précédé d'aucun testament," translated by Arendt herself as "our inheritance was left to us by no testament." For Arendt, this sentence perfectly illustrates the situation in which European peoples are left after the Second World War. It also illustrates the crisis in culture--the main subject of the sixth essay. Indeed, the absence of testament means the current breaking-off with tradition.

To characterize the way writers, men of letters and thinkers had lived the period of the French Résistance, Hannah Arendt speaks of a "treasure." Indeed René Char had stated during this period: "If I survive, I know that I have to break with the aroma of these essential years, silently reject my treasure." This treasure is the experience of freedom all intellectuals made during this unique period, when they left their traditional occupation, that is a life focused on their personal affairs and the quest of themselves. With the Resistance, these men had at last found themselves, they had discovered what is freedom. But with the Liberation, they had lost their treasure, in other words they had either to return to their past occupations or to be involved again in public life but defending ideologies and engaging themselves into endless polemics, which had nothing to do with the time of the Resistance movement.

The example of the French Resistance is one of the several historical experiences in which a treasure appears and then disappears. It was the case with the Revolutions of 1776 in the United States, 1789 in France or 1956 in Budapest. Although this treasure has no name, it was called public happiness in the United States in the eighteen century. Any time this treasure appeared, it did not remain, not because of historical events nor chance, "but because no tradition had foreseen its appearance," no tradition or no "testament" had been able to announce the coming and the reality of this treasure. Indeed tradition is what "selects and names, (...) hands down and preserves, (...) indicates where the treasures are and what their worth is."

Tradition and the Modern Age

According to Arendt, the origins of European philosophical thinking date back to Ancient Greece, with Aristotle and Plato. Plato had learned us that the truth was not present within the society and in public affairs, but in eternal ideas, as demonstrated in the allegory of the cave. On the contrary, Marx thought that the "truth is not outside the affairs of men and their common world but precisely in them." The end of Platonic and Aristotelean tradition of philosophy came with Marx, according to whom the philosopher had to turn away from philosophy in order to be involved in society and human affairs in order to change the world.

Marx's own attitude to the tradition of political thought was one of conscious rebellion. Crucial among [certain key statements containing his political philosophy] are the following: "Labor created man". "Violence is the midwife of every old society pregnant with a new one", hence: violence is the midwife of history. Finally, there is the famous last thesis on Feuerbach: "The philosophers have only interpreted the world differently; the point is, however, to change it", which, in the light of Marx's thought, one could render more adequately as: The philosophers have interpreted the world long enough; the time has come to change it. For this last statement is in fact only a variation of another: "You cannot *aufheben* philosophy without realizing it".

For Arendt, Marxist philosophy considers that man creates himself, that his humanity is the result of his own activity, and that what distinguishes man from animal is not reason but labor. Thus Marx challenges the traditional praise of reason. Moreover, for Marx violence is the leading force that determines human relations, while for the traditional thought it is the most disgraceful of human actions and the symbol of tyranny. To Marx, violence or rather the possession of the means of violence is the constituent element of all forms of government; the state is the instrument of the ruling class by means of which it oppresses and exploits, and the whole sphere of political action is characterized by the use of violence. The Marxian identification of violence with action implies another fundamental challenge of tradition.

Source (edited): "http://en.wikipedia.org/wiki/Between_Past_and_Future"

Croatian Journal of Philosophy

The *Croatian Journal of Philosophy* is a peer-reviewed academic journal of philosophy, publishing articles of diverse currents in English. The journal publishes three issues per year with the support of the Republic of Croatia's Ministry of Culture and the Ministry of Science, Education, and Sports. All issues are available in electronic format from the Central and Eastern European Online Library and the Philosophy Documentation Center.

Indexing

The *Croatian Journal of Philosophy* is abstracted and indexed in Article@INIST, Arts & Humanities Citation Index, International Bibliography of Book Reviews of Scholarly Literature (IBR), International Bibliography of Periodical Literature (IBZ), The Philosopher's Index, Philosophy Research Index, and the Répertoire bibliographique de la philosophie.

Source (edited): "http://en.wikipedia.org/wiki/Croatian_Journal_of_Philosophy"

Essays and Aphorisms on the Higher Man

Essays and Aphorisms on the Higher Man is the work of the American writer and philosopher, Emile Benoit (writer). The Foreword Clarion Review writes that "History has shown examples of man trying to pull himself out of his ignorant bliss and stagnancy, from the philosopher kings and Renaissance man to Nietzsche's Superman. A scant number of individuals have dared to become something more by the unremitting quest for knowledge gained from the arts, religion, philosophy, etc., and the implementation of this knowledge across the broad spectrum of their lives and the lives of others…[H]umanity can go beyond Kant, Hume, Nietzsche's Superman, and the selfishness of Sartre's existential humanism. In a sense, he or she can become a "higher man." Benoit writes, "The evolution of the species will be when man can incorporate and digest all of his religions and live wholly, honestly and peacefully with himself and others…when he accepts all the religions, arts, and sciences as expressions of human greatness; a time when even the truth will no longer be an eternal proposition but simply an expression of mankind's prominence at making the incomprehensible understood – if but only briefly." As Benoit writes in the preface of the book, his intention is "to inspire, rather than impose, to incite rather than allow man to settle into a comfortable repose, delighted with himself." The book has won critical acclaim from reviewers as well as New York Times bestselling authors. In a review from ForeWord (magazine) Lee Gordon writes: "With the brevity of Confucius, the beauty, depth, wit and wisdom of the poet Rumi, and his own succinct, lyrical language, Benoit writes about the human condition."

Source (edited): "http://en.wikipedia.org/wiki/Essays_and_Aphorisms_on_the_Higher_Man"

Thomas Aquinas

Thomas Aquinas, O.P. (/əˈkwaɪnəs/ *ə-kwy-nəs*; Aquino, 1225 – Fossanova, 7 March 1274), also **Thomas of Aquin** or **Aquino**, was an Italian Dominican priest of the Catholic Church, and an immensely influential philosopher and theologian in the tradition of scholasticism, known as **Doctor Angelicus**, **Doctor Communis**, or **Doctor Universalis**. "Aquinas" is not a surname (hereditary surnames were not then in common use in Europe), but is a Latin adjective meaning "of Aquino", his place of birth. He was the foremost classical proponent of natural theology, and the father of Thomism. His influence on Western thought is considerable, and much of modern philosophy was conceived as a reaction against, or as an agreement with his ideas, particularly in the areas of ethics, natural law and political theory.

Thomas is held in the Catholic Church to be the model teacher for those studying for the priesthood. The works for which he is best-known are the *Summa Theologica* and the *Summa Contra Gentiles*. As one of the 33 Doctors of the Church, he is considered the Church's greatest theologian and philosopher. Pope Benedict XV declared: "This (Dominican) Order ... acquired new luster when the Church declared the teaching of Thomas to be her own and that Doctor, honored with the special praises of the Pontiffs, the master and patron of Catholic schools."

Biography

Early years and desire to become a Dominican (1225–1240)

Thomas was born in Aquino c.January 28, 1225, according to some authors in his father's, the Count Landulf of Aquino, castle placed in Roccasecca, in the same Contea di Aquino (Kingdom of Sicily, in the present-day: Lazio). Through his mother, Theodora Countess of Theate, Thomas was related to the Hohenstaufen dynasty of Holy Roman emperors. Landulf's brother Sinibald was abbot of the original Benedictine abbey at Monte Cassino. While the rest of the family's sons pursued a military career, the family intended for Thomas to follow his uncle into the abbacy; this would have been a normal career path for a younger son of southern Italian nobility.

At the age of five, Thomas began his early education at Monte Cassino but after the military conflict that broke out between the Emperor Frederick II and Pope Gregory IX spilled into the abbey in early 1239, Landulf and Theodora had Thomas enrolled at the *studium generale* (university) recently established by Frederick in Naples. It was here that Thomas was probably introduced to Aristotle, Averroes and Maimonides, all of whom would influence his theological philosophy. It was also during his study at Naples that Thomas came under the influence of John of St. Julian, a Dominican preacher in Naples, who was part of the active effort by the Dominican order to recruit devout followers. Here his teacher in arithmetic, geometry, astronomy, and music was Petrus de Ibernia.

The Castle of Monte San Giovanni Campano

At age nineteen, Thomas resolved to join the Dominican Order. Thomas's change of heart did not please his family, who had expected him to become a Benedictine monk. In an attempt to prevent Theodora's interference in Thomas's choice, the Dominicans arranged for Thomas to be removed to Rome, and from Rome, sent to Paris. On his way to Rome, his brothers, per Theodora's instructions, seized him as he was drinking from a spring and took him back to his parents at the castle of Monte San Giovanni Campano. He was held for two years in the family homes at Monte San Giovanni and Roccasecca in an attempt to prevent him from assuming the Dominican habit and to push him into renouncing his new aspiration. Political concerns prevented the Pope from ordering Thomas's release, extending the detention, a detention which Thomas spent tutoring his sisters and communicating with members of the Dominican Order. Family members became desperate to dissuade Thomas, who remained determined to join the Dominicans. At one point, two of his brothers hired a prostitute to seduce him, but he drove her away, wielding a burning stick. According to legend, that night two angels appeared to him as he slept and strengthened his determination to remain celibate. By 1244, seeing that all of her attempts to dissuade Thomas had failed, Theodora sought to save the family's dignity, arranging for Thomas to escape at night through his window. In her mind, a secret escape from detention was less damaging than an open surrender to the Dominicans. Thomas was sent first to Naples and then to Rome to meet Johannes von Wildeshausen, the Master General of the Dominican Order.

Paris, Cologne, Albert Magnus, and first Paris regency (1245–1259)

In 1245, Thomas was sent to study at the University of Paris' Faculty of Arts where he most likely met Dominican scholar Albertus Magnus, then the Chair of Theology at the College of St. James in Paris. When Albertus was sent by his superiors to teach at the new *studium generale* at Cologne in 1248, Thomas followed him, declining Pope Innocent IV's offer to appoint him abbot of Monte Cassino as a Dominican. Albertus then appointed the reluctant Thomas *magister studentium*. When Thomas failed his first theological disputation, Albertus prophetically exclaimed: "We call him the dumb ox, but in his teaching he will one day produce such a bellowing that it will be heard throughout the world."

Thomas taught in Cologne as an apprentice professor (*baccalaureus biblicus*), instructing students on the books of the Old Testament and writing *Expositio super Isaiam ad litteram* (*Literal Commentary on Isaiah*), *Postilla super Ieremiam* (*Commentary on Jeremiah*) and *Postilla super Threnos* (*Commentary on Lamentations*). Then in 1252 he returned to Paris to study for the master's degree in theology. He lectured on the Bible as an apprentice professor, and upon becoming a *baccalaureus Sententiarum* (bachelor of the *Sentences*) devoted his final three years of study to commenting on Peter Lombard's *Sentences*. In the first of his four theological syntheses, Thomas composed a massive commentary on the *Sentences* entitled *Scriptum super libros Sententiarium* (*Commentary on the Sentences*). Aside from his masters writings, he wrote *De ente et essentia* (*On Being and Essence*) for his fellow Dominicans in Paris.

In the spring of 1256, Thomas was appointed regent master in theology at Paris and one of his first works upon assuming this office was *Contra impugnantes Dei cultum et religionem* (*Against Those Who Assail the Worship of God and Religion*), defending the mendicant orders which had come under attack by William of Saint-Amour. During his tenure from 1256 to 1259, Thomas wrote numerous works, including: *Questiones disputatae de veritate* (*Disputed Questions on Truth*), a collection of twenty-nine disputed questions on aspects of faith and the human condition prepared for the public university debates he presided over on Lent and Advent; *Quaestiones quodlibetales* (*Quodlibetal Questions*), a collection of his responses to questions posed to him by the academic audience; and both *Expositio super librum Boethii De trinitate* (*Commentary on Boethius's De trinitate*) and *Expositio super librum Boethii De hebdomadibus* (*Commentary on Boethius's De hebdomadibus*), commentaries on the works of 6th century philosopher Anicius Manlius Severinus Boethius. By the end of his regency, Thomas was working on one of his most famous works, *Summa contra Gentiles*.

Naples, Orvieto, Rome, and Santa Sabina (1259–1269)

Around 1259, Thomas returned to Naples where he lived until he arrived in Orvieto around September 1261. In Orvieto, he was appointed conventual lector, in charge of the education of friars unable to attend a *studium generale*. During his stay in Orvieto, Thomas completed his *Summa contra Gentiles*, and wrote the *Catena Aurea* (*The Golden Chain*). He also wrote the liturgy for the newly created feast of Corpus Christi and produced works for Pope Urban IV concerning Greek Orthodox theology, e.g. *Contra errores graecorum* (*Against the Errors of the Greeks*). In 1265 he was ordered by the Dominican Chapter of Agnani to establish a *studium* for the Order in Rome at the priory of Santa Sabina: "Fr. Thome de Aquino iniungimus in remissionem peccatorum quod teneat studium Rome, et volumus quod fratribus qui stant secum ad studendum provideatur in necessariis vestimentis a conventibus de quorum predicatione traxerunt originem. Si autem illi studentes inventi fuerint negligentes in studio, damus potestatem fr. Thome quod ad conventus suos possit eos remittere" (Acta Capitulorum Provincialium, Provinciae Romanae Ordinis Praedicatorum, 1265, n. 12). He remained there from 1265 until he was called back to Paris in 1268. It was in Rome that Thomas began his most famous work, *Summa Theologica*, and wrote a variety of other works like his unfinished *Compendium Theologiae* and *Responsio ad fr. Ioannem Vercellensem de articulis 108 sumptis ex opere Petri de Tarentasia* (*Reply to Brother John of Vercelli Regarding 108 Articles Drawn from the Work of Peter of Tarentaise*). In his position as head of the *studium*, conducted a series of important disputations on the power of God, which he compiled into his *De potentia*.

The quarrelsome second Paris regency (1269–1272)

In 1268 the Dominican Order assigned Thomas to be regent master at the University of Paris for a second time, a position he held until the spring of 1272. Part of the reason for this sudden reassignment appears to have arisen from the rise of "Averroism" or "radical Aristotelianism" in the universities. In response to these perceived evils, Thomas wrote two works, one of them being *De unitate intellectus, contra Averroistas* (*On the Unity of Intellect, against the Averroists*) in which he blasts Averroism as incompatible with Christian doctrine. During his second regency, he finished the second part of the *Summa* and wrote *De virtutibus* and *De aeternitate mundi*, the latter of which dealt with controversial Averroist and Aristotelian *beginninglessness* of the world. Disputes with some important Franciscans such as Bonaventure and John Peckham conspired to make his second regency much more difficult and troubled than the first. A year before Thomas re-assumed the regency at the 1266–67 Paris disputations, Franciscan master William of Baglione accused Thomas of encouraging Averroists, calling him the "blind leader of the blind". Thomas called these individuals the *murmurantes* (Grumblers). In reality, Thomas was deeply disturbed by the spread of Averroism and was angered when he discovered Siger of Brabant teaching Averroistic interpretations of Aristotle to Parisian students. On 10 December 1270, the bishop of Paris, Etienne Tempier, issued an edict condemning thirteen Aristotlelian and Averroistic propositions as heretical and excommunicating anyone who continued to support them. Many in the ecclesiastical community, the so-called Augustinians, were fearful that this introduction of Aristotelianism and the more extreme Averroism might somehow contaminate the purity of the Christian faith. In what appears to be an attempt to counteract the growing fear of Aristotelian thought, Thomas conducted a series of disputations between 1270 and 1272: *De virtutibus in communi* (*On Virtues in General*), *De virtutibus cardinalibus* (*On Cardinal Virtues*), *De spe* (*On Hope*).

Final days and "Straw" (1272–1274)

In 1272 Thomas took leave from the University of Paris when the Dominicans from his home province called upon him to establish a *studium generale* wherever he liked and staff it as he pleased. He chose to establish the institution in Naples, and moved there to take his post as regent master. He took his time at Naples to work on the third part of the *Summa* while giving lectures on various religious topics. On 6 December 1273 Thomas was celebrating the Mass of St. Nicholas when, according to some, he heard Christ speak to him. Christ asked him what he desired, being pleased with his meritorious life. Thomas replied "Only you Lord. Only you." After this exchange something happened, but Thomas never spoke of it or wrote it down. Because of what he saw, he abandoned his routine and refused to dictate to his *socius* Reginald of Piperno. When Reginald begged him to get back to work, Thomas replied: "Reginald, I cannot, because all that I have written seems like straw to me." (*mihi videtur ut palea*). What exactly triggered Thomas's change in behavior is believed to be some kind of supernatural experience of God. After taking to his bed, he did recover some strength.

Looking to find a way to reunite the Eastern Orthodox churches with the Catholic Church (the Eastern Orthodox had parted ways with the Catholic Church in A.D. 1054 over doctrinal disputes) Pope Gregory X convened the Second Council of Lyon to be held on 1 May 1274 and summoned Thomas to attend. At the meeting, Thomas's work for Pope Urban IV concerning the Greeks, *Contra errores graecorum*, was to be presented. On his way to the Council, riding on a donkey along the Appian Way, he struck his head on the branch of a fallen tree and became seriously ill again. He was then quickly escorted to Monte Cassino to convalesce. After resting for a while, he set out again, but stopped at the Cistercian Fossanova Abbey after again falling ill. The monks nursed him for several days, and as he received his last rites he prayed: "I receive Thee, ransom of my soul. For love of Thee have I studied and kept vigil, toiled, preached and taught..." He died on 7 March 1274 while giving commentary on the Song of Songs.

Condemnation of 1277

In 1277, the same bishop of France, Etienne Tempier, who had issued the condemnation of 1270 issued another, more extensive condemnation. One aim of this condemnation was to clarify that God's absolute power transcended any principles of logic that Aristotle or Averroes might place on it. More specifically, it contained a list of 219 propositions that the bishop had determined to violate the omnipotence of God, and included in this list were twenty Thomistic propositions. Their inclusion badly damaged Thomas's reputation for many years.

In *The Divine Comedy*, Dante sees the glorified spirit of Thomas in the Heaven of the Sun with the other great exemplars of religious wisdom. Dante asserts that Thomas died by poisoning, on the order of Charles of Anjou; Villani (ix. 218) cites this belief, and the *Anonimo Fiorentino* describes the crime and its motive. But the historian Ludovico Antonio Muratori reproduces the account made by one of Thomas's friends, and this version of the story gives no hint of foul play.

Thomas's theology had begun its rise to prestige. Two centuries later, in 1567, Pope Pius V proclaimed St. Thomas Aquinas a Doctor of the Church and ranked his feast with those of the four great Latin fathers: Ambrose, Augustine of Hippo, Jerome, and Gregory. However, in the same period the Council of Trent would still turn to Duns Scotus before Thomas as a source of arguments in defence of the Church. Even though Duns Scotus was more consulted at the Council of Trent, Thomas had the honor of having his *Summa Theologica* placed on the altar alongside the Bible and the Decretals.

In his encyclical of 4 August 1879, Pope Leo XIII stated that Thomas's theology was a definitive exposition of Catholic doctrine. Thus, he directed the clergy to take the teachings of Thomas as the basis of their theological positions. Leo XIII also decreed that all Catholic seminaries and universities must teach Thomas's doctrines, and where Thomas did not speak on a topic, the teachers were "urged to teach conclusions that were reconcilable with his thinking." In 1880, Saint Thomas Aquinas was declared patron of all Catholic educational establishments.

Canonization

When the devil's advocate at his canonization process objected that there were no miracles, one of the cardinals answered, "*Tot miraculis, quot articulis*"—"there are as many miracles (in his life) as articles (in his *Summa*)," viz., thousands. Fifty years after the death of Thomas, Pope John XXII, seated in Avignon, pronounced Thomas a saint.

In a monastery at Naples, near the cathedral of St. Januarius, a cell in which he supposedly lived is still shown to visitors. His remains were placed in the Church of the Jacobins in Toulouse in 1369. Between 1789 and 1974, they were held in Basilique de Saint-Sernin, Toulouse. In 1974, they were returned to the Church of the Jacobins, where they have remained ever since.

In the General Roman Calendar of 1962, in the Roman Catholic Church, Thomas was commemorated on 7 March, the day of death. However, in the General Roman Calendar of 1969, even though the norm in the Roman Catholic Church is to remember saints on the day of their death, Thomas's memorial was transferred to 28 January, the date of the translation of his relics to Toulouse.

Saint Thomas Aquinas is honored with a feast day on the liturgical of the Episcopal Church in the United States of America on January 28.

Thomas was a theologian and a Scholastic philosopher. He had such respect for Aristotle that in the *Summa*, he often cites Aristotle simply as "the Philosopher." Much of his work bears upon philosophical topics, and in this sense may be characterized as philosophical. Thomas's philosophical thought has exerted enormous influence on subsequent Christian theology, especially that of the Roman Catholic Church, extending to Western philosophy in general. Thomas stands as a vehicle and modifier of Aristotelianism and Neoplatonism.

Commentaries on Aristotle

Thomas wrote several important commentaries on Aristotle, including On the Soul, Nicomachean Ethics and Metaphysics. His work is associated with William of Moerbeke's translations of Aristotle from Greek into Latin.

Epistemology

Thomas believed "that for the knowledge of any truth whatsoever man needs divine help, that the intellect may be moved by God to its act." However, he believed that human beings have the natural capacity to know many things without special divine revelation, even though such revelation occurs from time to time, "especially in regard to such (truths) as pertain to faith."

Revelation

Thomas believed that truth is known through reason (natural revelation) and faith (supernatural revelation). *Supernatural* revelation has its origin in the inspiration of the Holy Spirit and is made available through the teaching of the prophets, summed up in Holy Scripture, and transmitted by the Magisterium, the sum of which is called "Tradition". *Natural* revelation is the truth available to all people through their human nature; certain truths all men can attain from correct human reasoning. For example, he felt this applied to rational ways to know the existence of God.

Though one may deduce the existence of God and his Attributes (One, Truth, Good, Power, Knowledge) through reason, certain specifics may be known only through special revelation (such as the Trinity). In Thomas's view, special revelation is equivalent to the revelation of God in Jesus Christ. The major theological components of Christianity, such as the Trinity and the Incarnation, are revealed in the teachings of the Church and the Scriptures and may not otherwise be deduced.

Supernatural revelation (faith) and natural revelation (reason) are complementary rather than contradictory in nature, for they pertain to the same unity: truth.

Creation

As a Catholic, Thomas believed that God is the "maker of heaven and earth, of all that is visible and invisible." Like Aristotle, Thomas posited that life could form from non-living material or plant life, a theory of ongoing abiogenesis known as spontaneous generation:
Since the generation of one thing is the corruption of another, it was not incompatible with the first formation of things, that from the corruption of the less perfect the more perfect should be generated. Hence animals generated from the corruption of inanimate things, or of plants, may have been generated then.
Additionally, Thomas considered Empedocles' theory that various mutated species emerged at the dawn of Creation. Thomas reasoned that these species were generated through mutations in animal sperm, and argued that they were not unintended by nature; rather, such species were simply not intended for perpetual existence. This discussion is found in his commentary on Aristotle's Physics:
The same thing is true of those substances which Empedocles said were produced at the beginning of the world, such as the 'ox-progeny', i.e., half ox and half man. For if such things were not able to arrive at some end and final state of nature so that they would be preserved in existence, this was not because nature did not intend this [a final state], but because they were not capable of being preserved. For they were not generated according to nature, but by the corruption of some natural principle, as it now also happens that some monstrous offspring are generated because of the corruption of seed.

Ethics

Thomas's ethics are based on the concept of "first principles of action." In his *Summa Theologica*, he wrote:
Virtue denotes a certain perfection of a power. Now a thing's perfection is considered chiefly in regard to its end. But the end of power is act. Wherefore power is said to be perfect, according as it is determinate to its act.
Thomas defined the four cardinal virtues as prudence, temperance, justice, and fortitude. The cardinal virtues are natural and revealed in nature, and they are binding on everyone. There are, however, three theological virtues: faith, hope, and charity. These are supernatural and are distinct from other virtues in their object, namely, God:
Now the object of the theological virtues is God Himself, Who is the last end of all, as surpassing the knowledge of our reason. On the other hand, the object of the intellectual and moral virtues is something comprehensible to human reason. Wherefore the theological virtues are specifically distinct from the moral and intellectual virtues.
Furthermore, Thomas distinguished four kinds of law: eternal, natural, human, and divine. *Divine law* is the decree of God that governs all creation. *Natural law* is the human "participation" in the *eternal law* and is discovered by reason. *Natural law*, of course, is based on "first principles":
. . . this is the first precept of the law, that good is to be done and promoted, and evil is to be avoided. All other precepts of the natural law are based on this . . .
The desires to live and to procreate are counted by Thomas among those basic (natural) human values on which all human values are based. However, Thomas condemned non-procreative sexual activity. This lead him to view masturbation, oral sex, and even coitus interruptus, as being worse than incest and rape when the act itself is considered (apart from the abuse suffered by the violated party). He also objected to sexual positions other than the missionary position, on the assumption that they made conception more difficult.

Human law is positive law: the natural law applied by governments to societies. Divine law is the specially revealed law in the scriptures.

Thomas also greatly influenced Catholic understandings of mortal and venial sins.

Thomas denied that human beings have any duty of charity to animals because they are not persons. Otherwise, it would be unlawful to use them for food. But this does not give us license to be cruel to them, for "cruel habits might carry over into our treatment of human beings."

Thomas contributed to economic thought as an aspect of ethics and justice. He dealt with the concept of a just price, normally its market price or a regulated price sufficient to cover seller costs of production. He argued it was immoral for sellers to raise their prices simply because buyers were in pressing need for a product.

Intentionality

The pioneer of neurodynamics, cognitive neuroscientist Walter Freeman, considers the work of Thomas important in remodeling intentionality, the directedness of the mind toward what it is aware of.

Psychology

Aquinas maintains that a human is a single material substance. He understands the soul as the form of the body, which makes a human being the composite of the two. Thus, only living, form-matter composites can truly be called human; dead bodies are "human" only analogously. One actually existing substance comes from body and soul. A human is a single material substance, but still should be understood as having an immaterial soul, which continues after bodily death.

Ultimately, humans are animals; the animal genus is body; body is material substance. When embodied, a human person is an "individual substance in the category rational animal." The body belongs to the essence of a human being. In his *Summa Theologica*, Aquinas clearly states his position on the nature of the soul; defining it as "the first principle of life." The soul is not corporeal, or a body; it is the act of a body. Because the intellect is incorporeal, it does not use the bodily organs, as "the operation of anything follows the mode of its being."

The human soul is perfected in the body, but does not depend on the body, because part of its nature is spiritual. The body-soul composite has matter and spirit. In this way, the soul differs from other forms, which are only found in matter, and thus depend on matter. Typically, matter exists only through form (by being organized by it), but the soul, as form of the body, does not depend on matter in this way. This is all thanks to the dual nature of humanity, which bridges the spiritual and material worlds.

The soul is not matter, not even incorporeal or spiritual matter. If it were, it would not be able to understand universals, which are immaterial. A receiver receives things according to the receiver's own nature, so in order for soul (receiver) to understand (receive) universals, it must have the same nature as universals. Yet, any substance that understands universals may not be a matter-form composite. So, humans have intellectual souls which are abstract forms of the body and a human is one existing, single material substance (which comes from body and soul). This conclusion entails that the soul is the body's form; that is, "something one in nature can be formed from an intellectual substance and a body," and "a thing one in nature does not result from two permanent entities unless one has the character of substantial form and the other of matter."

The soul as form can be understood when one compares Aquinas' definition of matter (that which of itself exists incompletely), with his definition of form (that which gives existence to matter). An item is matter if it is changeable and can become different than it is; matter is always potentially something else. For example, bronze matter is potentially a statue, or also potentially a cymbal. When Aquinas says the body is of matter, it means the material body is only potentially a human being (without the intellectual soul). Matter must be understood as the matter of something. The form of something is that whose presence in some matter is that matter's being that thing. For matter to be the thing, some form of the thing must be present in it. Consequently, a human's matter's being live human tissue consists in a human soul's being wholly present in each part of the human. The soul is a substantial form; it is a part of a substance, but it is not a substance itself. The soul exists separately from the body, and continues, after death, in many of the capacities we think of as human. Substantial form is what makes a thing a member of the species to which it belongs, and substantial form is also the structure or configuration that provides the object with the abilities that make the object what it is. For humans, those abilities are those of the rational animal.

Theology

17th century sculpture of Thomas Aquinas

Thomas viewed theology, or the *sacred doctrine*, as a science, the raw material data of which consists of written scripture and the tradition of the Catholic Church. These sources of data were produced by the self-revelation of God to individuals and groups of people throughout history. Faith and reason, while distinct but related, are the two primary tools for processing the data of theology. Thomas believed both were necessary — or, rather, that the *confluence* of both was necessary — for one to obtain true knowledge of God. Thomas blended Greek philosophy and Christian doctrine by suggesting that rational thinking and the study of nature, like revelation, were valid ways to understand truths pertaining to God. According to Thomas, God reveals himself through nature, so to study nature is to study God. The ultimate goals of theology, in Thomas's mind, are to use reason to grasp the truth about God and to experience salvation through that truth.

Nature of God

Thomas believed that the existence of God is neither obvious nor improvable. In the *Summa Theologica*, he considered in great detail five reasons for the existence of God. These are widely known as the *quinque viae*, or the "Five Ways."

Concerning the nature of God, Thomas felt the best approach, commonly called the *via negativa*, is to consider what God is not. This led him to propose five statements about the divine qualities:

1. God is simple, without composition of parts, such as body and soul, or matter and form.
2. God is perfect, lacking nothing. That is, God is distinguished from other beings on account of God's complete actuality. Thomas defined God as the '*Ipse Actus Essendi subsistens*,' subsisting act of being.
3. God is infinite. That is, God is not finite in the ways that created beings are physically, intellectually, and emotionally limited. This infinity is to be distinguished from infinity of size and infinity of number.
4. God is immutable, incapable of change on the levels of God's essence and character.
5. God is one, without diversification within God's self. The unity of God is such that God's essence is the same as God's existence. In Thomas's words, "in itself the proposition 'God exists' is necessarily true, for in it subject and predicate are the same."

In this approach, he is following, among others, the Jewish philosopher Maimonides.

Following St. Augustine of Hippo, Thomas defines sin as "a word, deed, or desire, contrary to the eternal law." It is important to note the analogous nature of law in Thomas's legal philosophy. Natural law is an instance or instantiation of eternal law. Because natural law is that which human beings determine according to their own nature (as rational beings), disobeying reason is disobeying natural law and eternal law. Thus eternal law is logically prior to reception of either "natural law" (that determined by reason) or "divine law" (that found in the Old and New Testaments). In other words, God's will extends to both reason and revelation. Sin is abrogating either one's own reason, on the one hand, or revelation on the other, and is synonymous with "evil" (privation of good, or *privatio boni*). Thomas, like all Scholastics, generally argued that the findings of reason and data of revelation cannot conflict, so both are a guide to God's will for human beings.

Nature of the Trinity

Thomas argued that God, while perfectly united, also is perfectly described by Three Interrelated Persons. These three persons (Father, Son, and Holy Spirit) are constituted by their relations within the essence of God. The Father generates the Son (or the Word) by the relation of self-awareness. This eternal generation then produces an eternal Spirit "who enjoys the divine nature as the Love of God, the Love of the Father for the Word."

This Trinity exists independently from the world. It transcends the created world, but the Trinity also decided to communicate God's self and God's goodness to human beings. This takes place through the Incarnation of the Word in the person of Jesus Christ and through the indwelling of the Holy Spirit (indeed, the very essence of the Trinity itself) within those who have experienced salvation by God.

Prima causa – first cause

Thomas's five proofs for the existence of God take some of Aristotle's assertions concerning principles of being. For Thomas, God as prima causa (first cause) comes from Aristotle's concept of the unmoved mover and asserts that God is the ultimate cause of all things.

Nature of Jesus Christ

In the *Summa Theologica*, Thomas begins his discussion of Jesus Christ by recounting the biblical story of Adam and Eve and by describing the negative effects of original sin. The purpose of Christ's Incarnation was to restore human nature by removing "the contamination of sin", which humans cannot do by themselves. "Divine Wisdom judged it fitting that God should become man, so that thus one and the same person would be able both to restore man and to offer satisfaction." Thomas argued in favor of the satisfaction view of atonement; that is, that Jesus Christ died "to satisfy for the whole human race, which was sentenced to die on account of sin."

Thomas argued against several specific contemporary and historical theologians who held differing views about Christ. In response to Photinus, Thomas stated that Jesus was truly divine and not simply a human being. Against Nestorius, who suggested that Son of God was merely conjoined to the man Christ, Thomas argued that the fullness of God was an integral part of Christ's existence. However, countering Apollinaris' views, Thomas held that Christ had a truly human (rational) soul, as well. This produced a duality of natures in Christ. Thomas argued against Eutyches that this duality persisted after the Incarnation. Thomas stated that these two natures existed simultaneously yet distinguishably in one real human body, unlike the teachings of Manichaeus and Valentinus.

In short, "Christ had a *real body* of the same nature of ours, a *true rational soul*, and, together with these, *perfect Deity*." Thus, there is both unity (in his one *hypostasis*) and diversity (in his two natures, human and Divine) in Christ.

Echoing Athanasius of Alexandria, he said that "The only begotten Son of God...assumed our nature, so that he, made man, might make men gods."

Goal of human life

In Thomas's thought, the goal of human existence is union and eternal fellowship with God. Specifically, this goal is achieved through the beatific vision, an event in which a person experiences perfect, unending happiness by seeing the very essence of God. This vision, which occurs after death, is a gift from God given to those who have experienced salvation and redemption through Christ while living on earth.

This ultimate goal carries implications for one's present life on earth. Thomas stated that an individual's will must be ordered toward right things, such as charity, peace, and holiness. He sees this as the way to happiness. Thomas orders his treatment of the moral life around the idea of happiness. The relationship between will and goal is antecedent in nature "because rectitude of the will consists in being duly ordered to the last end [that is, the beatific vision]." Those who truly seek to understand and see God will necessarily love what God loves. Such love requires morality and bears fruit in everyday human choices.

Treatment of heretics

Thomas Aquinas belonged to the Dominican Order (formally *Ordo Praedicatorum*, the Order of Preachers) who attempted the peaceful conversion of the Albigensian heretics. In the *Summa Theologica*, he wrote:

With regard to heretics two points must be observed: one, on their own side; the other, on the side of the Church. On their own side there is the sin, whereby they deserve not only to be separated from the Church by excommunication, but also to be severed from the world by death. For it is a much graver matter to corrupt the faith which quickens the soul, than to forge money, which supports temporal life. Wherefore if forgers of money and other evil-doers are forthwith condemned to death by the secular authority, much more reason is there for heretics, as soon as they are convicted of heresy, to be not only excommunicated but even put to death. On the part of the Church, however, there is mercy which looks to the conversion of the wanderer, wherefore she condemns not at once, but "after the first and second admonition," as the Apostle directs: after that, if he is yet stubborn, the Church no longer hoping for his conversion, looks to the salvation of others, by excommunicating him and separating him from the Church, and furthermore delivers him to the secular tribunal to be exterminated thereby from the world by death.(*Summa*, II–II, Q.11, art.3.)

Heresy was a capital offense against the secular law of most European countries of the 13th century. Thomas's suggestion specifically demands that heretics be handed to a "secular tribunal" rather than magisterial authority. That Thomas specifically says that heretics "deserve... death" is concerning his theology, where all sinners do not deserve life ("For the wages of sin is death; but the free gift of God is eternal life in Christ Jesus our Lord"). He elaborates on his opinion regarding heresy in the next article, when he says:

In God's tribunal, those who return are always received, because God is a searcher of hearts, and knows those who return in sincerity. But the Church cannot imitate God in this, for she presumes that those who relapse after being once received, are not sincere in their return; hence she does not debar them from the way of salvation, but neither does she protect them from the sentence of death. (*Summa*, op. cit., art.4.)

The afterlife and resurrection

A grasp of Aquinas's psychology is essential for understanding his beliefs around the afterlife and resurrection. Thomas, following Church doctrine, accepts that the soul continues to exist after the death of the body. Because he accepts that the soul is the form of the body, then he also must believe that the human being, like all material things, is form-matter composite. Substantial form (the human soul) configures prime matter (the physical body) and is the form by which a material composite belongs to that species it does; in the case of human beings, that species is rational animal. So, a human being is a matter-form composite that is organized to be a rational animal. Matter cannot exist without being configured by form, but form can exist without matter—which allows for the separation of soul from body. Aquinas says that the soul shares in the material and spiritual worlds, and so has some features of matter and other, immaterial, features (such as access to universals). The human soul is different from other material and spiritual things; it is created by God, but also only comes into existence in the material body.

Human beings are material, but the human person can survive the death of the body through continued existence of the soul, which persists. The human soul straddles the spiritual and material worlds, and is both a configured subsistent form as well as a configurer of matter into that of a living, bodily human. Because it is spiritual, the human soul does not depend on matter and may exist separately. Because the human being is a soul-matter composite, the body has a part in what it is to be human. Perfected human nature consists in the human dual nature, embodied and intellecting.

Resurrection appears to require dualism, which Thomas rejects. Yet, Aquinas believes the soul persists after the death and corruption of the body, and is capable of existence, separated from the body between the time of death and the resurrection. Aquinas believes in a different sort of dualism, one guided by Christian scripture. Aquinas knows that human beings are essentially physical, but that that physicality has a spirit capable of returning to God after life. For Aquinas, the rewards and punishment of the afterlife are not *only* spiritual. Because of this, resurrection is an important part of his philosophy on the soul. The human is fulfilled and complete in the body, so the hereafter must take place with souls enmattered in resurrected bodies. In addition to spiritual reward, humans can expect to enjoy material and physical blessings. Because Aquinas's soul requires a body for its actions, during the afterlife, the soul will also be punished or rewarded in corporeal existence.

Aquinas states clearly his stance on resurrection, and uses it to back up his philosophy of justice; that is, the promise of resurrection compensates Christians who suffered in this world through a heavenly union with the divine. He says, "If there is no resurrection of the dead, it follows that there is no good for human beings other than in this life." Resurrection provides the impetus for people on earth to give up pleasures in this life. Thomas believes the human who has prepared for the afterlife both morally and intellectually will be rewarded more greatly; however, all reward is through the grace of God. Aquinas insists beatitude will be conferred according to merit, and will render the person better able to conceive the divine. Aquinas accordingly believes punishment is directly related to earthly, living preparation and activity as well. Aquinas's account of the soul focuses on epistemology and metaphysics, and because of this he believes it gives a clear account of the immaterial nature of the soul. Aquinas conservatively guards Christian doctrine, and thus maintains physical and spiritual reward and punishment after death. By accepting the essentiality of both body and soul, he allows for a heaven and hell described in scripture and church dogma.

Modern influence

Many modern ethicists both within and outside the Catholic Church (notably Philippa Foot and Alasdair MacIntyre) have recently commented on the possible use of Thomas's virtue ethics as a way of avoiding utilitarianism or Kantian "sense of duty" (called deontology). Through the work of twentieth century philosophers such as Elizabeth Anscombe (especially in her book *Intention*), Thomas's principle of double effect specifically and his theory of intentional activity generally have been influential.

In recent years, the cognitive neuroscientist Walter Freeman proposes that Thomism is the philosophical system explaining cognition that is most compatible with neurodynamics, in a 2008 article in the journal *Mind and Matter* entitled "Nonlinear Brain Dynamics and Intention According to Aquinas."

Thomas's aesthetic theories, especially the concept of *claritas*, deeply influenced the literary practice of modernist writer James Joyce, who used to extol Thomas as being second only to Aristotle among Western philosophers. The influence of Thomas's aesthetics also can be found in the works of the Italian semiotician Umberto Eco, who wrote an essay on aesthetic ideas in Thomas (published in 1956 and republished in 1988 in a revised edition).

Claims of levitation

For centuries, there have been recurring claims that Thomas had the ability to levitate. For example, G. K. Chesterton wrote that, "His experiences included well-attested cases of levitation in ecstasy; and the Blessed Virgin appeared to him, comforting him with the welcome news that he would never be a Bishop."

Source (edited): "http://en.wikipedia.org/wiki/Thomas_Aquinas"

Inquiry: An Interdisciplinary Journal of Philosophy

Inquiry: An Interdisciplinary Journal of Philosophy is a peer-reviewed academic journal of philosophy published bimonthly by Routledge. It was established in 1958 by Ingemund Gullvåg and Jacob Meløe in the spirit of Arne Naess and the so-called Oslo school in Norwegian philosophy and covers all areas of philosophy.

Abstracting and indexing

Inquiry is abstracted and indexed in Arts and Humanities Citation Index, Current Contents/Arts & Humanities, Humanities Index, International Bibliography of the Social Sciences, Philosopher's Index, Social Sciences Citation Index, and Sociological Abstracts.

Source (edited): "http://en.wikipedia.org/wiki/Inquiry:_An_Interdisciplinary_Journal_of_Philosophy"

Jürgen Habermas bibliography

Habermas during a discussion in the Munich School of Philosophy 2008

The works of the German sociologist and philosopher **Jürgen Habermas** (born June 18, 1929) includes books, papers, contributions to journals, periodicals, newspapers, lectures given at conferences and seminars, reviews of works by other authors, and dialogues and speeches given in various occasions. Working in the tradition of critical theory and pragmatism. Habermas is perhaps best known for his theory on the concepts of 'communicative rationality' and the 'public sphere'. His work focuses on the foundations of social theory and epistemology, the analysis of advanced capitalistic societies and democracy, the rule of law in a critical social-evolutionary context, and contemporary politics—particularly German politics. Habermas's theoretical system is devoted to revealing the possibility of reason, emancipation, and rational-critical communication latent in modern institutions and in the human capacity to deliberate and pursue rational interests.

This list is primarily based on *Mapping Habermas from German to English: A Bibliography of Primary Literature 1952-1995* edited by Demetrios Douramanis, *Jürgen Habermas: A Bibliography* by René Görtzen, and Luca Corchia's *Jürgen Habermas. A Bibliography: Works and Studies (1952-2010)*, a bibliography based on direct consultation of the original editions and their translations, with their internal references; as well as research carried out by other scholars.

The catalog of Habermas production includes books, collections, interviews, prefaces to later editions of his own books, papers, contributions to journals, periodicals, newspapers, lectures given at conferences and seminars, reviews of works by other authors, dialogues and speeches given in various occasions.

Furthermore, Habermas' publications are often collections of writings which have been taken and reordered chronologically in this bibliography. The chronology is determined by the publication dates of Habermas's German language books. Articles that do not appear in these books are included as works in their own right. Insofar as most of the writings collected in Habermas's books find their origin in journals, newspapers, edited books and magazines, or were delivered as lectures or discussion and occasional papers, information on their origin is given in the footnotes.

- —. *Zur Logik der Sozialwissenschaften*, in *Philosophische Rundschau* 14, No.5 (February), Tübingen, Mohr, 1967, **LSW**. Expanded edition 1970 and 1982. Frankfurt am Main: Suhrkamp Verlag
- —. *Technik und Wissenschaft als 'Ideologie'*. Frankfurt am Main: Suhrkamp Verlag, 1968, **TWI**.
- —. *Erkenntnis und Interesse*. Frankfurt am Main: Suhrkamp Verlag, 1968, **EI**. (With a New Postscript) 1973.

Works

1952

- —. *Gottfried Benns neue Stimme*, in *Frankfurter Allgemeine Zeitung*, 19.6.1952, p. 6.
- —. *Im Lichte Heideggers*, in *Frankfurter Allgemeine Zeitung*, 12.7.1952, p. 12.
- —. *Wider den moralpädagogischen Hochmut der Kulturkritik*, in *Die Literatur*, 13, 15.9.1952, p. 6.
- —. *Des Hörspiels Mangel ist seine Chance*, in *Frankfurter Allgemeine Zeitung*, 15.9.1952, p. 4.
- —. *Die akustische Bühne. Hörspielnotizen zu Adamov, Dürrenmatt und Huber*, in *Frankfurter Allgemeine Zeitung*, 27.11.1952, p. 4.

1953

- —. *Der musikalische Stil des Films. Ein Vortrag und zwei Filme von Jean Mitry*, in *Frankfurter Allgemeine Zeitung*, 19.1.1953, p. 4.
- —. *Die Ironie der Holz und Gipsköpfe. Bei Gelegenheit des Internationalen Puppenspielzyklus in Bonn*, in *Frankfurter Allgemeine Zeitung*, 29.1.1953, p. 6.
- —. *Der Moloch und die Künste. Gedanken zur Entlarvung der Legende von der technischen Zweckmäßigkeit*, in *Frankfurter Allgemeine Zeitung*, 30.5.1953.
- —. *Die farbigen Schatten aus Szetschuan. Notizen zum zweiten Bonner Puppenspielzyklus*, Puppenspielzyklus in *Frankfurter Allgemeine Zeitung*, 14.7.1953, p. 8.
- —. *Mit Heidegger gegen Heidegger denken. Zur Veröffentlichung von Vorlesungen aus dem Jahre 1935*, *Frankfurter Allgemeine Zeitung*, 25.7.1953, published as *Martin Heidegger: Zur Veröffentlichung von Vorlesungen aus dem Jahre 1935* in J. Habermas, *Philosophisch-politische Profile (PPP)* Frankfurt am Main: Suhrkamp Verlag, 1971, revised 1981, pp. 67-75.

Notes and references

Notes
References
Bibliography
Source (edited): "http://en.wikipedia.org/wiki/J%C3%BCrgen_Habermas_bibliography"

Laughter (Bergson)

Laughter is the title of a collection of three essays written by French philosopher Henri Bergson, first published in 1900. It was written in French, the original title is *Le Rire. Essai sur la signification du comique* ("Laughter, an essay on the meaning of the comic").

Publication

The three essays were first published in the French review *Revue de Paris*. A book was published in 1924 by the Alcan publishing house. It was reprinted in 1959 by the Presses Universitaires de France, on the occasion of the hundredth anniversary of the birth of Bergson.

In a foreword published in 1900, but suppressed in 1924, Bergson explains that through the three articles, he wanted to study the laughter, especially the laughter caused by comic, and to determine the principal categories of comic situations, to determine the laws of comic. He also added a list of works and studies about laughter and comic.

In the preface written in 1924 to replace the initial foreword, Bergson explains that his method is entirely new because it consists in determining the process of comic instead of analyzing the effects of comic. He specifies that his method does not contradict the results of the other one, but he assumes that it is more rigorous from a scientific point of view. He adds a larger bibliography.

First essay

The first essay is made up of three parts:
1. *Du comique en général* (Of comic in general)
2. *Le comique des formes et le comique des mouvements* (Comic of forms and comic of movements)
3. *Force d'expansion du comique* (Force of expansion of comic)

In a short introduction, Bergson announces that he will try to determine what is comic, but he does not want to give a rigid definition of the word, he wants to deal with comic as part of human life. His ambition is also to have a better knowledge of society, of the functioning of human imagination and of collective imagination, but also of art and life.

General facts on comic

Bergson begins to note three facts on comic:
- comic is strictly a human phenomenon. A landscape cannot be

a source of laughter, and when humans make fun of animals, it is often because they recognize some human behaviour in them. Man is not only a being that can laugh, but also a being that is a source of laughter.
- laughter requires an indifference, a detachment from sensibility and emotion: it is more difficult to laugh when one is fully aware of the seriousness of a situation.
- it is difficult to laugh alone, it is easier to laugh collectively. One who is excluded from a group of people does not laugh with them, there is often a complicity in laughter. Thus comic is not a mere pleasure of the intellect, it is a human and social activity, it has a social meaning.

The social role of laughter

Bergson now assumes that comic requires the use of intelligence instead of sensibility, and he tries to determine what is the real role of intelligence in a comic situation. He takes the example of a man falling down in the street in front of passers-by. Laughter is caused by an accidental situation, caused by a movement. The source of comic is the presence of a rigidity in life. Life is defined by Bergson a perpetual movement, it is characterized by flexibility and agility. Comic situations, such as that of a falling man, are situations where movement is not flexible.

However, comic is not only based upon unusual situations, but also upon characters and individuals. Bergson takes the example of absent-minded people, a common source of comic. People tend to associate individuals with a comic character, which increases comic. In addition, when we make fun of somebody for one of his vices, it is because the individual is unaware of his own vice while we are aware of it. Thus laughter forces people to be better and to suppress their vices, because laughter makes them be conscious of them. This is why Bergson asserts that laughter has a moral role, it is a factor of uniformity of behaviours, it eliminates ludicrous and eccentric attitudes : « Beyond actions and attitudes that are automatically punished by their natural consequences, there remains a certain inflexibility of the body, of the mind and of the character that society would like to eliminate to obtain a greater elasticity and a better sociability of its members. This inflexibility is the comic, laughter is the punishment ».

Comic and forms of materiality

Laughter can be caused by ugliness, but ugliness is not always comic. To laugh about ugliness, we need to have a naive, immediate, original approach, not to think. We also have to focus on a specific feature of the person and to associate the person with this feature. It is the same with cartoonists, who exaggerate physical and natural features of people. Our imagination see in everyone the efforts of the soul to dynamise materiality, the soul or the mind give flexibility, agility and animation to the rigid body and to materiality. However the body tend to rigidify itself, and it produces a comic effect: « When materiality succeeds in fixing the movement of the soul, in hindering its grace, it obtains a comic effect. To define comic in comparison to its contrary, we should oppose it to grace instead of beauty. It is stiffness rather than ugliness ».

Comic of gesture and movements

Bergson concludes as an immediate consequence of the previous chapter that « attitudes, gestures and movements of the human body are subject to laughter precisely in the way that body makes us think to a simple machine ». Humans tend to laugh when they see the effect of a machine within the human body. This is why when we concentrate our attention on a particular gesture made by a speaker to better express his thinking, we automatically find it comic whereas this movement in itself is not comic. We also laugh when someone imitate somebody else, because to imitate somebody, the imitator reproduces the most mechanical, the most unconscious movements and gestures of the person. This is also the case with the parody of an activity. For Bergson, this explains also why, as Pascal had noted, when we see two faces that look like very much, we find it comic, while the faces alone are not comic. And finally: « This is because really lively life is not supposed to repeat itself. Where there is repetition, complete similarity, we suspect that there is mechanism behind life. That diversion of life towards mechanism is the real cause of laughter. »

Comic and human imagination

At the beginning of chapter five, Bergson thinks again about his method of analysis. He recalls that to look for a unique method of comic does not make sense. However, there is a central cause of comic, and all comic situation are derived from it. This central cause is mechanism applied to life, and all comic effects are articulated around this cause by our imagination. There are three main directions in which our imagination is oriented to produce comic effects, three general laws:
- a lot of things are comic *en droit* (de jure) whereas they are not comic *en fait* (de facto), because common use and collective habits generalize these comic situations. Hence the mind needs to break with fashion to revive and to note the comic of the situation, not to create it, Bergson insists. He takes the example of clothes: fashionable clothes do not make us laugh, because we are used to seeing them, while we automatically make fun of someone who wears old-fashioned clothes. Also the application of social conventions and rules are comic situation because these regulations and applied automatically, mechanically. « A mechanism inserted into nature, an automatic regulation of society, these are the two kinds of funny effects at which we are ending up. »
- contrary to the body, the soul is perfectly flexible, always in activity. However, we tend to attribute these qualities to the body, we considerer it as flexible and ignore his resistance, its materiality. But when we are fully aware that the body is a weigh, a burden for the soul, the situation is comic. Hence, « is comic any incident which attracts our

attention on the physique of a person while the mind is active ». There is a comic effect when our attention is diverted from the mind to the physique.

- we laugh every time somebody looks like a material thing, every time we are under the impression that someone is a thing.

Notes and links

Source (edited): "http://en.wikipedia.org/wiki/Laughter_(Bergson)"

Liberty and Nature: An Aristotelian Defense of Liberal Order

Liberty and Nature: An Aristotelian Defense of Liberal Order is political philosophy book written by Douglas B. Rasmussen and Douglas J. Den Uyl.
Source (edited): "http://en.wikipedia.org/wiki/Liberty_and_Nature:_An_Aristotelian_Defense_of_Liberal_Order"

Norms of Liberty: A Perfectionist Basis for Non-Perfectionist Politics

Norms of Liberty: A Perfectionist Basis for Non-Perfectionist Politics is political philosophy book written by Douglas B. Rasmussen and Douglas J. Den Uyl.

Table of contents

Analytic Contents
  Preface
  Part One: Liberalism and the Political Order
    1. Liberalism in Crisis
    2. Liberalism and Ethics
    3. Liberalism's Past and Precendents
    4. Why Individual Rights? Rights as Metanormative Principles
    5. The Natural Right to Private Property
  Part Two: A Deep Structure for Liberalism
    6. Individualistic Perfectionism
    7. Defending Individualistic Perfectionism
    8. Natural Law and the Common Good
    9. Self-Ownership
  Part Two: Defending Liberalism
    10. Communitarian and Conservative Critics
    11. The Structure of the Argument for Individual Rights
    12. Defending Individualistic Non-Perfectionist Politics
  Epilogue: From Metanorms to Metaphysics
  Index

Availability

Norms of Liberty: A Perfectionist Basis for Non-Perfectionist Politics is available in paperback under ISBN 0-271-02701-0 (University Park, PA: Penn State University Press, 2005).
Source (edited): "http://en.wikipedia.org/wiki/Norms_of_Liberty:_A_Perfectionist_Basis_for_Non-Perfectionist_Politics"

Organon F

Organon F is a Slovak academic journal of philosophy focusing on analytical philosophy.
Source (edited): "http://en.wikipedia.org/wiki/Organon_F"

Philosophy and Theology

Philosophy and Theology is a peer-reviewed academic journal that publishes articles and reviews exploring connections between philosophy and theology. It was established in 1986 by Andrew Tallon at Marquette University and is the journal of the Karl Rahner Society. One issue of each volume is dedicated to Rahner's thought. Since 1997 the journal has been published on behalf of Marquette University by the Philosophy Documentation Center. All issues are available in electronic format.

Notable contributors

- Shlomo Avineri
- Avery Dulles
- Bernard Lonergan
- Karl Rahner
- Nicholas Rescher
- William Sweet

Source (edited): "http://en.wikipedia.org/wiki/Philosophy_and_Theology"

Re.press

re.press is a Melbourne (Australia) based open access publisher of contemporary philosophy (and some theory and poetry). re.press is an independent publisher that seeks to promote philosophical ideas through making many of its works available for free in electronic form (PDF downloads) in addition to hard-copy paperbacks.

History

re.press began publishing in 2006 with the edited collection "The Praxis of Alain Badiou" and since then has published authors such as Alain Badiou, G. W.F. Hegel, Graham Harman, Andrew Benjamin, Reza Negarestani and the poet Attar.

Open Access

re.press was one of the first publishers to offer books as open access or free downloads. There has been some discussion of the "re.press model" on the blogging network and whether this is a sustainable model.

Series

re.press publishes in three series: Anamnesis, Transmission and Anomaly. Anamnesis and Transmission publish philosophy and Anomaly publishes other works including poetry and speculative fiction. The Open Access free downloads seem to be confined to the Anamnesis and Transmission series.

Cover Art

According to re.press' website they are committed to "maximizing design values, boosting clarity and aesthetic qualities". This commitment is expressed through the use of Melbourne based artists on their covers. According to their website:

"re.press aims to publish the best philosophical works available, whether these emerge from well-established or from previously unknown thinkers, whether they are from the North or the South, the East or the West, whether they are Platonists or Hegelians, materialists or idealists. True thought is global, universal, transformative, shredding ideologies and opinions like the statues of old dictators. But true thought also begins locally, in images and signs that may as yet have no recognisable reference or import. re.press' head offices are located in the city of Melbourne, Australia. And Melbourne is, as the art-critic Norbert Loeffler has remarked, one of the great art-cities of the world - without anybody knowing it. Lacking the established power, media and reputation of traditional centres of world art, Melbourne forces its artists to sustain themselves otherwise. Aware of contemporary work from all over the world, local artists transmute it for their own, often-obscure purposes, into unprecedented forms. re.press seeks, like an insatiable kleptoparasite, to draw off some of this aesthetic power for its own ends, by using their images for its cover-art."
Source (edited): "http://en.wikipedia.org/wiki/Re.press"

Social Epistemology (journal)

Social Epistemology: A Journal of Knowledge, Culture and Policy is a quarterly academic journal. The journal was established in 1987 and is published by Routledge in collaboration with The Society for Social Studies of Science and the European Association for the Study of Science and Technology. *Social Epistemology* provides a forum for philosophical and social scientific inquiry that incorporates the work of scholars from a variety of disciplines who share a concern with the production, assessment and validation of knowledge. The journal covers both empirical research into the origination and transmission of knowledge and normative considerations which arise as such research is implemented, serving as a guide for directing contemporary knowledge enterprises.

Editor in chief

The founding editor in chief was Steve Fuller (University of Warwick, UK), who was succeeded in 1997 by Joan Leach (University of Queensland, Australia). Since 2009, James H. Collier (Virginia Tech) is the editor.
Source (edited): "http://en.wikipedia.org/wiki/Social_Epistemology_(journal)"

Studies in Logic, Grammar and Rhetoric

Studies in Logic, Grammar and Rhetoric is journal of philosophy, publishing articles of diverse streams in English.
Source (edited): "http://en.wikipedia.org/wiki/Studies_in_Logic,_Grammar_and_Rhetoric"

The Moral Landscape

The Moral Landscape: How Science Can Determine Human Values is a book by Sam Harris. In it, he promotes a science of morality and argues that many thinkers have long confused the relationship between morality, facts, and science. He aims to carve a third path between secularists who say morality is subjective (e.g. moral relativists), and religionists who say that morality is given by God and scripture. Harris contends that the only moral framework worth talking about is one where "morally good" things pertain to increases in the "well-being of conscious creatures". He then argues that, problems with philosophy of science and reason in general notwithstanding, 'moral questions' will have objectively right and wrong answers which are grounded in empirical facts about what causes people to flourish.

Challenging the age-old philosophical notion that we can never get an 'ought' from an 'is', Harris argues that moral questions are best pursued using, not just philosophy, but the methods of science. Thus, "science can determine human values" translates to "science can tell us which values lead to human flourishing". It is in this sense that Harris advocates that scientists begin conversations about a normative science of "morality".

Synopsis

Harris believes science has already begun to pin-down the causes of human "happiness", and that regulating this pursuit is the purpose of "social morality"

Sam Harris's case starts with two premises: "(1) some people have better lives than others, and (2) these differences are related, in some lawful and not entirely arbitrary way, to states of the human brain and to states of the world". The idea is that a person is simply describing material facts (many about their brain) when they describe possible "better" and "worse" lives for themselves. Granting this, Harris says we must conclude that there are facts about which courses of action will allow one to pursue a better life.

Harris attests to the importance of admitting that such facts exist, because he says this logic applies to groups of individuals as well. He suggests that there are better and worse ways for whole societies to pursue better lives. Just like at the scale of the individual, there may be multiple different paths and "peaks" to flourishing for societies - and many more ways to fail.

Harris then makes a pragmatic case that science could usefully define "morality" according to such facts (about people's wellbeing). Often his arguments point out the way that problems with this scientific definition of morality seem to be problems shared by all science, or reason and words in general. Harris also spends some time describing how science might engage nuances and challenges of identifying the best ways for individuals, and groups of individuals, to improve their lives. Many of these issues are covered below.

Philosophical case

Harris says science requires that one acknowledge certain values (e.g. curiosity)

Although Harris's book discusses the challenges that a science of morality must face, he also mentions that his scientific argument is unavoidably philosophical—but says that this is the case for almost all science. He mentions that modern science amounts to careful practice of accepted first philosophical principles like empiricism and physicalism, reminding the reader that science was once even called "natural philosophy". He further suggests that science has already very much settled on *values* in answering the question "what should I believe, and why should I believe it?". Harris says it should not be surprising that a scientific pursuit of morality is equally founded on bedrock assumptions (Basic norms).

The way he thinks science might engage moral issues draws on various philosophical positions like ethical realism (there are facts worth calling 'moral facts'), and ethical naturalism (these facts relate to the physical world). Harris says a science of morality may resemble Utilitarianism, but that the science is, importantly, more open-ended because it involves an evolving definition of well-being. Rather than committing to Reductive materialism, then, Harris recognizes the arguments of revisionists that psychological definitions themselves are contingent on research and discoveries. Harris adds that any science of morality must consider everything from emotions and thoughts to the actual actions and their consequences.

To Harris, moral propositions, and explicit values in general, are concerned with the flourishing of conscious creatures in a society. He argues that "Social morality exists to sustain cooperative social relationships, and morality can be objectively evaluated by that standard." Harris sees some philosophers' talk of strictly *private* morality as akin to unproductive discussion of some private, personal physics.

Harris also discusses how interchangeability of perspective might emerge as an important part of moral reasoning. He alludes to an 'unpleasant surprise principle', where someone realizes they have been supporting an ineffective moral norm (e.g. reported cases of Jew-hunting Nazis discovering that they themselves were of Jewish descent).

Science and moral truths

Harris identifies three projects for science as it relates to morality: (1) explaining why humans do what they do in the name of "morality" (e.g. traditional evolutionary psychology), (2) determining which patterns of thought and behaviour humans actually *should* follow (i.e. the science of morality), and (3) generally persuading humans to change their ways. Harris says that the first project is focussed only on describing what is, whereas projects (2) and (3) are focused on what should and could be, respectively. Harris's point is that this second, prescriptive project should be the focus of a science of morality. He mentions, however, that we should not fear an "Orwellian future" with scientists at every door - vital progress in the science of morality could be shared in much the same way as advances in medicine.

Harris says it is important to delineate project (1) from project (2), or else we risk committing a moralistic fallacy. He also highlights the importance of distinguishing between project (2) (asking what is right) from project (3) (trying to change behaviour). He says we must realize that the nuances of human motivation is a challenge in itself; humans often fail to do what they "ought" to do to even be successfully selfish - there is every reason to believe that discovering what is best for society would not change every member's habits overnight.

Harris does not imagine that people, even scientists, have always made the right moral decisions—indeed it is precisely his argument that many of them are wrong about moral facts. This is due to the many real challenges of good science in general, including human cognitive limitations and biases (e.g. loss aversion can sway human decisions on important issues like medicine). He mentions the research of Paul Slovic and others to describe just a few of these established mental heuristics that might keep us from reasoning properly. Although he mentions that training might temper the influence of these biases, Harris worries about research showing that incompetence and ignorance in a domain leads to confidence (the Dunning–Kruger effect).

Harris explains that debates and disagreement is a part of the scientific method, and that one side can certainly be wrong. He also explains that all the debates still available to science illustrates how much work could still be done, and how much conversation must continue.

Harris's positive beliefs

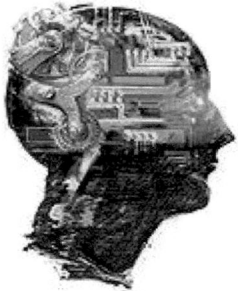

Harris rejects the idea of free will

The book is full of issues that Harris thinks are far from being empirically, morally grey areas. That is, besides saying that 'reasonable' thinking about moral issues amounts to scientific thinking. For instance, he references one poll that found that 36 percent of British Muslims think apostates should be put to death for their unbelief, and he says that these individuals are "morally confused". He also suggests it is obvious that loneliness, helplessness, and poverty are "bad", but that these are by no means as far as positive psychology has taken, and will take us.

In one section, called *The illusion of free will*, Harris argues that there is a wealth of evidence in psychology (e.g. the illusion of introspection) or specifically related to the neuroscience of free will that suggests that metaphysically free will does not exist. This, he thinks, is intuitive; "trains of thought...convey the apparent reality of choices, freely made. But from a deeper perspective...thoughts simply arise (what else could they do?)". He adds "The illusion of free will is itself an illusion". The implications of free will's non-existence may be a working determinism, and Harris warns us not to confuse this with fatalism.

One implication of a determined will, Harris says, is that it becomes unreasonable to punish people out of retribution—only behaviour modification and the deterrence of others still seem to be potentially valid reasons to punish. This, especially because behaviour modification is a sort of cure for the evil behaviours; Harris provides a thought experiment:

" Consider what would happen if we discovered a cure for human evil. Imagine, for the sake of argument...the cure for psychopathy can be put directly into the food supply like vitamin D...consider, for instance, the prospect of withholding the cure for evil from a murder as part of his punishment. Would this make any moral sense at all? "

Harris acknowledges a hierarchy of moral consideration (e.g. humans are more important than bacteria or mice). He says it follows that there could, in principle, be a species compared to which we are relatively unimportant (although he doubts such a species exists).

Harris supports the development of lie-detection technology and believes it would be, on the whole, beneficial for humanity. He also supports the formation of an explicit global civilization because of the potential for stability under a world government.

Religion: good or bad?

Consistent with Harris's definition of morality, he says we must ask whether religion increases human flourishing today (regardless of whether it increased it in the distant past). He argues that religions may largely be practiced because they fit well with human cognitive tendencies (e.g. animism). In Harris's view, religion and religious dogma is an impediment to reason, and he discusses the views of Francis Collins as one example.

Harris criticizes the tactics of secularists like Chris Mooney, who argue that science is not fundamentally (and certainly not superficially) in conflict with religion. Harris sees this as a very serious disagreement, that patronizingly attempts to pacify more devout theists. Harris claims that societies can move away from deep dependence on religion just as it has witchcraft, which he says was once just as deeply ingrained.

Reception

The Moral Landscape reached 9th in the New York Times Best Seller list for Hardcover Non-Fiction, and remained amongst the top 35 until 5 weeks later.

Reviews

Professional reviews of *The Moral Landscape* have been largely negative. Critics have found that Harris offers insufficient new information beyond offering the reader a science of utilitarianism, and called his treatment of a science of morality naive. Others found the whole project was distracted by Harris's ongoing rhetoric against religion. On the other hand, some critics allowed that "when [Harris] stays closest to neuroscience, he says much that is interesting and important...".

In his review for Barnes & Noble, Cal State Associate Professor of Philosophy Troy Jollimore allowed that the book "has some good, reasonable, and at times persuasive things to say" to people who are unfamiliar with moral skepticism, but "has little to say to those people who actually do know what the arguments are, and it will not help others become much better informed." Jollimore also worried that Harris wrongly presents complex issues as having simple solutions.

The philosopher Kwame Anthony Appiah, writing in *The New York Times*, criticized Harris for failing to articulate "his central claim" and identifying how science has "revealed" that human well-being has an objective component. Appiah concluded that Harris "ends up endorsing ... something very like utilitarianism, a philosophical position that is now more than two centuries old, ... that faces a battery of familiar problems," which Harris merely "push[es] ... aside."

Cognitive scientist and anthropologist Scott Atran criticized Harris for failing to engage with the philosophical literature on ethics and the problems in attempting to scientifically quantify human well being, noting that: "Nobel Prize–winner Daniel Kahneman studies what gives Americans pleasure—watching TV, talking to friends, having sex—and what makes them unhappy—commuting, working, looking after their children. So this leaves us where . . . ?" Dismissing the book, he writes "this work contains precious little science. There is, however, much playacting at science to justify a peculiar sort of Brave New World where atheism will help do away with female genital mutilation and lie detectors will preclude pleading the Fifth Amendment."

American novelist Marilynne Robinson, writing in *The Wall Street Journal*, sardonically noted that Harris fails to "articulate a positive morality of his own" but, had he done so, would have found himself in the company of the "Unitarians, busily cooperating on schemes to enhance the world's well being, as they have been doing for generations."

David Sexton of the London Evening Standard described Harris's claim to provide a science of morality as ' 'the most extraordinarily overweening claim and evidently flawed. Science does not generate its own moral values; it can be used for good or ill and has been. Harris cannot stand outside culture, and the "better future" he prophesies is itself a cultural projection.' '

John Horgan, journalist for the *Scientific American* blog and author of *The End of Science*, expressed deep skepticism regarding Harris's claims, pointing out "the harm — historical and recent — wreaked by scientists supposedly concerned with humanity's well-being." Horgan continued:

Harris further shows his arrogance when he claims that neuroscience, his own field, is best positioned to help us achieve a universal morality. ... Neuroscience can't even tell me how I can know the big, black, hairy thing on my couch is my dog Merlin. And we're going to trust neuroscience to tell us how we should resolve debates over the morality of abortion, euthanasia and armed intervention in other nations' affairs?

Writing in Canada's *National Post*, Peter Foster wrote that "Harris's assault on religion is vicious to the point of being deranged[,]" while he simultaneously "fails to register that the greatest horrors of the past century have all been perpetrated in the name of 'scientific' socialism...." Foster concluded,

Science may help us better examine moral values, but only if attached to historical knowledge and philosophical wisdom. Mr. Harris might consider removing the beam from his own liberal eye before he pretends to deal with the conservative mote that he finds so annoying in the eyes of others.

Bill Whitehouse wrote *Epistle to a Sam Harris Nation: Debunking the Moral Landscape*, and wrote "Sam Harris has harsh words for religious extremists -- as well he should. However, he apparently fails to understand how his own position incorporates a brand of irreligious fundamentalism which is inclined to be just as blind and unyielding as the religious people whom he wishes to criticize."

Atheist science fiction writer and philosopher Russell Blackford said "The Moral Landscape is an ambitious work that will gladden the hearts, and strengthen the spines, of many secular thinkers" but that he had "serious reservations about a good book". Harris responded to some of his criticisms (see below).

But the atheist philosopher Simon Blackburn, reviewing the book, describes Harris as "a knockabout atheist" who "joins the prodigious ranks of those whose claim to have transcended philosophy is just an instance of their doing it very badly", pointing out that "if Bentham's hedonist is in one brain state and Aristotle's active subject is in another, as no doubt they would be, it is a moral, not an empirical, problem to say which is to be preferred.". And H. Allen Orr in the New York Review of Books finds that 'Despite Harris's bravado about "how science can determine human values," The Moral Landscape delivers nothing of the kind'

Response to reviews

A few months after the book's release, Sam Harris wrote a follow-up at *The Huffington Post* in response to what he says are "cloudbursts of vitriol and confusion". In this response, Harris expresses regret that few directly engage his theses. Harris says that he does not want to lend credibility to many of his critics, but explains that he is committed to spreading ideas, and says about negative reviews that "not only do they discourage smart people from reading a book, they can lead them to disparage it as though they had discovered its flaws for themselves." A case in point, he cites Colin McGinn (whom Harris does admire), who criticized his ideas based solely on the reviews of others.

Harris is skeptical of reviewers Marilynne Robinson and John Horgan, saying they are paranoid and generally missing the point by focusing on non sequiturs (the claim that a science of morality necessarily leads to Nazism, seemingly added "for good measure"). He also says that Kwame Anthony Appiah fails to raise any issues not addressed in the book. Harris is most critical, however, of Deepak Chopra, whose comments at The San Francisco Chronicle were made without reading the book, and based solely on a promotional Q&A published by Harris.

In the end, Harris's Follow-Up Response applies to three reviews: Thomas Nagel's, Troy Jollimore's, and Russel Blackford's (Harris focused his response on Blackford's criticisms—whom he says encompassed the most legitimate criticisms of the others).

Response to Blackford

After summarizing his book's arguments, Harris adds a point he says was not sufficiently discussed in the book. He proposes that the boundary between aesthetic (e.g. I love chocolate) and moral imperatives (it's wrong to kill) may not be as categorical as we think, and it may be that moral issues are simply aesthetic issues with higher stakes. To Harris, this possibility fits well with his belief that morality can only be reasonably understood by referring to facts about minds, and thus people's brains.

Harris again uses a metaphor from his book to recast the main criticisms against his position (replacing "morality" and "well-being", with "medicine" and "health"). The main criticisms become: (*The Value Problem*) There is no scientific basis to say we should value health; (*The Persuasion Problem*) If a person does not care about health, there is no way for science to argue that they are wrong when it comes to medicine; (*The Measurement Problem*) Even if the purpose of medicine is health, "health" cannot be completely defined, and therefore cannot be studied scientifically. Harris argues that this metaphor, although imperfect, makes it more clear how to disarm these three types of critique.

Harris addresses the *Value problem* by maintaining that some presupposition of values is necessary for any science, and that his science of morality is simply no different. He thus yields Blackford's point that "*that initial presupposition does not come from science,*" but Harris does not see this as a problem. For example, science presupposes logical coherence and respect for evidence - without which science could not proceed. Harris maintains that a critic who rejects such basic norms of a discussion, whether it is that "science should be coherent" or that "morality depends on maximizing flourishing", cannot be taken seriously. Harris is *not* saying that everyone *must* value health, morality, science or even reasonable discussion (indeed, one could always refuse to engage in these pursuits). Harris rather argues that reasonable discussion of these topics requires certain assumptions - and we should not expect reasonable discussion of morality to be any different. He yields that fuzzy terms like health and flourishing admit of reasonable disagreement, but says that these terms are not so fuzzy as to allow extreme deviations. That is, science may not be certain whether it is healthier to be more flexible or to be able to jump higher, but science does seem to be able to call "unhealthy" a raging case of smallpox.

In response to the *measurement problem*, Harris criticizes the idea that a science of morality falls apart without an iron-clad metric or "unit of well-being". He says this is an unrealistic constraint, and one that is not placed on other sciences (e.g. there is no "unit of depression", and yet depression is certainly a scientific topic).

Sam Harris finishes his response by disagreeing with Blackford's last point: that conceptions of morality that are relative and even nihilistic do not prevent people from criticizing moral systems that causes suffering or violence. Harris says "Unless you understand that human health is a domain of genuine truth claims -- however difficult "health" may be to define—it is impossible to think clearly about disease. I believe the same can be said about morality. And that is why I wrote a book about it."

Debate with William Lane Craig

Dr William Lane Craig, a philosopher of science and religion and Christian theologian recently debated Sam Harris on the topic "Does Good come from God?". Craig maintained that there is nothing worth calling "Morality" unless it is the system that originates from God, while Harris supported the view that a science of morality (a naturalistic moral theory) is superior in various ways.

Nathan Shneider of Religion Dispatches online magazine gave the whole debate an unfavorable review, arguing that the speakers failed to address each other's issues satisfactorily. Shneider likewise describes a great deal of disappointment in the audience. He noted that each speakers' pace was different, with Craig flawlessly, but nevertheless "charging" through too many points to consider, whereas Harris spoke slower.

Craig made many objections. He suggested that Harris is making a more contentious claim than he admits when he equates morality with wellbeing. Craig also argued that the moral landscape cannot be identical to the continuum of human well-being and that Sam Harris's moral theory was logically incoherent; Craig describes how
"On the next to last page of his book (page 190), Harris makes the telling admission that if people like rapists, liars, and thieves could be just as happy as good people, then his moral landscape would no longer be a moral land-

scape...Since it's possible that human well-being and moral goodness are not identical, it follows necessarily that human well-being and moral goodness are not the same, as Harris has asserted....By granting that it's possible that the continuum of well-being is not identical to the moral landscape, Harris' view becomes logically incoherent."

Craig may be rebutting a straw man, however. In "The Moral Landscape" Harris explains on those pages that "if evil turned out to be a reliable path to happiness as goodness is, my argument about the moral landscape would still stand, as would the likely utility of neuroscience for investigating it." This is his main contention throughout the book, and it is then that he adds that "It would no longer be an especially 'moral' landscape; rather it would be a continuum of well-being, upon which saints and sinners would occupy equivalent peaks." It is precisely Harris's point that the question "Are Sinners as happy as Saintly people?" is an important empirical one. Furthermore, it may turn out that so-called 'Sinners' are just as happy as so-called 'Saints', and although Harris doubts this interesting possibility is true, this fact would not hurt Harris's case. This is because his thesis is that one sinner's reaching a peak of wellbeing does not rule out the possibility that it will cause others to suffer; a life of behavior like rape is not morally justifiable (i.e. having considered the wellbeing of all conscious creatures involved) compared to a life of empathy.

Craig also criticized the fact that Harris's theory says that metaphysical moral responsibility does not exist at all, and that the system is weaker for it. Harris discusses such issues in his book. Harris calls notions of moral obligations and "oughts", when they do not relate to wellbeing, "an artificial and needlessly confusing way to think about moral choice" adding that this is a way of thinking that depends on Abrahamic religion. Harris explains elsewhere that "we do not require a metaphysical repository of right and wrong, or actions that are mysteriously right or wrong *in themselves.*" To Harris, the science of morality does not require more than social obligations, and indeed he believes they are the only kind that really exist.

Craig later wrote that Harris's moral theory "leads naturally to eugenics... On Harris' view if torturing a little girl to death would somehow happen to lead to greater well-being of conscious creatures, then not only is it permissible, but you are morally obligated to torture her to death.... Harris is aware of these problems (remember his example of the doctor who could save five lives by harvesting the organs of one healthy patient?), and his attempts to avert the consequences of his theory are utterly unconvincing..." Harris addresses ideas related to eugenics in his book when he explains "Many readers may also fear that the case I am making is vaguely, or even explicitly, utopian. It isn't, as should become clear in due course." Harris is at least clear that he is far from advocating an 'Orwellian' society, and he does not advocate drastic actions based on a science of morality - but says there should be papers available on the topic (as in the field of medicine).

Harris is critical of Craig's debating style, which he felt attempted to define some topics as "irrelevant" from the outset (although they may not be), and contained too many straw men and irrelevancies for Harris to take the time to correct without basically abandoning his prepared remarks. Craig, on the other hand, felt that Harris did not try hard enough to address his questions.

Other commentaries

In an article for *The San Francisco Chronicle*, Deepak Chopra, author of several self-help books and one-time debating opponent of Harris, wondered whether Harris "is writing a satire on morality" and commented that Harris's "naiveté ... raises suspicion about his connection to psychological reality."

Praise from colleagues

In advance of publication, four personal and professional acquaintances of the author, Richard Dawkins, Ian McEwan, Steven Pinker, and Lawrence Krauss, offered their praise for the book. They each serve on the Advisory Board of Harris's Project Reason, and their praise appears as blurbs (released by the book's publisher on Harris's website and reproduced on the book's dust jacket). Dawkins said,

I was one of those who had unthinkingly bought into the hectoring myth that science can say nothing about morals. To my surprise, The Moral Landscape has changed all that for me. It should change it for philosophers too. Philosophers of mind have already discovered that they can't duck the study of neuroscience, and the best of them have raised their game as a result...".

McEwan wrote that "Harris breathes intellectual fire into an ancient debate. Reading this thrilling, audacious book, you feel the ground shifting beneath your feet. Reason has never had a more passionate advocate." Pinker said that Harris offers "a tremendously appealing vision, and one that no thinking person can afford to ignore." Krauss opined that Harris "has the rare ability to frame arguments that are not only stimulating, they are downright nourishing, even if you don't always agree with him!" Krauss predicted that "readers are bound to come away with previously firm convictions about the world challenged, and a vital new awareness about the nature and value of science and reason in our lives."

Source (edited): "http://en.wikipedia.org/wiki/The_Moral_Landscape"

The Philosophic Thought of Ayn Rand

The Philosophic Thought of Ayn Rand is a collection of essays on Ayn Rand's philosophy Objectivism edited by Douglas J. Den Uyl and Douglas B. Rasmussen. It includes essays by Antony Flew, Robert Hollinger Charles King,

Tibor R. Machan, Erick Mack, Wallace Matson, Jack Wheeler, and the editors covering Rand's views of metaphysics, epistemology, ethics, and politics.

Table of contents
Preface
  I. Metaphysics and Epistemology
  1. *Ayn Rand's Realism* by Douglas J. Den Uyl and Douglas B. Rasmussen
  2. *Rand on Concepts* by Wallace Matson
  3. *Ayn Rand's Epistemology in Historical Perspective* by Robert Hollinger Charles King
  II. Ethics
  4. *Life, Teleology, and Eudaimonia in the Ethics of Ayn Rand* by Douglas J. Den Uyl and Douglas B. Rasmussen
  5. *Rand and Aristotle: A Comparison of Objectivist and Aristotelian Ethics* by Jack Wheeler
  6. *Life and the Theory of Value: The Randian Argument Reconsidered* by Charles King
  7. *The Fundamental Moral Elements of Rand's Theory of Rights* by Erick Mack
  III. Politics
  8. *Capitalism* by Douglas J. Den Uyl and Douglas B. Rasmussen
  9. *Selfishness and the Unintended Consequences of Intended Action* by Antony Flew
  10. *Reason, Individualism, and Capitalism: The Moral Vision of Ayn Rand* by Tibor R. Machan
  Conclusion
  The Contributors
  Index

Availability
The Philosophic Thought of Ayn Rand is available in paperback under ISBN 0252014073 (Champaign, IL: University of Illinois Press, 1987).
Source (edited): "http://en.wikipedia.org/wiki/The_Philosophic_Thought_of_Ayn_Rand"

The Post Card: From Socrates to Freud and Beyond

The Post Card: From Socrates to Freud and Beyond is a 1980 book by French philosopher Jacques Derrida. It is a "satire of epistolary literature." After *Glas* (1974), it's sometimes considered Derrida most "literary" book.

Content

The "obscene" medieval depiction of Socrates and Plato.

The first half of the book, titled *L'envoi*, contains a series of love letters addressed to his loved one. In one of the letters, dated 6 June 1977, Derrida tells about his time spent in London with Jonathan Culler and Cynthia Chase, which had been recently married. They showed Derrida and exposition of hundreds of card reproductions, among which was the medieval depiction of Socrates and Plato, which seized Derrida's attention. After describing Plato's posture in the picture, and the various possible actions that he may be performing at Socrates's back (riding a skateboard, conducting a tram), Derrida says

" The card immediately seemed to me, how to put it, obscene. [...] For the moment, myself, I tell you that I see Plato getting an erection in Socrates' back and see the insane hubris of his prick, an interminable, disproportionate erection ... slowly sliding, still warm, under Socrates' right leg [...] Imagine the day, when we will be able to send sperm by post card. [... and finally, Plato] wants to emit ... to sow the entire earth, to send the same fertile card to everyone.

Source (edited): "http://en.wikipedia.org/wiki/The_Post_Card:_From_Socrates_to_Freud_and_Beyond"

The Sublime Object of Ideology

The Sublime Object of Ideology is a book by the Slovenian philosopher and cultural theorist Slavoj Žižek, first published in 1989. The book, which Žižek believes to be one of his best, essentially makes thematic the Kantian notion of the sublime in order to liken ideology to an experience of something that is absolutely vast and forceful beyond all perception and objective intelligibility.

Source (edited): "http://en.wikipedia.org/wiki/The_Sublime_Object_of_Ideology"

Think: A Compelling Introduction to Philosophy

Think: A Compelling Introduction to Philosophy is an introduction to philosophy book written by Simon Blackburn. It covers subjects such as epistemology, philosophy of the mind, free will and philosophy of religion.

Source (edited): "http://en.wikipedia.org/wiki/Think:_A_Compelling_Introduction_to_Philosophy"

Truth and Method

Truth and Method (*Wahrheit und Methode*) is the major philosophical work by Hans-Georg Gadamer, first published in 1960.

The book draws heavily on the work of Wilhelm Dilthey, and Romantic hermeneutics. It rejects as unachievable the goal of objectivity, and instead suggests that meaning is created through intersubjective communication.

The book is regarded as Gadamer's magnum opus, and has influenced many philosophers and sociologists, notably Jürgen Habermas.

Gadamer's philosophical project, as explained in *Truth and Method*, was to elaborate on the concept of "philosophical hermeneutics", which Heidegger initiated but never dealt with at length. Gadamer's goal was to uncover the nature of human understanding. In the book Gadamer argued that "truth" and "method" were at odds with one another. He was critical of two approaches to the human sciences (*Geisteswissenschaften*). On the one hand, he was critical of modern approaches to humanities that modelled themselves on the natural sciences (and thus on rigorous scientific methods). On the other hand, he took issue with the traditional German approach to the humanities, represented for instance by Friedrich Schleiermacher and Wilhelm Dilthey, which believed that correctly interpreting a text meant recovering the original intention of the author who wrote it.

In contrast to both of these positions, Gadamer argued that people have a 'historically effected consciousness' (*wirkungsgeschichtliches Bewußtsein*) and that they are embedded in the particular history and culture that shaped them. Thus interpreting a text involves a fusion of horizons where the scholar finds the ways that the text's history articulates with their own background. *Truth and Method* is not meant to be a programmatic statement about a new 'hermeneutic' method of interpreting texts. Gadamer intended *Truth and Method* to be a description of what we always do when we interpret things (even if we do not know it): "My real concern was and is philosophic: not what we do or what we ought to do, but what happens to us over and above our wanting and doing".

Truth and Method was published twice in English, and the revised edition is now considered authoritative. The German-language edition of Gadamer's Collected Works includes a volume in which Gadamer elaborates his argument and discusses the critical response to the book. Finally, Gadamer's essay on Celan (entitled "Who Am I and Who Are You?") has been considered by many—including Heidegger and Gadamer himself—as a "second volume" or continuation of the argument in *Truth and Method*.

Source (edited): "http://en.wikipedia.org/wiki/Truth_and_Method"

Word and Object

Word and Object is a 1960 book of epistemology by Willard Van Orman Quine. In it, Quine develops his thesis of the Indeterminacy of translation.

Source (edited): "http://en.wikipedia.org/wiki/Word_and_Object"

Xueren

Xueren (English: *The Scholar*) was an influential Chinese independent intellectual journal that ran from 1991 to 2000. It was founded and edited by Chen Pingyuan, Wang Hui, and Wang Shouchang under the sponsorship of a Japanese foundation. In order to work around censorship conditions in the Chinese publishing industry that make it more difficult for periodicals to get approval than books, *Xueren* was published as a "series" in the latter format. Other journals that have taken the same approach include *Res Publica* and *Horizons*.

Scholar Chaohua Wang locates *Xueren*'s origins in "the self-examination of intellectuals intimately involved in the ferment of the eighties":

The project of its editors [. . .] was to retrieve the history of modern Chinese scholarship (*xueshu shi*), a tradition they felt was in danger of being obscured or forgotten under the pressure of imported theories. In doing so, they wanted to clarify their own intellectual identity and responsibilities. What was their position in a historical chain of scholarly development? When and how should a scholar speak out on public issues?

Co-founder Wang Hui characterizes his and his colleagues' motivations similarly, but without a critical approach toward "imported theories" in academe as a primary component of their intellectual project, and with more of an eye toward directly socially relevant goals. According to him, *Xueren* was created to facilitate an effort by young intellectuals to "reconsider" modern Chinese history in the wake of the failure of the 1989 democracy movement, a "process of reflection" that

included serious reconsideration of modern history, conscientious rethinking of attempts to carry out radical reform on the basis of Western models, close investigation of the Chinese historical legacy and its contemporary significance, and necessary critiques of certain of the consequences of radical political action.

However, Wang Hui states that *Xueren* "did not pursue any particular academic agenda."

Example table of contents

The 648-page seventh issue of *Xueren* (May 1995) printed the following table of contents in English (though all articles were in Chinese):

Source (edited): "http://en.wikipedia.org/wiki/Xueren"

Ai City

Ai City (アイ・シティ) is a Japanese science fiction manga created by **Shuuhou Itahashi** (板橋しゅうほう *Itahashi Shuuhou*), a.k.a. **SYUFO**, it was turned into an anime film later.

Plot

1983: off-duty policeman Reiden picked up suspicious "father and daughter" (who appear close in age), Kei and Ai on his car. Reiden is involved in fighting with them and the female fighter K2 who chased them. Kei who is drawn out his latent ability to the maximum by a Legendary "Trigger" Ai blows away K2. Then, the night sky split and strange space is showing from the slit. Their enemy is the secret society "Fraud" of para-psionics commanded by Kuu Ragua Lee. Kei, Ai and Reiden meet the assassinators whom "Fraud" sends out one after another.

Characters

Ai's companions

I2 (Ai)

Ai is Headmeters who escaped from Fraud with Kei; (but she doesn't have the operation yet). The original name is "I2". She is a clone of Kei's lover Etsuko (= "I") killed by Fraud, and adores Kei as a father.

Fraud suspects that she is legendary "Trigger" who draws out others' dormant faculty and amplifies it, and so pursues her.

"2" of "I2" means "The second generation of the clone of Headmeters I". However, nobody of Headmeters knew who are "I" and "I2". And there is no information about the two persons also in the memory bank of Fraud's computer, and "Headmeters I" is a missing number. It is not clear why they recognized "I" and "I2", but the two people did not exist actually.

K (Kei)

Kei is Headmeters who escaped from Fraud to defend Ai. He was anesthetized suddenly and was made to undergo the operation for Headmeters on college days. And, he was given the code name "K". He was even proud of being Headmeters, but he became despondent because his lover Etsuko died from the same operation as him. Then, a girl appeared. She is just like Etsuko, but is ten years younger than Etsuko. She introduced herself as Ai- "I2"-. "I" was a code name of Etsuko. Kei decided to behave as her father.

Kei has both ability of Headmeters and Tuned-man exceptionally, because Kuu Ragua Lee, the leader of Fraud, operated on Kei in person. However, he is a defect product as Headmeters, and he has only the faculty for incomplete mind reading. The number of his headmeter has risen only to level 5 by the shock of Etsuko's death, but the number rises to infinite (∞) when Ai draws out his latent abilities. His performance as Tuned-man is less than 1/10 of the output of Yi or Lyan, but Fraud performed the operation which is different from them on the body of Kei. Sensors which are embedded on the 108 vital points of his whole body control his muscles and internal organs, and brain, and he can always utilize his whole muscles 100% (people usually use them only about 20%).

Cat

The stray cat which touched the topology wall, and lost the tail. Ai brings along the cat after she treated the injury.

Reiden Yoshioka

The obliging policeman involved in fighting of Kei and Ai vs. Fraud. 34 years old. He is automania, and his own car is Alpina based on BMW cars. He is in a dilemma between his wife Akemi and K2 currently charmed by him.

K2

K2 is Kei's feminized clone who was born by the chromosome manipulation. She is a high-ranking Headmeters of Fraud who is the same level as Mr. J in capability, and commanded the pursuit corps to Kei and Ai.

She loves Kei by fervent narcissism and demands him to love her. Then, she wants to kill Ai who monopolizes his love. However, she lost memory and regressed to her infantile state of mind by touching the topology wall. And she took to Reiden who saved her. She recovers her memory later, but she does not change her mind

Lee

Lee is an old security guard of a supermarket. He looks after Ai from Kei. He is a very kind old man, but is a mysterious man who is actually Headmeters of level 100.

Residents of floor 1983
Akemi Yoshioka
Akemi is a wife of Reiden, and she dominates him. She is possessed by Alloy and is made the puppet by it.

Sugiura
One of hoodlum group of 3s. He is a little man with suspenders.
Alloy possesses him and manipulates him any way it wants.
They bear a grudge against that Reiden reported their injustice in the university entrance exam to the police, and they ambush him at his home and attack him. They had parents hush up the rape and the violence till then.

Miyasaka
One of hoodlum group of 3s. He is a big-boned man. He is pushed away on a road by Sugiura controlled by Alloy, and is run over by a car.

Takenaka
One of hoodlum group of 3s. He is a foppish man who wears sunglasses, dyed hair brown and has a permanent. He shoots Reiden with a gun, but the bullet is teleported to the inside of his body, and he dies.

Residents of floor 2183
Kuu Ragua Lee
The leader of "Fraud" which is the highest consultative body of "Floor 2183", and also manages "Floor 1983". Supported by Headmeters with super-natural power, he is in opposition to the chief delegate Lai Lou Chin. He himself is Headmeters, and his level is 100.
He is a skinhead and a brawny big man. He equips his head with the metal electronic device which covers his eyes, mouth, and his forehead.
He believed that he was the governing classes who have managed the human beings of Floor 1983 who will live in 1983 fixed forever. But, he notices that he is also a captive managed by higher-ranking managers (inspectors) like them. Then, he decides to challenge them to fighting.

J (Mr. J)
Mr. J is a high-ranking Headmeters of Fraud and his level is 40. He is a sexless youth of long hair.
He is Kuu Ragua Lee's page boy, and admires and loves him. He always fears that Kuu Ragua Lee loses the concern about him.
He commands the operational unit which pursues Kei and Ai.

A (Miss A)
Miss A is a leader of Headmeters, is Kuu Ragua Lee's right-hand woman, and is a daughter of the Coedes family. She is a muscular woman. There is her younger brother "B" in Headmeters.

Yi
Yi is a secret agent of Fraud. He is a Tuned-man who was converted by Fraud with fighting power at the same level as a tank. He can shoot rays from his finger-tip.
He is dressed in black from head to toe. He wears Mao suit, the glasses of a round frame and a black hat.
He makes a combination with Lyan and chases Kei and others together.

Lyan
Lyan is a partner of Yi and is Tuned-man converted by Fraud as well as Yi. His clothes are full of black like Yi, too. He is killed by "Cat" which had power amplified by Ai.

Talkative dolls
"Talkative doll" is a general term for human robots (androids) which serve as an operator in Fraud headquarters. Their appearance resembles a naked middle-age man with a skinhead.

Lai Lou Chin
Lai Lou Chin is a chief delegate of "Floor 2183" and is the only person who opposes the leader of Fraud, Kuu Ragua Lee. He is a poor-looking old man of a bobbed hair style. He always soaks in a capsule filled with special solution in the nude. The capsule is set in the position ranging from the body to the head of the large-sized humanoid robot. Actually, the robot serves as a substitute for the body of Lai Lou Chin, and the capsule has the function to prevent "mind reading" of Headmeters. He is called "Enema head" by Miss A, because the form of the capsule resembles a disposable syringe.

Residents of the upper floor
Alloy
Alloy is in the floor upper than the floor where Ai and Kei are, and sent only speculation into lower floors from there. The identity of Alloy is a thing invented based on "Program alloy" which is against Ai and tries to incorporate the gene in itself when it finds the gene that the program does not have. Alloy was invented by incorporating the program in a monster cell discovered by chance. Alloy stores billions of human beings' gene in the cell.
Since Alloy is an infinite form, it interferes in the world by getting into an organism and controlling the consciousness of that. However, the host of which Alloy influenced consciousness becomes very suggestive.
Alloy possesses "Cat", a staff of Fraud, Sugiura, Yoshioka, Akemi, the artificial body of Lai Lou Chin in sequence, and handles their body.
Alloy can draw out potential capacities of those whom Alloy touches and possessed like Ai.

Residents in A.D. 1983
Lee Kuwabara
Kuwabara is the head of Kasuga lab which existed in Shizuoka Izu in Japan once. He won fame as a professor of the bionics department of Los Angeles Institute of Technology. However, he was expelled from the bionics society, because he repeated medical experimentation on a living person to make a person with supernatural power artificially. When he was out of work, Sosuke Kasuga, his best friend and the head of Kasuga lab, gave him a job. Kuwabara assumed the head of the Kasuga lab after Sousuke's death, but Kuwabara betrayed Sosuke and his son after all, and returned to the society thanks to the program that they had studied.
He is the original of Kuu Ragua Lee and old Lee. The two are his clone.

Kasuga
Kasuga is the son of Sosuke Kasuga, the former head of Kasuga lab, and is the research worker.
He lost his father and wife and daughter

in a traffic accident at the same time in 1980.
He completed "Program Ai" which Sosuke had studied.
He is the original of Kei.

Terms
Floor
"Floor" is a cylindrical world of a radius of 440km which extends concentrically with centering on "Fraud Building (=The Pillar of God)" as center point and is surrounded by topology walls.
Fraud
"Fraud" is para-psychicers' groups, they are considered to be a national prime consultative body in Floor 2183.
Kuu Ragua Lee violated custom, and established headquarters inside of "The Pillar of God" where he calls "Fraud Building". He lives in there.
Headmeters
"Headmeters" are members of Fraud using para-supernatural power.
They analyze others' brain waves by many electronic devices buried in their body and read their minds (para-telepathy). And they control a magnetic field and float in the air and move an object (para-levitation and para-psychokinesis). And they predict what will happen in the near future at high hitting ratio by communicating with the city computer directly (para-precognition).
When they show their ability, their forehead displays the number suitable for the degree.
They occasionally equip the power supporter which is the heavy armaments for anti-Tuned-man warfare.
Tuned-man (Cyborg)
"Tuned-men" are combat cyborgs to whom the artificial muscle, the metal skeleton, etc. are transplanted, and they are equal to a tank in fighting power.
It is especially easy to read their minds for Headmeters.
Diver
"Diver" is a pet name of new and powerful mobile sky soldier or combat flying boat that Lai Lou Chin lent to Kuu Ragua Lee. Diver is a military escort for Kuu Ragua Lee to counter a new enemy, Alloy. Diver is a disk type and is propelled by a jet engine. Diver divides into 2 parts, and the upper part (Diver1) transforms into a combat humanoid robot. The lower part (Diver2) can be used as a flying boat as it is after separation.

Film adaption
An eponymous OVA was produced in 1986, and was shown at movie theaters affiliated with Toho on July 26, 1986. The film was directed by Kōichi Mashimo.

Outline
it is sometime in the future and the anime starts off with Kei and Ai running for their lives. Ai is a girl who holds a terrible secret which could destroy the current world. The world is now populated by Headmeters, people who have psychic powers and their strength is shown on their forehead when they fight. However, Kei was an experimental subject and his strength never went above level 5 while other surpasses his ability effortlessly. In escaping, when in desperate moments, Kei could increase his ability to infinity when Ai is in trouble. And then the one who is after her have a deep secret, aided by a small dwarflike man living in a robotic suit. Eventually Ai is captured and Kei, a Sherlock Holmes detective and another Headmeter who was converted to the good side when Kei unleashed his horrible powers through Ai must go and rescue her. Together they must save Ai and the secret which she holds. What is the secret of Ai?? Who is she?

Characters
Ai Ai is a girl who holds a terrible secret which could destroy the current world.
Kei a human who is a test subject for the headmeters he escapes their grasp. Kei was an experimental subject and his strength never went above level 5 while other surpasses his ability effortlessly. In escaping, when in desperate moments, Kei could increase his ability to infinity when Ai is in trouble.
Reiden The private detective who helps Kei and Ai. He is a former police officer.
K2 Headmeters, she becomes an ally of Ai and Kei.
Kuu Ragua Lee Headmeters, he is a leader of Fraud.
Lai Lou Chin Old Headmeters with artificial body.
Alloy Gene polymer
Tee
Mr. J Headmeters
Yi Tuned-man
Ryan Tuned-man
Source (edited): "http://en.wikipedia.org/wiki/Ai_City"

Blade Runner

Blade Runner is a 1982 American science fiction film directed by Ridley Scott and starring Harrison Ford, Rutger Hauer, and Sean Young. The screenplay, written by Hampton Fancher and David Peoples, is loosely based on the novel *Do Androids Dream of Electric Sheep?* by Philip K. Dick.

The film depicts a dystopian Los Angeles in November 2019 in which genetically engineered organic robots called replicants—visually indistinguishable from adult humans—are manufactured by the powerful Tyrell Corporation; as well as by other "mega–manufacturers" around the world. Their use on Earth is banned and replicants are exclusively used for dangerous, menial or leisure work on Earth's off-world colonies. Replicants who defy the ban and return to Earth are hunted down and "retired" by police special operatives known as "Blade Runners". The plot focuses on a brutal and cunning group of recently escaped replicants hiding in Los Angeles and the burnt out expert blade runner, Rick Deckard (Harrison Ford), who reluctantly agrees to take on one more assignment to hunt them down.

Blade Runner initially polarized critics: some were displeased with the pacing, while others enjoyed its thematic complexity. The film performed poorly in North American theaters but, despite the box office failure of the film, it has since become a cult classic and is now widely regarded as one of the best movies ever made. *Blade Runner* has been hailed for its production design, depicting a "retrofitted" future, and it remains a leading example of the neo-noir genre. *Blade Runner* brought the work of author Philip K. Dick to the attention of Hollywood and several later films were based on his work. Ridley Scott regards *Blade Runner* as "probably" his most complete and personal film. In 1993 *Blade Runner* was selected for preservation in the United States National Film Registry by the Library of Congress as being "culturally, historically, or aesthetically significant".

Seven versions of the film have been shown for various markets as a result of controversial changes made by film executives. A rushed director's cut was released in 1992 after a strong response to workprint screenings. This, in conjunction with its popularity as a video rental, made it one of the first films released on DVD, resulting in a basic disc with mediocre video and audio quality. In 2007 Warner Bros. released the 25th anniversary digitally remastered Final Cut by Scott in selected theaters, and subsequently on DVD, HD DVD, and Blu-ray Disc.

Plot

In Los Angeles, November 2019, retired police officer Rick Deckard (Harrison Ford) is detained at a noodle bar by officer Gaff (Edward James Olmos). Gaff takes Deckard to see his former supervisor, Bryant (M. Emmet Walsh). Deckard's former job, as a "blade runner", was to track down replicants, bioengineered robots, and "retire" them. Bryant tells Deckard that several late-model replicants have escaped, and have come to Earth illegally. These replicants are Tyrell Corporation Nexus-6 models and have a four-year life as a fail-safe, to prevent them from developing emotions. They may have come to Earth to try to have their lives extended.

Bryant shows Deckard a video of another blade runner, Holden (Morgan Paull), administering a Voight-Kampff test, which distinguishes humans from replicants based on their empathic response to questions. The subject of the test, Leon (Brion James), shoots Holden when it becomes likely he will be exposed. Bryant wants Deckard to return to work to retire Leon and three other replicants—Roy Batty (Rutger Hauer), Zhora (Joanna Cassidy) and Pris (Daryl Hannah). Deckard attempts to shirk the duty, but reluctantly agrees after Bryant issues a veiled threat.

Deckard is teamed with Gaff and sent to the Tyrell Corporation to ensure that the Voight-Kampff test works on Nexus-6 models. While he is there Deckard discovers that Tyrell's (Joe Turkel) assistant Rachael (Sean Young) is an experimental replicant who believes she is human; Rachael's consciousness has been enhanced with childhood memories from Tyrell's niece. As a result, a more extensive Voight-Kampff test is required to identify her as a replicant.

The replicants attempt to meet with Tyrell. Their first attempt leads Roy and Leon to the eye-manufacturing laboratory of Chew (James Hong). Under duress, Chew directs them to J.F. Sebastian (William Sanderson), a gifted designer who works closely with Tyrell. Rachael visits Deckard at his apartment to prove her humanity to him by showing him a family photo. She leaves in tears after Deckard tells her that her memories are implants. Pris meets J.F. Sebastian at his apartment in the Bradbury Building, where he lives with manufactured companions.

At Leon's apartment, Deckard finds an image of Zhora in Leon's photos, and some sort of scale in the bathtub. Deckard visits a replicant animal vendor and learns that it came from a snake made by Abdul Ben Hassan (Ben Astar). Hassan directs Deckard to a strip club where Zhora works. Deckard "retires" Zhora, whose death is witnessed by Leon. Deckard meets with Bryant shortly after and is told to add Rachael to his list of retirements, as she has disappeared from the Tyrell Corporation headquarters. Deckard spots Rachael in a crowd but is attacked by Leon. Rachael saves Deckard by killing Leon. The two return to Deckard's apartment, where Deckard promises not to hunt Rachael. Later they share an intimate moment; Rachael then tries to leave, but Deckard forcibly compels her to kiss him and ask for sex.

Roy arrives at Sebastian's apartment and tells Pris they are the only ones left alive. They gain Sebastian's help after explaining their plight. Sebastian reveals that they share their short lifetime; Sebastian suffers from a genetic disorder that accelerates his aging. Under the pretext of Sebastian informing Tyrell of a winning move in a game of correspondence chess, Roy and Sebastian enter Tyrell's penthouse. Roy demands more life from his maker, but Tyrell explains that a way to accomplish this was never found. Roy asks absolution for his sins, confessing that he has done "questionable things". Tyrell dismisses Roy's guilt, praising Roy's advanced design and his accomplishments. He tells Roy to "revel in his time", to which Roy responds "Nothing the god of biomechanics wouldn't let you into Heaven for". Roy then holds Tyrell's head in his hands, kisses him, and then kills him. Sebastian runs for the elevator with Roy following. Roy rides the elevator down alone; Sebastian is not seen again.

Deckard arrives at Sebastian's apartment and is ambushed by Pris, managing to kill her just as Roy returns. Roy punches through a wall, grabbing Deckard's right arm and breaks two of his fingers in retaliation for "retiring" Zhora and Pris. Roy releases Deckard and gives him time to run before hunting him through the building. The symptoms of Roy's limited life worsen and his right hand begins failing; he jabs a nail through it to regain control. Roy forces Deckard to the roof where, as Deckard attempts to escape, he leaps across to another building but falls short and ends up hanging from a rain-slicked girder. As Deckard loses his grip Roy, having made the same leap effortlessly, seizes his arm and hauls him onto the roof. As Roy's life ends he delivers a soliloquy on his life: "I've seen things you people wouldn't believe: Attack ships on fire off the shoulder of Orion; I've watched C-beams glitter in the dark near the Tannhauser Gate. All those moments will be lost in time, like tears in rain. Time to die."

Gaff arrives and shouts over to Deckard, "It's too bad she won't live but then again, who does?". Deckard returns to his apartment to find Rachael alive and sleeping in his bed; as they leave Deckard finds an origami unicorn, a calling card left by Gaff. Depending on the version, the film ends with Deckard and Rachael either leaving the apartment block to an uncertain future or driving through an idyllic pastoral landscape.

Technology

Spinner

Police spinners flying above Los Angeles city in 2019.

"Spinner" is the generic term for the fictional flying cars used in the film. A Spinner can be driven as a ground-based vehicle, take off vertically, hover, and cruise using jet propulsion much like the Vertical Take-Off and Landing (VTOL) aircraft currently in use today. They are used extensively by the police to patrol and survey the population, and it is clear that despite restrictions wealthy people can acquire spinner licenses. The vehicle was conceived and designed by Syd Mead who described the spinner as an "aerodyne" – a vehicle which directs air downward to create lift, though press kits for the film stated that the spinner was propelled by three engines: "conventional internal combustion, jet and anti-gravity". Mead's conceptual drawings were transformed into 25 working vehicles by automobile customizer Gene Winfield.

A Spinner is on permanent exhibit at the Science Fiction Museum and Hall of Fame in Seattle, Washington.

Voight-Kampff machine

Description from the original 1982 *Blade Runner* press kit.
The Voight-Kampff machine (or device) is a fictional interrogation tool, originating in the book where it is spelled Voigt-Kampff. The Voight-Kampff is a polygraph-like machine used by Blade Runners to assist in the testing of an individual to determine if he or she is a replicant. It measures bodily functions such as respiration, "blush response", heart rate, and eye movement in response to emotionally provocative questions. In the film two replicants take the test, Leon and Rachael, and Deckard tells Tyrell that it usually takes 20 to 30 cross-referenced questions to distinguish a replicant; in contrast with the book, where it is stated it only takes "six or seven" questions to make a determination. In the film it takes more than one hundred questions to determine if Rachael is a replicant.

Casting and characters

Casting the film proved troublesome, particularly for the lead role of Deckard. Screenwriter Hampton Fancher envisioned Robert Mitchum as Deckard and wrote the character's dialogue with Mitchum in mind. Director Ridley Scott and the film's producers "spent months" meeting and discussing the role with Dustin Hoffman, who eventually departed over differences in vision. Harrison Ford was ultimately chosen for several reasons, including his performance in the *Star Wars* films, Ford's interest in the story of *Blade Runner*, and discussions with Steven Spielberg who was finishing *Raiders of the Lost Ark* at the time and strongly praised Ford's work in the film. According to production documents, a long list of actors were considered for the role, including, but not limited to, Gene Hackman, Sean Connery, Jack Nicholson, Paul Newman, Clint Eastwood, Tommy Lee Jones, Arnold Schwarzenegger, Al Pacino, and Burt Reynolds.

Casting the roles of Rachael and Pris was also challenging and a lengthy series of screen tests were filmed with numerous actresses auditioning for the roles. Morgan Paull played the role of Deckard during the screen tests with actresses who were auditioning for the role of Rachael and Pris. Paull was cast as Deckard's fellow bounty hunter Holden based on his performances in the tests. Among the actresses tested for the role of Rachael was Nina Axelrod, who was Paull's recommendation. Stacey Nelkin tried out for Pris but was instead given another role in the film, which was ultimately cut before filming. Both Axelrod's and Nelkin's screen tests are featured in the 2007 documentary *Dangerous Days: Making Blade Runner*. Sean Young was picked to play Rachael, Tyrell's assistant, a replicant with memories that belonged to Tyrell's niece. Daryl Hannah played Pris, a "basic pleasure model" replicant, and the development of her relationship with Roy Batty is shown as a symbol of the replicants' underlying humanity.

One role that was not difficult to cast was Rutger Hauer as Roy Batty, the violent yet thoughtful leader of the replicants. Scott cast Hauer without having met him, based solely on Hauer's performances in other films Scott had seen. Hauer's portrayal of Batty was regarded by Philip K. Dick as, "the perfect Batty—cold, Aryan, flawless". Of the many films Hauer has done, *Blade Runner* is his favorite. As he explained in a live chat in 2001, "BLADE RUNNER needs no explanation. It just IZZ [*sic*]. All of the best. There is nothing like it. To be part of a real MASTERPIECE which changed the world's thinking. It's awesome." Joe Pantoliano, who later played the role of Cypher in *The Matrix*, was considered for the role of Sebastian.

Coming off the success of *Star Wars* (1977), *The Empire Strikes Back* (1980) and *Raiders of the Lost Ark* (1981), Ford was looking for a role with dramatic depth. After Steven Spielberg praised Ford, he was hired for *Blade Runner*. In 1992, Ford revealed, "*Blade Runner* is not one of my favorite films. I tangled with Ridley." Apart from friction with the director, Ford also disliked the voiceovers: "When we started shooting it had been tacitly agreed that the version of the film that we had agreed upon was the version without voiceover narration. It was a f**king [*sic*] nightmare. I thought that the film had worked without the narration. But now I was stuck re-creating that narration. And I was obliged to do the voiceovers for people that did not represent the director's interests." "I went kicking and screaming to the studio to record it."

In 2006 Scott was asked "Who's the biggest pain in the arse you've ever worked with?", he replied: "It's got to be Harrison ... he'll forgive me because now I get on with him. Now he's become charming. But he knows a lot, that's the problem. When we worked together it was my first film up and I was the new kid on the block. But we made a good movie." Ford said of Scott in 2000: "I admire his work. We had a bad patch there, and I'm over it." In 2006 Ford reflected on the production of the film saying: "What I remember more than anything else when I see *Blade Runner* is not the 50 nights of shooting in the rain, but the voiceover ... I was still obliged to work for these clowns that came in writing one bad voiceover after another." Ridley Scott confirmed in the summer 2007 issue of *Total Film* that Harrison Ford contributed to the *Blade Runner* Special Edition DVD, having already done his interviews. "Harrison's fully on board", said Scott.

Edward James Olmos played Gaff and used his diverse ethnic background, and some in-depth personal research, to help create the fictional "Cityspeak" language his character uses in the film. His initial addresses to Deckard at the noodle bar is partly in Hungarian and means, "Horse dick! No way. You are the Blade ... Blade Runner." M. Emmet Walsh lived up to his reputation as a great character actor with the role of Captain Bryant, a hard-drinking, sleazy, and underhanded police veteran typical of the film noir genre. Joe Turkel was Dr. Eldon Tyrell, a corporate mogul who built an empire on genetically manipulated humanoid slaves. William Sanderson was cast as J. F. Sebastian, a quiet and lonely genius who provides a compassionate yet compliant portrait of humanity. J. F. is able to sympathize with the replicants' short lifespan because he has "Methuselah Syndrome" (possibly a form of progeria), a genetic disease that causes faster aging and a short lifespan.

Brion James played Leon Kowalski, a replicant masquerading as a waste disposal engineer; he shoots a Blade Runner to escape, establishing the physical threat the replicants pose to their would-be captors. Joanna Cassidy was a special-ops, undercover and assassin replicant model called Zhora. Cassidy portrays a strong female who has seen the worst humanity has to offer. Morgan Paull plays Holden, the Blade Runner initially assigned to the case. James Hong as Hannibal Chew, an elderly Asian geneticist specializing in synthetic eyes. Hy Pyke conveyed the sleazy bar owner Taffey Lewis with ease and in a single take, something almost unheard-of with Scott whose drive for perfection resulted at times in double-digit takes.

The film also used a number of then less well-known actors such as Daryl Hannah and Sean Young.

Production

The Bradbury Building in Los Angeles was a filming location.

Interest in adapting Philip K. Dick's novel *Do Androids Dream of Electric Sheep?* developed shortly after its 1968 publication. According to Dick, director Martin Scorsese was interested in filming the novel, but never optioned it. Producer Herb Jaffe optioned it in the early 1970s, but Dick wasn't impressed with the screenplay: "Robert Jaffe, who wrote the screenplay, flew down here to Orange County. I said to him then that it was so bad that I wanted to know if he wanted me to beat him up there at the airport or wait till we got to my apartment." The screenplay by Hampton Fancher was optioned in 1977.

Producer Michael Deeley became interested in Fancher's draft and convinced director Ridley Scott to use it to create his first American film. Scott had previously declined the project, but after leaving the slow production of *Dune*, wanted a faster-paced project to take his mind off his older brother's recent death. He joined the project on February 21, 1980, and managed to push up the promised Filmways financing from US$13 million to $15 million. Fancher's script focused more on environmental issues and less on issues of humanity and faith, which had featured heavily in the novel and Scott wanted changes. Fancher found a cinema treatment by William S. Burroughs for Alan E. Nourse's novel *The Bladerunner* (1974), entitled *Blade Runner (a movie)*. Scott liked the name, so Deeley obtained the rights to the titles. Eventually he hired David Peoples to rewrite the script and Fancher left the job over the issue on December 21, 1980, although he later returned to contribute additional rewrites.

Having invested over $2.5 million in pre-production, as the date of commencement of principal photography neared, Filmways withdrew financial backing. In ten days Deeley had secured $21.5 million in financing through a three way deal between The Ladd Company (through Warner Bros.), the Hong Kong-based producer Sir Run Run Shaw, and Tandem Productions.

Some of the costumes used in the movie, such as Zhora's raincoat and Sean Young's dark suit (Science Fiction Museum and Hall of Fame, Seattle)

Philip K. Dick became concerned that no one had informed him about the film's production, which added to his distrust of Hollywood. After Dick criticized an early version of Hampton Fancher's script in an article written for the Los Angeles *Select TV Guide*, the studio sent Dick the David Peoples rewrite. Although Dick died shortly before the film's release, he was pleased with the rewritten script, and with a twenty-minute special effects test reel that was screened for him when he was invited to the studio. Despite his well known skepticism of Hollywood in principle, Dick enthused to Ridley Scott that the world created for the film looked exactly as he had imagined it. He said, "I saw a segment of Douglas Trumbull's special effects for *Blade Runner* on the KNBC-TV news. I recognized it immediately. It was my own interior world. They caught it perfectly." He also approved of the film's script, saying, "After I finished reading the screenplay, I got the novel out and looked through it. The two reinforce each other, so that someone who started with the novel would enjoy the movie and someone who started with the movie would enjoy the novel." The motion picture was dedicated to Dick.

Blade Runner has numerous deep similarities to Fritz Lang's *Metropolis*, including a built up urban environment, in which the wealthy literally live above the workers, dominated by a huge building—the Stadtkrone Tower in *Metropolis* and the Tyrell Building in *Blade Runner*. Special effects supervisor David Dryer used stills from *Metropolis* when lining up *Blade Runner*'s miniature building shots.

Ridley Scott credits Edward Hopper's painting *Nighthawks* and the French science fiction comic magazine *Métal Hurlant* ("Heavy Metal"), to which the artist Moebius contributed, as stylistic mood sources. He also drew on the landscape of "Hong Kong on a very bad day", and the industrial landscape of his one-time home in the North East of England. Scott hired Syd Mead as his concept artist who, like Scott, was influenced by *Métal Hurlant*. Moebius was offered the opportunity to assist in the pre-production of *Blade Runner*, but he declined so that he could work on René Laloux's animated film *Les Maîtres du temps*—a decision he later regretted. Lawrence G. Paull (production designer) and David Snyder (art director) realized Scott's and Mead's sketches. Douglas Trumbull and Richard Yuricich supervised the special effects for the film. Principal photography of *Blade Runner* began on March 9, 1981, and ended four months later.

Interpretation

Dr. Tyrell polarizing his office window to control the Sun implies the god-like powers of the Tyrell Corporation. The dark and shadowy film-noir cinematography are clearly visible.

Although *Blade Runner* is ostensibly an action film, it operates on multiple dramatic and narrative levels. It is indebted to film noir conventions: the femme fatale; protagonist-narration (removed in later versions); dark and shadowy cinematography; and the questionable moral outlook of the hero—in this case, extended to include reflections upon the nature of his own humanity. It is a literate science fiction film, thematically enfolding the philosophy of religion and moral implications of human mastery of genetic engineering in the context of classical Greek drama and hubris. It also draws on Biblical images, such as Noah's flood, and literary sources, such as *Frankenstein*. Linguistically, the theme of mortality is subtly reiterated in the chess game between Roy and Tyrell, based on the famous Immortal game of 1851 though Scott has said that was coincidental.

Blade Runner delves into the implications of technology on the environment and on society by reaching to the past, using literature, religious symbolism, classical dramatic themes, and film noir. This tension between past, present, and future is mirrored in the retrofitted future of *Blade Runner*, which is high-tech and gleaming in places but decayed and old elsewhere. Ridley Scott was interviewed in 2002 by reporter Lynn Barber of *The Observer* where he described the film as: "extremely dark, both literally and metaphorically, with an oddly masochistic feel". Director Scott said he "liked the idea of exploring pain" in the wake of his brother's skin cancer death: "When he was ill, I used to go and visit him in London, and that was really traumatic for me."

An aura of paranoia suffuses the film: corporate power looms large; the police seem omnipresent; vehicle and warning lights probe into buildings; and the consequences of huge biomedical power over the individual are explored—especially the consequences for replicants of their implanted memories. Control over the environment is depicted as taking place on a vast scale, hand in hand with the absence of any natural life, with artificial animals substituting for their extinct predecessors. This oppressive backdrop explains the frequently referenced migration of humans to extra-terrestrial ("off-world") colonies. The dystopian themes explored in *Blade Runner* are an early example of cyberpunk concepts expanding into film. Eyes are a recurring motif, as are manipulated images, calling into question reality and our ability to accurately perceive and remember it.

These thematic elements provide an atmosphere of uncertainty for *Blade Runner*'s central theme of examining humanity. In order to discover replicants an empathy test is used, with a number of its questions focused on the treatment of animals—it seems to be an essential indicator of someone's "humanity". The replicants appear to show compassion and concern for one another and are juxtaposed against human characters who lack empathy while the mass of humanity on the streets is cold and impersonal. The film goes so far as to put in doubt whether Deckard is human, and forces the audience to re-evaluate what it means to be human.

The question of whether Deckard is intended to be a human or a replicant has been an ongoing controversy since the film's release. Both Michael Deeley and Harrison Ford wanted Deckard to be human while Hampton Fancher preferred ambiguity. Ridley Scott has confirmed that in his vision Deckard is a replicant. Deckard's unicorn dream sequence, inserted into the Director's Cut, coinciding with Gaff's parting gift of an origami unicorn is seen by many as showing that Deckard is a replicant—as Gaff could have accessed Deckard's implanted memories. The interpretation that Deckard is a replicant is challenged by others who believe the unicorn imagery shows that the characters, whether human or replicant, share the same dreams and recognize their affinity, or that the absence of a decisive answer is crucial to the film's main theme. The inherent ambiguity and uncertainty of the film, as well as its textual richness, have permitted viewers to see it from their own perspectives.

Adapting the novel

Philip K. Dick refused an offer of $400,000 to write a novelization of the *Blade Runner* screenplay, saying: "[I was] told the cheapo novelization would have to appeal to the twelve-year-old audience" and "[it] would have probably been disastrous to me artistically." He added, "That insistence on my part of bringing out the original novel and not doing the novelization—they were just furious. They finally recognized that there was a legitimate reason for reissuing the novel, even though it cost them money. It was a victory not just of contractual obligations but of theoretical principles." *Do Androids Dream of Electric Sheep?* was eventually reprinted as a tie-in, with the film poster as a cover and the original title in parentheses below the *Blade Runner* title.

Reception

Blade Runner was released in 1,290 theaters on June 25, 1982. That date was chosen by producer Alan Ladd, Jr. because his previous highest-grossing films (*Star Wars* and *Alien*) had a similar opening date (May 25) in 1977 and 1979, making the date his "lucky day". The gross for the opening weekend was a disappointing $6.15 million. A significant factor in the film's rather poor box office performance was that its release coincided with other science fiction film releases, including *The Thing*, *Star Trek II: The Wrath of Khan*, and, most significantly, *E.T. the Extra-Terrestrial*, which dominated box office revenues that summer.

Film critics were polarized as some felt the story had taken a back seat to special effects and that it was not the action/adventure the studio had advertised. Others acclaimed its complexity and predicted it would stand the test of time.

In the United States, a general criticism was its slow pacing that detracts from other strengths; Sheila Benson from the *Los Angeles Times* called it "Blade crawler", while Pat Berman in State and Columbia Record described it as "science fiction pornography". Roger Ebert praised the visuals of both the original *Blade Runner* and the *Director's cut* versions and recommended it for that reason; however, he found the human story clichéd and a little thin. In 2007, upon release of *The Final Cut*, Ebert somewhat revised his original opinion of the film and added it to his list of Great Movies, while noting, "I have been assured that my problems in the past with *Blade Runner* represent a failure of my own taste and imagination, but if the film was perfect, why has Sir Ridley continued to tinker with it?"

Accolades

Blade Runner has won and been nominated for the following awards: Recognitions for *Blade Runner* include:

Cultural influence

A police spinner flying beside huge advertising-laden skyscrapers. These special effects are benchmarks that have influenced many subsequent science-fiction films.

While not initially a success with North American audiences, the film was popular internationally and became a cult film. The film's dark style and futuristic designs have served as a benchmark and its influence can be seen in many subsequent science fiction films, anime, video games, and television programs. For example Ronald D. Moore and David Eick, the producers of the re-imagining of *Battlestar Galactica*, have both cited *Blade Runner* as one of the major influences for the show. *Blade Runner* continues to reflect modern trends and concerns, and an increasing number consider it one of the greatest science fiction films of all time. *Blade Runner* is also cited as an important influence to both the style and story of the *Ghost in the Shell* film series, which itself has been highly influential to the future-noir genre.

The film was selected for preservation in the United States National Film Registry in 1993 and is frequently used in university courses. In 2007 it was named the 2nd most visually influential film of all time by the Visual Effects Society.

Blade Runner is one of the most musically sampled films of the 20th century and inspired the Grammy nominated song "More Human than Human" by White Zombie. The 2009 album, *I, Human*, by Singaporean band Deus Ex Machina makes numerous references to the genetic engineering and cloning themes from the film, and even features a track entitled "Replicant".

Blade Runner has influenced adventure games such as; *Rise of the Dragon*, *Snatcher*, *Beneath a Steel Sky*, *Flashback: The Quest for Identity*, *Bubblegum Crisis* (and its original anime films), the role-playing game *Shadowrun*, the first-person shooter *Perfect Dark*, and the *Syndicate* series of video games. The film is also cited as a major influence on Warren Spector, designer of the computer-game *Deus Ex*, which displays evidence of the film's influence in both its visual rendering and plot. The look of the film, darkness, neon lights and opacity of vision, is easier to render than complicated backdrops, making it a popular choice for game designers.

Blade Runner has also been the subject of parody, such as the comics *Blade Bummer* by *Crazy* comics, *Bad Rubber* by Steve Gallacci, and the *Red Dwarf* 2009 twenty-first anniversary three-part miniseries, "Back To Earth".

Blade Runner curse

Among the folklore that has developed around the film over the years has been the belief that the film was a curse to the companies whose logos were displayed prominently as product placements in some scenes. While they were market leaders at the time, more than half experienced disastrous setbacks during the next decade. RCA, which at one time was the United States' leading consumer electronics and communications conglomerate, was bought out by one-time parent General Electric in 1985, and dismantled. Atari dominated the home video game market when the film came out, but never recovered from the next year's downturn in the industry and, by the 1990s, had ceased to represent anything more than a brand, a back catalogue of games, and some legacy computers. Atari today is an entirely different firm, using the former company's name. Cuisinart similarly went bankrupt in 1989, though it lives on under new ownership. The Bell System monopoly was broken up that same year and most of the resulting Regional Bell operating companies have since changed their names and merged back with each other, and other companies, to form the new AT&T. Pan Am suffered from the terrorist bombing and destruction of Pan Am Flight 103 and, after a decade of mounting losses, finally went bankrupt in 1991 with the falloff in overseas travel caused by the Gulf War. The Coca-Cola Company suffered losses during its failed introduction of New Coke in 1985, but soon afterwards regained its market share.

Future Noir

Before the film's principal photography began, *Cinefantastique* magazine commissioned Paul M. Sammon to write an article about *Blade Runner*'s production which became the book *Future Noir: The Making of Blade Runner* (referred to as the "*Blade Runner* Bible" by many of the film's fans). The book chronicles the evolution of *Blade Runner* as a film and focuses on film-set politics, especially the British director's experiences with his first American film crew; of which producer Alan Ladd, Jr. has said, "Harrison wouldn't speak to Ridley and Ridley wouldn't speak to Harrison. By the end of the shoot Ford was 'ready to kill Ridley', said one colleague. He really would have taken him on if he hadn't been talked out of it." *Future Noir* has short cast biographies and quotations about their experiences in making *Blade Runner*, as well as many photographs of the film's production and preliminary sketches. The cast chapter was deleted from the first edition, though it is available online. A second edition of *Future Noir* was published in 2007.

Soundtrack

The *Blade Runner* soundtrack by Vangelis is a dark melodic combination of classic composition and futuristic synthesizers which mirrors the film-noir retro-future envisioned by Ridley Scott. Vangelis, fresh from his Academy Award winning score for *Chariots of Fire*, composed and performed the music on his synthesizers. He also made use of various chimes and the vocals of collaborator Demis Roussos. Another memorable sound is the haunting tenor sax solo "Love Theme" by British saxophonist Dick Morrissey, who appeared on many of Vangelis' albums. Ridley Scott also used "Memories of Green" from Vangelis' album *See You Later* (an orchestral version of which Scott would later use in his film *Someone To Watch Over Me*).

Along with Vangelis' compositions and ambient textures, the film's sound scape also features a track by the Japanese Ensemble Nipponia ('Ogi No Mato' or 'The Folding Fan as a Target' from the Nonesuch Records release "Traditional Vocal And Instrumental Music") and a track by harpist Gail Laughton ("Harps of the Ancient Temples" from Laurel Records).

Despite being well received by fans and critically acclaimed and nominated in 1983 for a BAFTA and Golden Globe as best original score, and the promise of a soundtrack album from Polydor Records in the end titles of the film, the release of the official soundtrack recording was delayed for over a decade. There are two official releases of the music from *Blade Runner*. In light of the lack of a release of an album, the New American Orchestra recorded an orchestral adaptation in 1982 which bore little resemblance to the original. Some of the film tracks would in 1989 surface on the compilation *Vangelis: Themes*, but not until the 1992 release of the Director's Cut version would a substantial amount of the film's score see commercial release.

These delays and poor reproductions led to the production of many bootleg recordings over the years. A bootleg tape surfaced in 1982 at science fiction conventions and became popular given the delay of an official release of the original recordings, and in 1993 "Off

World Music, Ltd." created a bootleg CD that would prove more comprehensive than Vangelis' official CD in 1994. A set with three CDs of *Blade Runner*-related Vangelis music was released on December 10, 2007. Titled *Blade Runner Trilogy*, the first CD contains the same tracks as the 1994 official soundtrack release, the second CD contains previously unreleased music from the movie, and the third CD is all newly composed music from Vangelis, inspired by, and in the spirit of the movie.

Versions

Seven different versions of *Blade Runner* have been shown. The original workprint version (1982, 113 minutes) was shown for audience test previews in Denver and Dallas in March 1982. It was also shown in 1990 and 1991 in Los Angeles and San Francisco as a *Director's Cut* without Scott's approval. Negative responses to the test previews led to the modifications resulting in the U.S. theatrical version, while positive response to the showings in 1990 and 1991 pushed the studio to approve work on an official director's cut. It was re-released with the 5-disc Ultimate Edition in 2007. A San Diego Sneak Preview was shown only once, in May 1982, and was almost identical to the *Domestic Cut* but contained three extra scenes.

The releases seen by most cinema audiences were: the U.S. theatrical version (1982, 116 minutes), known as the original version or *Domestic Cut*, released on Betamax and VHS in 1983 and laserdisc in 1987; the *International Cut* (1982, 117 minutes), also known as the "Criterion Edition" or "uncut version", which included more violent action scenes than the U.S. version. Although initially unavailable in the U.S., and distributed in Europe and Asia via theatrical and local Warner Home Video laserdisc releases, it was later released on VHS and Criterion Collection laserdisc in North America, and re-released in 1992 as a "10th Anniversary Edition".

The U.S. broadcast version (1986, 114 minutes) was the U.S. theatrical version edited by CBS to tone down the violence, profanity, and nudity to meet broadcasting restrictions.

The Ridley Scott-approved (1991, 116 minutes) *Director's Cut* was screened at the Los Angeles NuArt Theater and the San Francisco Castro Theater in September and October 1991 and was prompted by the unauthorized 1990–1991 workprint theatrical release. This *Director's Cut* was made available on VHS and laserdisc in 1993, and on DVD in 1997. Significant changes from the theatrical version include: the removal of Deckard's voice-over; re-insertion of a unicorn sequence; and removal of the studio-imposed happy ending. Scott provided extensive notes and consultation to Warner Bros. through film preservationist Michael Arick, who was put in charge of creating the *Director's Cut*.

Ridley Scott's *Final Cut* (2007, 117 minutes), or the "25th Anniversary Edition", was released by Warner Bros. theatrically on October 5, 2007, and subsequently released on DVD, HD DVD, and Blu-ray Disc in December 2007. This is the only version over which Ridley Scott had complete artistic control, as he was not directly in charge of the *Director's Cut*. In conjunction with the *Final Cut* cinema release, extensive documentary and other materials were produced for the DVD releases which culminated in a five-disc "Ultimate Collector's Edition" release by Charles de Lauzirika. A single disc version of the final cut in Blu-ray and DVD formats was released in 2010.

Derivative works

Documentaries

On the Edge of Blade Runner (2000, 55 minutes) was produced by Nobles Gate Ltd. (for Channel 4), was directed by Andrew Abbott and hosted/written by Mark Kermode. Interviews with production staff, including Scott, give details of the creative process and the turmoil during preproduction. Stories from Paul M. Sammon and Hampton Fancher provide insight into Philip K. Dick and the origins of *Do Androids Dream of Electric Sheep?*

Interwoven are cast interviews (with the notable exceptions of Harrison Ford and Sean Young), which convey some of the difficulties of making the film (including an exacting director and humid, smoggy weather). There is also a tour of some locations, most notably the Bradbury Building and the Warner Bros. backlot that became the LA 2019 streets, which look very different from Scott's dark vision. The documentary then details the test screenings and the resulting changes (the voice over, the happy ending, and the deleted Holden hospital scene), the special effects, the soundtrack by Vangelis, and the unhappy relationship between the filmmakers and the investors which culminated in Deeley and Scott being fired but still working on the film. The question of whether or not Deckard is a replicant surfaces.

Future Shocks (2003, 27 minutes) is a documentary by TVOntario (part of their *Film 101* series using footage compiled over the years for Saturday Night at the Movies). It includes interviews with executive producer Bud Yorkin, Syd Mead, and the cast, this time with Sean Young, but still without Harrison Ford. There is extensive commentary by science fiction author Robert J. Sawyer and from film critics, as the documentary focuses on the themes, visual impact and influence of the film. Edward James Olmos describes Ford's participation, and personal experiences during filming are related by Young, Walsh, Cassidy and Sanderson. They also relate a story about crew members creating T-shirts that took pot shots at Scott. The different versions of the film are critiqued and the accuracy of its predictions of the future are discussed.

Dangerous Days: Making Blade Runner (2007, 183 minutes) is a documentary directed and produced by Charles de Lauzirika for the 2007 Final Cut version of the film. It appears with every edition of *The Final Cut* on DVD, HD DVD and Blu-ray Disc, except for the 2010 single-disc DVD and Blu-Ray editions. (It is a DVD format disc, even in the HD DVD and Blu-ray Disc editions). It was culled from over 80 interviews, including Harrison Ford, Sean

Young, Rutger Hauer, Edward James Olmos, Jerry Perenchio, Bud Yorkin and Ridley Scott, and also contains several alternate and deleted shots within the context of the documentary itself. The documentary consists of eight chapters, each covering a portion of the film-making—or in the case of the final chapter, the film's controversial legacy.

All Our Variant Futures: From Workprint to Final Cut (2007, 29 minutes), produced by Paul Prischman, appears on Disc 5 of the *Blade Runner* Ultimate Collector's Edition and provides an overview of the film's multiple versions and their origins, as well as detailing the seven year-long restoration, enhancement and remastering process behind *The Final Cut*. Included are interviews with director Ridley Scott, restoration producer Charles de Lauzirika, restoration consultant Kurt P. Galvao, restoration VFX supervisor John Scheele and *Future Noir: The Making of Blade Runner* author Paul M. Sammon. Behind-the-scenes footage documenting the restoration—from archival work done in 2001 through the 2007 filming of Joanna Cassidy and Benjamin Ford for *The Final Cut*'s digital fixes—are seen throughout. A variety of other supplemental featurettes produced and directed by Charles de Lauzirika are included both the four- and five-disc collector's editions of *Blade Runner* released by Warner Home Video in 2007.

Sequels

K. W. Jeter, a friend of Philip K. Dick, has written three officially authorized *Blade Runner* novels that continue Deckard's story; attempting to resolve many of the differences between *Blade Runner* and *Do Androids Dream of Electric Sheep?*

- *Blade Runner 2: The Edge of Human* (1995)
- *Blade Runner 3: Replicant Night* (1996)
- *Blade Runner 4: Eye and Talon* (2000)

Ridley Scott apparently toyed with the idea of a sequel film, which would have been titled *Metropolis*. The project was ultimately shelved due to rights issues. A script was also written for a proposed sequel titled *Blade Runner Down*, which would have been based on Jeter's first sequel novel. At the 2007 Comic-Con Scott again announced that he was considering a sequel to the film. *Eagle Eye* co-writer Travis Wright worked with producer Bud Yorke for a few years on the project. His colleague John Glenn, who left the film by 2008, stated the script explores the nature of the off-world colonies as well as what happens to the Tyrell Corporation in the wake of its founder's death.

Blade Runner co-author David Peoples wrote the 1998 action film *Soldier*, which was referred to by him as a "sidequel", or spiritual successor, to the original film.

Prequel

In June 2009 *The New York Times* reported that Ridley Scott and his brother Tony Scott, were working on a prequel to *Blade Runner*. The prequel, *Purefold*, will be a series of 5–10 minute shorts, aimed first at the web and then perhaps television, and will be set at a point in time before 2019. Due to rights issues the series will not be linked too closely to the characters or events of the 1982 film.

On March 4, 2011, io9 reported that Bud Yorkin, the producer of *Blade Runner*, is now developing a sequel or prequel to the film. It was not announced whether this was connected to Ridley Scott or any of the other original filmmakers. It has been reported that Christopher Nolan, who has worked with Warner Bros. many times in the past, was wanted at the helm of any eventual prequel or sequel.

Comics

Archie Goodwin scripted the comic book adaptation, *A Marvel Comics Super Special: Blade Runner*, published in September 1982. The Jim Steranko cover leads into a 45-page adaptation illustrated by the team of Al Williamson, Carlos Garzon, Dan Green and Ralph Reese. This adaptation includes the narrative line, "Blade runner. You're always movin' on the edge".

In 2009 BOOM! Studios published a 24-issue miniseries comic book adaptation of *Do Androids Dream of Electric Sheep?*, the *Blade Runner* source novel. In April 2010 BOOM! Studios announced a follow up comic 'Dust To Dust, *written by Chris Robertson and drawn by Robert Adler, a four issue miniseries which started production on May 26, 2010.*

Video games

There are two video games based on the film, one for Commodore 64, Sinclair ZX Spectrum and Amstrad CPC (1985) by CRL Group PLC based on the music by Vangelis (due to licensing issues), and another action adventure PC game (1997) by Westwood Studios. The Westwood PC game featured new characters and branching storylines based on the *Blade Runner* world. Eldon Tyrell, Gaff, Leon, Rachael, Chew, and J.F. Sebastian are seen, and their voice files were recorded by the original actors. DNA Row, the Eye Works, the Police Headquarters, Howie Lee's, the Tyrell Corporation building, and J.F. Sebastian's hotel are faithfully replicated. The events portrayed in the 1997 game occur not after, but in parallel to those in the film. The player assumes the role of McCoy, another replicant-hunter working at the same time as Deckard. Although Deckard is seen in photo evidence and referred to in dialogue, Deckard and McCoy never meet, preserving the canon of the film and the independence of the game plot.

The PC game featured a non-linear plot, non-player characters that each ran in their own independent AI, and an unusual pseudo-3D engine (which eschewed polygonal solids in favor of voxel elements) that did not require the use of a 3D accelerator card to play the game.

Television series

Though not an official sequel to *Blade Runner* the TV movie *Total Recall 2070* was initially planned as a spin-off of the movie *Total Recall*, it would eventually be transformed into a hybrid of them both. The *Total Recall* film had, like *Blade Runner*, been based on a Philip K. Dick short story: "We Can Remember It for You Wholesale". There are

many similarities between the television series and the *Blade Runner* film. The series takes place in a dark, crowded, industrial, and cosmopolitan setting. David Hume is a senior detective for the Citizens Protection Bureau (CPB) who is partnered with Ian Farve, an Alpha Class android. The series focused on questions such as the nature of humanity and the rights of androids.
Source (edited): "http://en.wikipedia.org/wiki/Blade_Runner"

Come Find Yourself

Come Find Yourself is the first album released by the band Fun Lovin' Criminals. It was released on February 20, 1996.

Track listing
All tracks by Fun Lovin' Criminals, except where noted.
1. "The Fun Lovin' Criminal" - 3:11
2. "Passive/Aggressive" - 3:33
3. "The Grave and the Constant" - 4:46
4. "Scooby Snacks" - 3:04
5. "Smoke 'Em" - 4:45
6. "Bombin' the L" - 3:51
7. "I Can't Get with That" - 4:24
8. "King of New York" - 3:46
9. "We Have All the Time in the World" (John Barry, Hal David) - 3:41
10. "Bear Hug" - 3:27
11. "Come Find Yourself" - 4:19
12. "Crime and Punishment" - 3:19
13. "Methadonia" - 4:04
14. "I Can't Get with That (Schmoove Version)" - 5:34
15. "Coney Island Girl" - 1:28

Personnel
- Fun Lovin' Criminals – Producer
- Tim Latham – Engineer

Source (edited): "http://en.wikipedia.org/wiki/Come_Find_Yourself"

Cowboy Bebop

Cowboy Bebop (カウボーイビバップ *Kaubōi Bibappu*) is a 1998 Japanese anime series directed by Shinichirō Watanabe, written by Keiko Nobumoto, and produced by Sunrise. Its 26 episodes ("sessions") comprise a complete storyline: set in 2071, the series follows the adventures, misadventures and tragedies of a group of bounty hunters, or "cowboys", traveling on their spaceship, the *Bebop*. The series explores several concepts involving philosophy, including existentialism, loneliness, and existential ennui.

The series' art direction centers on American music and counterculture, especially the beat and jazz movements of the 1940s-60s and the early rock era of the 1950s-70s, which the original soundtrack by Yoko Kanno and The Seatbelts recreates.

Cowboy Bebop was a commercial success both in Japan and international markets, notably in the United States. After this reception, Sony Pictures released a feature film, *Knockin' on Heaven's Door* (2001), to theaters worldwide and followed up with an international DVD release. Two manga adaptations were serialized in Kadokawa Shoten's *Asuka Fantasy DX*.

Plot

Setting
In 2022, the explosion of an experimental hyperspace gateway severely damaged the Moon, resulting in a debris ring and meteor bombardments that eradicated a large portion of the population. As a result, many survivors abandoned the barely habitable Earth to colonize the inner planets, the asteroid belt and the moons of Jupiter.

The series is set in the year 2071, when the entire Solar System has been made accessible through reliable hyperspace gates. Mars has become the new central hub of human civilization, and interplanetary crime syndicates exert influence over the government and the *Inter-Solar System Police* (ISSP), limiting their effectiveness in dealing with crime. As a result, a bounty system similar to that in the Old West is established to deal with fugitives, terrorists, and other criminals; the bounty hunters involved are frequently termed "cowboys."

Story
Cowboy Bebop revolves around a crew of bounty hunters living in the spaceship named *Bebop*. They are a team of bounty hunters who travel the Solar System trying to apprehend bounties. Jet Black, the ship's captain and owner, partnered with Spike Spiegel for his diverse combat skills. During their travels, the *Bebop* gains new crew members Ein, Faye, and Edward.

Throughout the series *Bebop* crew members' pasts catch up with them, and the show regularly utilizes flashbacks to illustrate the history of the main characters. Spike's past as a syndicate enforcer is a major element of the series, while other episodes deal with Jet's previous occupation as an ISSP officer on Ganymede, and Faye's mysterious origins and significant debt problems. The day-to-day life of the crew is also explored throughout the series.

Characters

From left to right: Ein, Edward, Spike Spiegel, Jet Black and Faye Valentine

Spike Spiegel is a former member of the Red Dragon Crime Syndicate. Spike is a master in firearms and hand-to-hand combat, practicing Jeet Kune Do, and is also a skilled pilot. He flies a sleek custom-designed Mono Racer, red-painted, atmosphere-capable spacecraft called *Swordfish II*. Despite his outwardly carefree attitude, he is haunted by the memory of his time in the syndicate, particularly of his romantic relationship with a mysterious woman named Julia, and his conflict with archrival and former syndicate partner, Vicious. He is also an accomplished pickpocket.

Jet Black is a former ISSP officer and the owner of the *Bebop*. Once called "The Black Dog" by his fellow officers for his relentless nature, he left the ISSP after becoming fed up with the corruption and red tape of the organization, and turned to bounty hunting as a way to pursue justice. Despite the ability to have it replaced, he voluntarily bears a cybernetic arm as a reminder of what happened when he rushed into trouble without looking first. He owns both their main ship, Bebop, and his own small yellow ship called Hammerhead. The Hammerhead has been equipped with a claw and harpoon that can be used as a tow cable. Like Spike, he too is haunted by the memory of a woman, Alisa, his longtime girlfriend who left him without giving a reason.

Faye Valentine is a novice bounty hunter with a persistent gambling addiction. She joins the crew of the *Bebop* uninvited, to the consternation of Jet and Spike. Though she abandons the ship several times during the course of the series, her attachment to the crew always brings her back. These feelings are apparently reciprocated, as Jet and Spike always allow her to return despite claiming they're pleased to see her leave. She pilots a generic heavy spacecraft called *Red Tail* which is pale blue despite the name and has been heavily modified with armament and tracking sensors. Her gambling, cheating, and competitive skills are unrivaled except by Spike. Much of her past and her real last name are a mystery, however it appears that she was severely injured in a space shuttle accident and was then put into cold sleep until she could be healed. She emerges from the cryo sleep without her memories, which she eventually recovers. She finds her old house which was a large mansion, but it had since burnt down.

Edward is a young, eccentric computer genius and master hacker. She goes by the name "Radical Edward" when hacking. Ed is a girl, though her name and androgynous appearance suggest otherwise. She had followed the travels of the *Bebop* before encountering the ship, and agrees to help the crew track down a bounty-head in exchange for becoming a member of the crew. Although extremely intelligent, Ed is still a young child, and looks up to the crew of the Bebop as members of her family. She gave herself the fanciful name "Edward Wong Hau Pepulu Tivruskii 4th" after running away to an orphanage, but after her father is found, it is revealed that her real name is Françoise Appledelhi and spends much of her time with Ein.

Ein is a Pembroke Welsh Corgi and former lab animal identified as a "data dog" by the scientists who created him. The reason for this title is that the scientists used him for unspecified experiments, cyber-enhancing him to give him extraordinary data-sniffing and pattern-recognition abilities. It is suggested that he possesses enhanced intelligence, which he displays in subtle ways throughout the series, including showing the ability to speak to other animals, and possibly Ed, and perfectly hacking the 'Scratch' website in session #23. Despite his enhanced capabilities, the rest of the *Bebop* crew, with the exception of Ed, often fail to notice these qualities and treat Ein as an average pet.

Vicious – grim enforcer of the Red Dragon Crime Syndicate, a former friend of Spike's and now his sworn nemesis. Vicious sports an emaciated, embittered look, wields a katana for a weapon and is always accompanied by a strange, crow-like bird perched on his shoulder. He lives up to his name both through his violent actions and his two-timing scheming within the syndicate. With only five appearances throughout the entire show, Vicious is arguably the series' main antagonist, or at any rate the only recurring one.

Production

The balances of the atmospheres of the planets and the racial groups of the people in *Cowboy Bebop* mostly originate from Shinichiro Watanabe's ideas, with some collaboration from set designer Isamu Imakake, Shoji Kawamori, and Dai Satou. The staff of *Cowboy Bebop* established the particular atmospheres early in the production. Initially in the production, the ethnic groups were not solidly established. Watanabe wanted to have many racial groups appear in *Cowboy Bebop*.

Mars was the planet most often used in storylines in *Cowboy Bebop*. Satoshi Toba, the cultural and setting producer, explained that other planets "were unexpectedly difficult to use." Toba explained that each planet in *Cowboy Bebop* has unique features, and in the plotlines the producers had to take into account the characteristics of each planet. Toba explained that it was not possible for the staff of *Cowboy Bebop* to have a dramatic rooftop scene occur on Venus, so "we ended up normally falling back to Mars."

Distribution

In the United States, on September 2, 2001, *Cowboy Bebop* became the first anime title to be shown as part of the U.S. Cartoon Network's Adult Swim programming block. It was successful enough to be broadcast repeatedly for four years. It was rerun again in 2007, 2008, 2009, 2010, and 2011.. It is currently being shown on Adult Swim Video and on Adult Swim on Saturday nights. In the United Kingdom, *Cowboy Bebop* was first broadcast in 2002 as one of the highlights of the ill-fated "cartoon network for adults", CNX. From November 6, 2007, it was being repeated on AnimeCentral until the channel's closure in August 2008. In Australia, *Cowboy Bebop* was first broadcast on pay-TV in 2002 on Cartoon Network's Adult Swim. It has recently started broadcasting on the Sci Fi Channel on Foxtel. In Australia, *Cowboy Bebop* TV series was first broadcast on free-to-air-TV on ABC2 (the national digital public television channel) on January 2, 2007. It has been repeated several times, most recently starting from Monday, December 29, 2008 and finishing on Monday, June 22, 2009. *Cowboy Bebop: The Movie* also aired again on February 23, 2009, on SBS (a hybrid-funded Australian public broadcasting television network). In Canada, *Cowboy Bebop* was first broadcast on December 24, 2006, on Razer.

Japan

Cowboy Bebop almost did not appear on Japanese broadcast television due to its depictions of graphic violence. It was first sent to TV Tokyo, one of the main broadcasters of anime in Japan. The show had an aborted first run from April 3, 1998, until June 19, 1998, on TV Tokyo, broadcasting only episodes 2, 3, 7 to 15, and 18.

Later that year, the series was shown in its entirety from October 23 until April 23, 1999, on the satellite network WOWOW. Because of the TV Tokyo broadcast slot fiasco, the production schedule was disrupted to the extent that the last episode was delivered to WOWOW on the day of its broadcast. *Cowboy Bebop* won the Seiun Award in 2000.

The full series has also been broadcast across Japan by the anime television network Animax, which has also aired the series via its respective networks across Southeast Asia, South Asia and East Asia. *Cowboy Bebop* was popular enough that the movie, *Cowboy Bebop: Tengoku no Tobira* (*Knockin' on Heaven's Door*), was commissioned and released in Japan in 2001, and later released in the United States as *Cowboy Bebop: The Movie* in 2003.

Legacy

A 2004 poll in *Newtype USA*, the US edition of the Japanese magazine *Newtype*, asked its readers to rank the "Top 25 Anime Titles of All Time"; *Cowboy Bebop* placed second on a list that included such strong contenders as *Mobile Suit Gundam*. The American Anime magazine *Anime Insider* (No. 50, November 2007) ranked the 50 Best Anime by compiling lists of industry regulars and magazine staff, with *Cowboy Bebop* ranked as #1 of all time. In 2009, IGN published a list of the "Top 100 Animated Series", on which *Cowboy Bebop* placed 14th, making it the second highest ranking anime on the list.

In the U.S., Cartoon Network has regularly rotated *Cowboy Bebop* in and out of its Adult Swim block line-up. Adult Swim occasionally refers to Cowboy Bebop as "The greatest series we have ever aired."

T.H.E.M Anime Reviews said the series has "sophistication and subtlety that is practically one-of-a-kind", touting it as a masterpiece that "puts most anime...and Hollywood, to shame."

On May 16, 2006, IGN listed Cowboy Bebop in its article "Top Ten Anime Themes and Soundtracks of All-Time," as the number one soundtrack: "Yoko Kanno strikes again. From beginning to end this may be one of the best anime ever and certainly is tops when it comes to music."

In March 2009, the print and web editions of *The Onion*'s A.V. Club called *Cowboy Bebop* "rightly a huge hit", and listed it as a gateway series to understanding the medium of anime as a whole.

Cowboy Bebop has been released in three separate editions in North America.

The first release was sold in 2000 individually, and featured uncut versions of the original 26 episodes. In 2001, these DVDs were collected in the special edition *Perfect Sessions* which included the first 6 DVDs, the first *Cowboy Bebop* soundtrack, and a collector's box. At the time of release, the art box from the Perfect Sessions was made available for purchase on The Right Stuff International as a solo item for collectors who already owned the series.

The second release, *The Best Sessions*, was sold in 2002 and featured what Bandai considered to be the best 6 episodes of the series remastered in Dolby Digital 5.1 and DTS surround sound.

The third release, *Cowboy Bebop Remix*, was also distributed on 6 discs and included the original 26 episodes, with sound remastered in Dolby Digital 5.1 and video remastered under the supervision of Shinichiro Watanabe. This release also included various extras that were not present in the original release. Cowboy Bebop Remix was itself collected as the Cowboy Bebop Remix DVD Collection in 2008.

Music

One of the most notable elements of *Cowboy Bebop* is its music. Episodes are called "sessions", each of which follows a different musical theme, and episode titles are borrowed from notable album or song names (i.e. "Sympathy for the Devil", "Bohemian Rhapsody", "Honky Tonk Women", "My Funny Valentine") or make use of a genre name ("Mushroom Samba", "Heavy Metal Queen").

Performed by Yoko Kanno and The Seatbelts, a band Kanno assembled to perform music for the series, the jazz and blues themed soundtrack helps to define the show as much as the characters, writing, and animation. *Cowboy Bebop* was voted by IGN in 2006 as having the greatest soundtrack for an anime.

Tim Jensen produced lyrics on some songs:

- "Ask DNA" sung by Raj Ramayya

- "Gotta Knock a Little Harder" sung by Mai Yamane
- "Call Me, Call Me" sung by Steve Conte

Other media
- An official side story to *Cowboy Bebop* was released on the original website called *Cowboy Bebop: UT*. Taking place long before the series started, it features Ural and Victoria Terpsichore (V.T. from the episode "Heavy Metal Queen") when they were bounty hunters. The story is available at the site mirror hosted by jazzmess.com.
- Bandai released a *Cowboy Bebop* shoot 'em up video game in Japan for the PlayStation in 1998. A PlayStation 2 video game, *Cowboy Bebop: Tsuioku no Serenade*, was released in Japan, and the English version had been set for release in North America during the first quarter of 2006. However, in November 2007, GameSpot reported that the North American release had been canceled, likely due to the Bandai-Namco merger.
- Two short manga series based on the *Cowboy Bebop* property were released in the US by Tokyopop.

Live-action film

On July 22, 2008, *IF Magazine* published an article on its website regarding a rumor of a live-action *Cowboy Bebop* movie in development by 20th Century Fox. Producer Erwin Stoff said that the film's development was in the early stages, and that they had "just signed it". Keanu Reeves has been confirmed as playing the role of Spike Spiegel. *Variety* confirmed on January 15, 2009, that the production company Sunrise Animation will be "closely involved with the development of the English language project." The site also confirmed Kenji Uchida, Shinichiro Watanabe, and series writer Keiko Nobumoto as associate producers, series producer Masahiko Minami as a production consultant, and Peter Craig as screenwriter. It was originally slated for release in 2011, but problems with the budget have delayed its production. The script that was submitted was sent back for rewrite to reduce the cost and little has been heard about it since an interview with producer Joshua Long on October 15, 2010.

Continuation rumors

After the creation of the series, an interviewer asked Watanabe if he had any plans to create more *Cowboy Bebop* material. Watanabe responded by saying that he does not believe that he "should just keep on making *Cowboy Bebop* sequels for the sake of it." Watanabe added that ending production and "to quit while we're ahead when people still want more" is more "in keeping with the *Bebop* spirit". In a more recent interview from 2006 with *The Daily Texan* Watanabe was asked if there would ever be more *Cowboy Bebop*. Watanabe's answer was "someday...maybe, someday." Source (edited): "http://en.wikipedia.org/wiki/Cowboy_Bebop"

Donnie Darko

Donnie Darko is a 2001 American psychological thriller film written and directed by Richard Kelly and starring Jake Gyllenhaal, Drew Barrymore, Patrick Swayze, Maggie Gyllenhaal, Noah Wyle, Jena Malone, and Mary McDonnell. The film depicts the reality-bending adventures of the title character as he seeks the meaning and significance behind his troubling Doomsday-related visions.

The film is distributed by Newmarket Films. Budgeted with $4.5 million and filmed over the course of 28 days, the film missed breaking even at the box office, grossing just over $4.1 million worldwide. Since then, the film has received favorable reviews from critics and developed a large cult following, resulting in the director's cut receiving a two-disc, special edition release in 2004.

Plot

In October 1988, teenager Donnie Darko (Jake Gyllenhaal) has been seeing a psychiatrist because of his troubled history. Donnie sleepwalks, and he has visions of Frank (James Duval), a menacing, demonic-looking rabbit.

On October 2, Frank draws Donnie out of his room to tell him, in 28 days, 6 hours, 42 minutes, and 12 seconds, the world will end. While Donnie is outside, a jet engine crashes through his bedroom. The next morning, Dr. Fisher (Arthur Taxier) and Jim Cunningham (Patrick Swayze), a motivational speaker, find Donnie sleeping on a golf course. Donnie returns home to find police and firemen. No one knows where the jet engine has come from, since there were no planes flying in the vicinity, and no airline reported losing an engine.

The following day, Donnie meets Gretchen Ross (Jena Malone), a new student, who becomes one of the few people with whom Donnie can share his visions. His father, Eddie (Holmes Osborne), takes Donnie to his therapist, Dr. Lillian Thurman (Katharine Ross), and nearly runs over Roberta Sparrow (Patience Cleveland), a seemingly senile old woman known as "Grandma Death." Dr. Thurman increases Donnie's medication and begins hypnotherapy. Frank continues to appear to Donnie and manipulates him to commit a series of crimes. He also tells Donnie about time travel. Donnie floods the school, steals his father's gun, and burns the home of Cunningham, where firemen uncover a "kiddie porn dungeon".

Donnie and older sister Elizabeth (Maggie Gyllenhaal) throw a Halloween party while their mother, Rose (Mary McDonnell), and younger sister Sam (Daveigh Chase), are away at a dance competition. Gretchen comes to Donnie's house for safety because her mother has suddenly disappeared, likely because of her threatening stepfather, and it is implied she and Donnie have sex for the first time at the party. At midnight, Donnie realizes 28 days have passed and only 6 hours remain until the end of the world. Donnie visits "Grandma Death" along with Gretchen and two friends. They are assaulted by the high school bullies (Alex Greenwald and Seth Rogen); Gretchen is knocked unconscious. A car swerves to avoid "Grandma Death", but runs over Gretchen, killing her. As the bullies run off, a man wearing a rabbit costume emerges from the car. It is Elizabeth's boyfriend, Frank. Donnie, yelled at by Frank, shoots him with his father's stolen pistol. Donnie carries Gretchen's lifeless body home, places her in the family car and speeds away, watching as a tornado forms over the city. For once, Donnie seems at peace as a vortex engulfs the jet carrying his mother and sister. The storm causes an engine to fall off before Donnie transports it back in time to 28 days earlier using a wormhole.

But in an alternate scene, Donnie chooses to stay in bed. He laughs and turns over as if to sleep just as the jet engine crashes through his bedroom, causing a plank to impale him (on the DVD's outtakes). As his body is taken away the next morning, Gretchen passes by on her bike and is informed by a neighborhood boy about what has happened. Gretchen tells him that she did not know Donnie, and she gives a sympathetic wave to Rose.

The film's official interactive website http://www.donniedarkofilm.com/ further explains the plot, including the parallel timelines aspect.

Cast
- Jake Gyllenhaal as Donnie Darko
- Jena Malone as Gretchen Ross
- Mary McDonnell as Rose Darko
- Holmes Osborne as Eddie Darko
- Katharine Ross as Dr. Lilian Thurman
- Maggie Gyllenhaal as Elizabeth Darko
- Daveigh Chase as Sam Darko
- James Duval as Frank
- Drew Barrymore as Karen Pomeroy
- Patrick Swayze as Jim Cunningham
- Noah Wyle as Dr. Kenneth Monnitoff
- Beth Grant as Kitty Farmer
- Stuart Stone as Ronald Fisher
- Alex Greenwald as Seth Devlin
- Seth Rogen as Ricky Danforth
- Patience Cleveland as Roberta Sparrow/"Grandma Death"
- Jolene Purdy as Cherita Chen
- Ashley Tisdale as Kim
- Jerry Trainor as Lanky kid
- David St. James as Bob Garland

Production

Filming
Donnie Darko was filmed in 28 days on a budget of $4.5 million. It almost went straight to home video release but was publicly released by Drew Barrymore's production company, Flower Films.

The film was shot in California, with many of the school sequences shot at Loyola High School. The "Carpathian ridge" scenes were shot on the Angeles Crest Highway.

Music
In 2003, the piano-driven cover of the Tears for Fears' "Mad World", featured in the film as part of the end sequence was a hit for composer Michael Andrews and singer Gary Jules and a UK Christmas Number One.

One continuous sequence involving an introduction of Donnie's high school prominently features the song "Head over Heels" by Tears for Fears, Samantha's dance group, "Sparkle Motion", performs with the song "Notorious" by Duran Duran, and "Under the Milky Way" by The Church is played after Donnie and Gretchen emerge from his room during the party. "Love Will Tear Us Apart" by Joy Division also appears in the film diegetically during the party and shots of Donnie and Gretchen upstairs. However, the version included was released in 1995, although the film is set in 1988. The opening sequence is set to "The Killing Moon" by Echo & the Bunnymen. In the theatrical cut, the song playing during the Halloween party is "Proud to be Loud" by Pantera, a track released on their 1988 album, which would coincide with the time setting of the film. However, the band is credited as "The Dead Green Mummies".

In the re-released Director's cut version of the film, the music in the opening sequence is replaced by "Never Tear Us Apart" by INXS; "Under the Milky Way" is moved to the scene of Donnie and Eddie driving home from Donnie's meeting with his therapist; and "The Killing Moon" is played as Gretchen and Donnie return to the party from Donnie's parents' room.

Release
The limited release of the film occurred during the month after the September 11 attacks. It was subsequently held back for almost a year for international release, where it garnered more favorable reviews. From this point, a large cult following for the movie began. Its DVD release gained an increased American audience for the film.

Marketing
- *The Donnie Darko Book*, written by Richard Kelly, is a 2003 book about the film. It includes an introduction by Jake Gyllenhaal, the screenplay of the Donnie Darko Director's Cut, an in-depth interview with Kelly, facsimile pages from the *Philosophy of Time Travel*, photos and drawings from the film, and artwork it inspired.
- NECA released first a six-inch (15 cm) figure of Frank the Bunny and later a foot-tall (30 cm) 'talking' version of the same figure.

Home media
The film was originally released on VHS and DVD in March 2002. Strong DVD sales led Newmarket Films to release a "Director's Cut" on DVD in 2004. Bob Berney, President of Newmarket Films, described the film as "a runaway hit on DVD," citing United States sales of more than $10 million.

The film was released in the US on Blu-ray on February 10, 2009.

The film was released as a 2-disc Blu-ray special edition in the UK on July 19, 2010 by Metrodome Distribution and featuring both Original and Director's Cut. Also including commentaries from director Kelly and actor Gyllenhaal, Kelly and Kevin Smith, and Cast and Crew including Drew Barrymore.

Director's cut

The Director's cut of the film was released on May 29, 2004, in Seattle, Washington, at the Seattle International Film Festival and later in New York City and Los Angeles on July 23, 2004. This cut includes twenty minutes of extra footage, an altered soundtrack, and visual excerpts from the (nonexistent) book *The Philosophy of Time Travel*.

The director's cut DVD, released on February 15, 2005, includes the new footage and more soundtrack changes, as well as some additional features exclusive to the two-DVD set: the director's commentary assisted by Kevin Smith, excerpts from the storyboard, a 52-minute production diary, "#1 fan video", a "cult following" video interviewing British fans, and the new director's cut trailer. The director's cut DVD was released as a giveaway with copies of the British *Sunday Times* newspaper on February 19, 2006.

Reception

Box office performance

Donnie Darko had its first screening at the Sundance Film Festival on January 19, 2001, and debuted in United States theaters in October 2001 to a tepid response. Shown on only 58 screens nationwide, the film grossed $110,494 in its opening weekend. By the time the film closed in United States theaters on April 11, 2002, it had earned just $517,375. It ultimately grossed $4.1 million worldwide.

Despite its poor box office showing, the film began to attract a devoted fan base. It was originally released on VHS and DVD in March 2002. During this time, the Pioneer Theatre in New York City's East Village began midnight screenings of *Donnie Darko* that continued for 28 consecutive months.

Critical reception

The film received widespread critical acclaim — Rotten Tomatoes gave the film an 85% rating (the Director's Cut received 91%), while Metacritic gave it 71/100. Critic Andy Bailey billed *Donnie Darko* as a "Sundance surprise" that "isn't spoiled by the Hollywood forces that helped birth it." Jean Oppenheimer of *New Times (LA)* praised the film, saying, "Like gathering storm clouds, Donnie Darko creates an atmosphere of eerie calm and mounting menace -- stands as one of the most exceptional movies of 2001." Writing for ABC Australia, Megan Spencer called the movie, "menacing, dreamy, [and] exciting" and noted that "it could take you to a deeply emotional place lying dormant in your soul." At first when the movie was released, Roger Ebert gave the film a less than positive review but later gave a positive review of the director's cut.

Awards and nominations

- 2001 — Richard Kelly won with *Donnie Darko* for "Best Screenplay" at the Catalonian International Film Festival and at the San Diego Film Critics Society. Donnie Darko also won the "Audience Award" for Best Feature at the Sweden Fantastic Film Festival. The film was nominated for "Best Film" at the Catalonian International Film Festival and for the "Grand Jury Prize" at the Sundance Film Festival.
- 2002 — Donnie Darko won the "Special Award" at the Young Filmmakers Showcase at the Academy of Science Fiction, Fantasy and Horror Films. The movie also won the "Silver Scream Award" at the Amsterdam Fantastic Film Festival. Kelly was nominated for "Best First Feature" and "Best First Screenplay" with *Donnie Darko*, as well as Jake Gyllenhaal being nominated for "Best Male Lead," at the Independent Spirit Awards. The film was also nominated for the "Best Breakthrough Film" at the Online Film Critics Society Awards.
- 2003 — Jake Gyllenhaal won "Best Actor" and Richard Kelly "Best Original Screenplay" for *Donnie Darko* at the Chlotrudis Awards, where Kelly was also nominated for "Best Director" and "Best Movie."
- 2005 — *Donnie Darko* ranked in the top five on My Favourite Film, an Australian poll conducted by the ABC.
- 2006 — *Donnie Darko* ranks #9 in FilmFour's 50 Films to See Before You Die.

Other awards

- #14 on Entertainment Weekly's list of the 50 Best High School Movies
- #2 in *Empire*'s "Greatest Independent Films of All Time" list.

Sequel

A 2009 sequel, *S. Darko*, centers on Sam, Donnie's younger sister. Again played by Daveigh Chase, Sam begins to have strange dreams that hint at a major catastrophe. *Donnie Darko* creator Richard Kelly has stated that he has no involvement in this sequel, as he does not own the rights to the original. Chase and producer Adam Fields are the only creative links between it and the original film. The sequel received extremely negative reviews.

Adaptations

Marcus Stern, associate director of the American Repertory Theater, directed a stage adaptation of *Donnie Darko* at the Zero Arrow Theatre in Cambridge, Massachusetts, in the fall of 2007. It ran from October 27-November 18, 2007, with opening night fittingly scheduled near Halloween.

An article written by the production drama team stated that the director and production team planned to "embrace the challenge to make the fantastical elements come alive on stage." In 2004, Stern adapted and directed Kelly's screenplay for a graduate student production at the American Repertory Theatre's Institute for Advanced Theatre Training (I.A.T.T./M.X.A.T.).

A 60-second version was created for the Empire Film Awards by Tea Fuelled Art.

Source (edited): "http://en.wikipedia.org/wiki/Donnie_Darko"

Godkiller (series)

Godkiller is a transmedia series of graphic novels, illustrated films, and novels created by award-winning filmmaker Matt Pizzolo that tells the stories of human beings caught in the crossfire of warring *fallen gods*. The core series is a trilogy of feature-length illustrated films beginning with *Godkiller: Walk Among Us*, illustrated by Anna Muckcracker. Pizzolo and Muckcracker are currently at work on the second part of the trilogy *Godkiller: Tomorrow's Ashes*.

The October 2009 *illustrated film* DVD *Godkiller: Walk Among Us - Episode 1* quickly established itself as its distributor's all-time fastest selling release.

When Fulle Circle asked about the inspiration behind *Godkiller*, Pizzolo stated:

"I thought it would be fun to design a new mythology for fuck-ups and misfits. My goal with it is to present heroes that don't behave heroically because it's their job to maintain the status quo or because they're bored and want to rescue a princess, they act heroically because they're regular misfits who are trying to do the best they can for each other in an unjust, fucked-up world."

The illustrated film format Pizzolo developed with producer Brian Giberson for *Godkiller* merges sequential art with 3D CGI, motion graphics and dramatic voice performances in the style of a radio play.

Wired asked Pizzolo to explain the differences between motion comics and illustrated films:

"In illustrated films, we drive the pace of the storytelling with the dramatic voice performances and the sound design, so that allows us to showcase the illustrations in a way where you can really take a moment to absorb the art in the same way you can when reading a comic book... Motion comics are closer to a form of limited animation that uses comics as source material. Illustrated films are closer to the experimental cinema of Ralph Bakshi's work, Chris Marker's La jetée or animation like Liquid Television."

Pizzolo gave Bloody Disgusting additional thoughts on differences between motion comics and illustrated films: "The simple answer is illustrated-films are an attempt to merge comic book sequential art with cinematic storytelling, whereas motion comics seem more intent on re-purposing comic books into cartoons. And I don't mean to sound like a dick because I think motion comics are cool, these are just different. On first glance, they look very similar... and people might say *'it's moving comics on a screen, that's motion comics'* to which I say *'just because Seinfeld is moving people captured on 35mm film doesn't make it the same thing as Full Metal Jacket.'* On one level you could see motion comics and illustrated films as siblings like comics books vs graphics novels or TV shows vs feature films, but there are deeper distinctions. Basically, we're filmmakers so we're bringing a cinematic sensibility to this[...] We animate motion in the frame, but the need for motion is different in film... it's not like Michael Madsen bounces around the frame in Reservoir Dogs the way Wakko does in Animaniacs."

Publication/Production history

Core Series

The *Godkiller* series was devised to be simultaneously produced as a series of graphic novels and films (both utilizing the same sequential art) with the ultimate goal being a trilogy of feature-length films. Pizzolo and Muckcracker began by serializing *Godkiller: Walk Among Us* into a 6-issue comic book series (debuting in 2008) and a 3-episode film series (debuting in 2009) before the completed *Walk Among Us* feature film opened theatrically in 2010.

The *Walk Among Us* film was slated for a unique release of limited edition, bi-monthly DVDs starting September 29, 2009, followed by a theatrical run of the full feature in January 2010 and a DVD/Blu-ray release in March 2010.

Due to overwhelming demand far beyond studio expectations, the first DVD's street date was delayed until October 6, 2009 so enough DVDs could be supplied to the stores, including Best Buy, Borders Books, F.Y.E. and Suncoast, among many more retailers.

Pizzolo and Muckcracker are currently working on the second part of the trilogy, *Godkiller: Tomorrow's Ashes*. The new series is slated to be released in mid 2011, followed soon after by the next wave of films. The complete *Tomorrow's Ashes* feature-length film is expected to premiere theatrically in 2011.

Additional Series

Godkiller: Silent War

Pizzolo is currently writing pre-apocalyptic prequel *Godkiller: Silent War*, an urban fantasy novel series which debuted as episodic e-books & audiobooks on the special features of the *Godkiller: Walk Among Us* dvds.

Pizzolo explained the dramatic structure to *Dread Central*:

"*Godkiller* is split into two periods... there's the pre-nuke world of *Silent War* and there's the post-nuke world of the graphic novel and illustrated film *Walk Among Us*. So *Silent War* is only a prequel insofar as it happens beforehand, but its events drive the *Walk Among Us* story, and many of the same characters appear in both. I'm super excited that the two stories can roll out together in this integrated way--everything about this project is unorthodox and crazy, hopefully everyone will enjoy the ride."

The Long Knives

Though not an official prequel, Pizzolo has indicated that his upcoming graphic novel series The Long Knives takes place in a shared universe with Godkiller and deals with several key Godkiller characters during the breakdown of society that precedes *Godkiller: Walk Among Us*. *The Long Knives* is a Giallo-style horror illustrated by newcomer

Ana Ludeshka.

Ludeshka told *Bloody-Disgusting*: "I was very shocked when I first read the Long Knives script. And not only because of the blood and the gore. There's no mercy in this story. It burns like cold things burn."

Plot

Godkiller: Silent War

[Pre-nuke period] In the near future, 17-year-old Joe Junior and his girlfriend Bee run a speakeasy in the basement of an abandoned NYC church where they serve narcotic drinks to underagers while providing sanctuary and black-market employment to draft dodgers. When Joe is recruited by an armed cult of populist assassins, he is thrust into a secret world of international cabals, alien conspiracies, and the countdown to Armageddon.

Godkiller: Walk Among Us

[Post-nuke period] Set in the future after an economic collapse, a nuclear holy war and an alien invasion, *Godkiller: Walk Among Us* follows orphan Tommy as he searches for a new heart for his ill sister, Lucy.

Illustrated Film format

Pizzolo developed the concept of an *illustrated film* with his producing partner Brian Giberson, mixing elements of anime, radio drama, video games, and motion comics. Utilizing the original artwork from the comic book, the *illustrated film* adds motion animation, visual effects, elaborate sound design, music, and voice-acting performances.

Explaining the decision to develop the new filmmaking format, Pizzolo told *Bloody Disgusting*: "When we decided to make an anime adaptation of the comic book, I couldn't see how a traditional animated approach would do justice to Anna's incredibly lush and detailed illustrations. It made perfect sense to adapt the medium to suit her art, rather than vice versa."

Pizzolo clarified further in an interview with *Horror News*: "There are lots of reasons [Godkiller was made as an illustrated film], but I think the most important one was really being inspired by Anna Muckcracker's gorgeous artwork. Brian Giberson (my partner at Halo-8) and I had been experimenting with the illustrated film format for a while, but we might still have gone with traditional animation for Godkiller since it's really risky to experiment with a crazy story and a new filmmaking format at the same time. But once I saw Anna's art I knew that no traditional form of animation could do justice to the grimy, textured, surreal aesthetic she created. It was really an artistic choice, because from a business point of view it's just so risky."

According to *Fangoria*, "Lance Henriksen, Bill Moseley and Tiffany Shepis are the genre stalwarts lending their vocal talents to the project; also on board in that capacity are underground cinema queen Lydia Lunch and singers Justin Pierre (of Motion City Soundtrack) and Davey Havok (of AFI)."

Pizzolo and Giberson unveiled a preview clip of the *Godkiller illustrated film* during the "Comic Books & Indie Movies" panel at Comic-Con International's Wondercon in San Francisco on February 28, 2009.

According to *Shock Till You Drop*, "Danielle Harris (known for her turns in the Halloween franchise), Katie Nisa (Threat), and Nicki Clyne (Battlestar Galactica) have joined previously announced cast members Lance Henriksen, Bill Moseley, Tiffany Shepis, Justin Pierre (singer of Motion City Soundtrack), Lydia Lunch (Richard Kern's 'Hardcore Collection'), and Davey Havok (AFI) in the cast of the 'illustrated film' adaptation *Godkiller*, written and directed by award-winning filmmaker Matt Pizzolo (Threat) based on the comic book he created with illustrator Anna Muckcracker."

Pizzolo, Giberson and actresses Danielle Harris and Tiffany Shepis presented two exclusive preview clips of the *Godkiller illustrated film* at Fangoria's Weekend of Horrors in Los Angeles on April 18, 2009.

Immediately following the preview clip debut at Weekend of Horrors, Fangoria posted the first exclusive online clip of *Godkiller* on its website. The film will release on 20 April 2010 over Halo 8 Enterntainment in Chicago as part of the Comic-Con C2E2.

Discography

Godkiller has been released in episodic and collected versions in various configurations:
Source (edited): "http://en.wikipedia.org/wiki/Godkiller_(series)"

Les Temps modernes

The first issue of **Les Temps modernes** (*Modern Times*), the most important cultural review of the period after World War II, appeared in October 1945. It was known as the review of Jean-Paul Sartre. *Les Temps Modernes* filled the void left by the disappearance of the most important pre-war literary magazine, *La Nouvelle Revue Française* (*The New French Review*), considered to be André Gide's magazine, which was shut down after the liberation of France because of its collaboration with the occupation.

Les Temps modernes was first published by Gallimard and is published by Gallimard today. In between, the magazine changed hands three times: Julliard (January 1949 to September 1965), Presses d'aujourd'hui (October 1964 to March 1985), Gallimard (April 1985 to the present).

The first editorial board consisted of Sartre (director), Raymond Aron, Simone de Beauvoir, Michel Leiris, Maurice Merleau-Ponty, Albert Ollivier, and Jean Paulhan. All published many articles for the magazine. Among Sartre's contributions were "*La nationalisation de la littérature*" ("The Nationalisation of Literature"), "*Matérialisme et révolution*" ("Materialism and Revolution"), and "*Qu'est-ce-que la littérature?*"

("What is Literature?"). Simone de Beauvoir first published "*Le Deuxième Sexe*" ("The Second Sex") in *Les Temps modernes*.

In the preface to the first edition, Sartre stated the review's purpose: to publish *littérature engagée*. This philosophy of literature expresses a basic creed of existentialism--that an individual is responsible for making conscious decisions to commit socially useful acts. Thus, literature in the magazine would have a utilitarian component; it would not be just culturally valuable (art for art's sake). Other intellectuals, such as André Gide, André Breton, and Louis Aragon, disapproved of this orientation. Sartre's response: "*Le monde peut fort bien se passer de la littérature. Mais il peut se passer de l'homme encore mieux.*" ("The world can easily get along without literature. But it can get along even more easily without man.")

The works of many new writers who would later become famous appeared in *Modern Times*. They include Richard Wright, Jean Genet, Nathalie Sarraute, Boris Vian, and Samuel Beckett.

Political divisions between board members soon surfaced. Raymond Aron quit in 1945 to become an editor at *Le Figaro* because of *Les Temps Moderne's* support of Communism. At the time of the Korean War, Merleau-Ponty resigned. Originally more supportive of Communism than Sartre, he moved progressively to the right as Sartre moved to the left. At the time, Sartre still endorsed Communism in his writings but in private expressed his reservations.

Sartre disapproved of Camus for seeing both sides in the Algerians' rebellion against their French colonial masters (The Algerian War--1954–62). In his bitterness against Camus, Sartre selected Francis Jeanson, who did not like the works of Camus, to review the Camus novel *L'Homme Révolté* (*The Rebel*). When Camus responded to the review with hurt feelings, Sartre put the final blow to a friendship that had lasted for years. He said, "*Vous êtes devenu la proie d'une morne démesure qui masque vos difficultés intérieures. . . . Tôt ou tard, quelqu'un vous l'eût dit, autant que ce soi moi.*" ("You have become the victim of an excessive sullenness that masks your internal problems. . . . Sooner or later, someone would have told you, so it might as well be me.")

Les Temps Modernes enjoyed its greatest influence in the sixties. At this time, it had over 20,000 subscribers. During the Algerian War, it strongly supported the National Liberation Front, the primary group in the ultimately successful battle against the French. It fiercely denounced the extensive use of torture by the French forces. For this, it was censured and its premises seized.

From its inception to the present day, the review has published 582 regular issues and many special issues. The special issues include Sartre's 1946 description of the United States, an attempt to discredit the myths that many of the French held about this country. In 1955, Claude Lanzmann described Sartre's Marxist philosophy in an issue called "*La Gauche*" ("The Left"). An issue on "*La révolte hongroise*" ("The Hungarian Revolution") (1956–57) denounced Soviet repression. In 1967, at the time of the Six-Day War, an issue, "*Le conflit israélo-arabe*" ("The Israeli-Arab conflict"), contained articles by both Israelis and Arabs.

Les Temps Modernes continues to publish articles consistent with the philosophy of Sartre, with the intent of informing its readers about the world as it is. And it continues to publish important authors who are not generally known. In 2001, a special edition was devoted to Serge Doubrovsky.

The current chief editor of *Les Temps Modernes* is Claude Lanzmann. The editorial board consists of Juliette Simont (Editorial Assistant to Claude Lanzmann), Adrien Barrot, Jean Bourgault, Joseph Cohen, Michel Deguy, Liliane Kandel, Jean Khalfa, Patrice Maniglier, Robert Redeker, Marc Sagnol, Gérard Wormser, Raphael Zagury-Orly. It is a bimonthly magazine. About 3,000 copies are printed.
Source (edited): "http://en.wikipedia.org/wiki/Les_Temps_modernes"

Madlax

Madlax (マドラックス *Madorakkusu*) is a 26-episode Japanese anime television series produced in 2004 by the Bee Train animation studio. Kōichi Mashimo directed *Madlax* and the soundtrack was composed by Yuki Kajiura. The DVD version was released by ADV Films in North America and the United Kingdom and by Madman Entertainment in Australia and New Zealand.

The story revolves around two young women who seemingly have little in common and do not know of the other's existence at the beginning. The titular Madlax is a legendary mercenary and assassin in the fictional civil war-torn country of Gazth-Sonika, who cannot remember her past or indeed her real name before twelve years ago, when the war started. The other protagonist is Margaret Burton, the sole heir of a wealthy aristocratic family in the peaceful European country Nafrece. Twelve years before the story begins, an airliner Margaret and her mother were on crashed over Gazth-Sonika, and its passengers, as well as Margaret's father who led the rescuers, have been missing ever since. Margaret, however, mysteriously traveled back to Nafrece on her own, losing her memories prior to her return; the only thing she recalls is a single word, "Madlax". With this thread linking the two girls, they both independently start investigating the powerful crime syndicate Enfant after its enigmatic mastermind shows interest in both of them.

Madlax was produced as a spiritual successor to the studio's earlier project, *Noir*, and together with *El Cazador de la Bruja*, these series constitute a trilogy exploring the "girls-with-guns" genre. The production of *Madlax* began in

2002 but it wasn't until Yōsuke Kuroda joined the project that the series took its final form. While the critics noted the resulting similarities between *Noir* and *Madlax*, they also acknowledged the differences, such as the latter's less episodic and more plot-driven style and, in particular contrast to the predominantly realistic *Noir*, incorporation of many supernatural elements, which the audience must often interpret without further explanation.

Plot

The first half of the series alternates between the two leads. Madlax is one of the most efficient special ops agents for hire in the war-torn Gazth-Sonika, while Margaret Burton is a sleepy, clumsy amnesiac living in Nafrece, a country styled after France. When a "picture book", presumably given to Margaret by her late father, attracts the attention of international criminal network Enfant, she discovers that the origins of the book lie in Gazth-Sonika. Enfant's top operative, Carrossea Doon, tracks Margaret down but tips off his superiors in the wrong direction, towards Madlax, who has been causing Enfant trouble for some time. Meanwhile, Vanessa Rene, Margaret's former tutor whose parents died because of Gazth-Sonikan war, discovers that her current employer, Bookwald Industries, covertly supports the war by supplying both sides with firearms and starts investigating its true cause. Her investigation brings her to Gazth-Sonika, where Madlax is hired as her bodyguard, and together, they uncover data that proves that Enfant orchestrated the entire conflict. Enfant eventually intercepts them and they are forced into hiding. Back in Nafrece, Margaret decides to help Vanessa and travels to Gazth-Sonika, accompanied by her devoted and sometimes overprotective maid Elenore Baker and Carrossea Doon.

Eventually, Madlax and Margaret meet and embark on a search for Quanzitta Marison, a Gazth-Sonikan mystic who supposedly knows about Margaret's book, Enfant's involvement with it, and Enfant itself. Lady Quanzitta does indeed tell them about Enfant and its plans to plunge the entire world into a total war, starting with Gazth-Sonika. She reveals that Enfant's leader Friday Monday possesses supernatural powers connected to the three ancient books, one of which belongs to Margaret. Margaret uses her own supernatural abilities and that of her book to return her lost memories. Carrossea, who has been aiding Margaret, requests that his memories be restored as well despite warnings not to do so; he discovers that he, in fact, died 12 years ago and held on to life only by sheer force of will to protect Margaret. Carrossea disappears, and Margaret is captured by Monday who intends to use her abilities to advance his own plans.

Unable to shoot her father in self-defence, Margaret expelled her wish to survive from herself, creating Madlax, who pulled the trigger for her. Laetitia (originally her doll) was created to seal off the memory of this event, preventing the two from merging.

While Margaret and Carrossea perform the ritual, Madlax is attacked by Limelda Jorg, a Gazth-Sonikan sniper who holds a grudge against Madlax ever since she failed to stop an assassination by Madlax earlier in the show. Limelda kills Vanessa while targeting Madlax, sending the latter into clinical depression. Elenore and Lady Quanzitta's servant Nakhl manage to restore Madlax's will to live and persuade her to save Margaret, and the three storm Enfant's headquarters together. During the assault, Elenore is killed and Margaret, now under Monday's control, shoots Madlax. Believing her to be dead, Monday commences a ritual to unleash people's inhibitions and trigger worldwide anarchy; but Margaret's memories return and she snaps out of his mind control. Only now does the audience learn the back-story: back in 1999, Monday drove Margaret's father insane with his powers and she was forced to kill her own father. To escape the horrible truth of her patricide, Margaret split herself into three personae: the "memory keeper" Laetitia, the sinful Madlax, and the innocent Margaret herself. Margaret then fuses her three personae back together to undo the ritual she previously performed with Monday, saving the world from insanity. Madlax, who should no longer exist after the fusion, appears and guns down Monday. It becomes apparent that Margaret has once again split herself into three, judging that after twelve years, she no longer has the right to make decisions for her other personae.

Themes

Madlax has gained fame among the shōjo-ai fandom for its implied lesbian content. The main source of such speculations in the series is the relationship between Madlax, Vanessa Rene, and Limelda Jorg.

Madlax is set against the backdrop of Gazth-Sonikan war and the first episodes contrast the tranquil Nafrece with the war-torn Gazth-Sonika; later, the story moves completely to the combat zone, focusing on the central characters, such as Limelda Jorg, and their suffering. In an interview, the director Mashimo stated that "[t]he story is about portraying inner struggles of people, while showing what life is like in this place of madness and this other place of peace". Accordingly, the series' title is a portmanteau of two English words, "mad" and "re*lax*ed", mirroring the authors' intention to portray the two extremes of human being.

Madlax also plays as the story of

Margaret Burton's search for her psychological identity. Based on the Mashimo Menu theme titles available to her, Yuki Kajiura has suggested an interpretation that while searching for her memories, Margaret meets the other characters ("Gatekeepers") one after another and learns about the lifestyles ("Gates") they represent. In the end, she finds her own "Gate", which is the new identity that finally replaces the one she lost twelve years ago.

Production
Writing
According to the director Kōichi Mashimo, he envisioned *Noir* and *Madlax* as part of a trilogy exploring the girls-with-guns genre, and soon after the release of the latter, he confirmed having plans to produce the third installment, which would later become *El Cazador de la Bruja*. In late 2002, Mashimo invited Shigeru Kitayama, the producer of *Noir* who once came up with its original idea, to discuss a new series entitled *Madlax*. Kitayama greatly expanded Mashimo's original screenplay plan, but it was not until Yōsuke Kuroda was put in charge of the script that the series took its final appearance. It took Kuroda around one year to finish the screenplays for all 26 episodes, during which he was constantly encouraged by Mashimo to add his own original ideas to their initial plan. Kuroda has admitted that at the time he received Mashimo's invitation, he felt frustrated after his first project has been canceled by the publisher, so he decided to make *Madlax* "really extravagant", blending as many genres at once as he could. Kōichi Mashimo, furthermore, admitted that the most unusual plot twists, like Margaret and Madlax's connection to each other, were invented by Kuroda and him while drunk.

Character design
By comparison with *Noir*, *Madlax* features a much larger primary cast, including multiple recurring male characters, an element nearly absent in the former. It was not so in the original screenplay draft written by Mashimo and Kitayama: for example, "Madlax" was Margaret's own nickname and Charlie (Vanessa's colleague at Bookwald Industries) had one of the central roles similar to Speedy's in *Avenger*. Only the "draft" characters' names remained of them when Kuroda has rewritten the script. A total of three character designers collaborated on *Madlax* cast: Satoshi Ohsawa (who also worked on *Noir* cast) created the central heroines Margaret and Madlax; Minako Shiba drew Friday Monday and Carrossea Doon; and Satoko Miyachi was entrusted with the "mysterious" characters, Laetitia and Poupee.

Several seiyūs who voiced characters in *Madlax* have participated in earlier projects by studio Bee Train, for example, Houko Kuwashima and Aya Hisakawa who played Kirika Yuumura and Chloe in *Noir* also voiced Margaret Burton and Limelda Jorg. Kotono Mitsuishi (Mireille Bouquet in *Noir*), on the other hand, has received only a minor role (Margaret's mother in episode 21), while the titular lead of *Madlax* was voiced by Sanae Kobayashi, previously involved with *.hack//Liminality* (Mai Minase). Masashi Ebara (Friday Monday) also had a major role in *Liminality* (Junichiro Tokuoka). Monica Rial (Kirika Yuumura in the English translation of *Noir*) worked on the translation of the screenplay for the ADV Films release.

Music
Like with many of studio Bee Train's other works, the entire *Madlax* soundtrack was composed by the acclaimed Yuki Kajiura, making it her and Kōichi Mashimo's fifth project together. In an interview Kajiura recalls having written the score in a hotel high-rise to save studio costs, and that this change in location helped her to explore different styles of music.

Kajiura and Yuuka Nanri's duo FictionJunction Yuuka recorded the series' opening and ending themes, "Fragments of an Eye" (瞳の欠片 *Hitomi no Kakera*) and "Inside Your Heart", respectively, as well as two insert songs: "nowhere" and "I'm here". Aside from the opening sequence, "Fragments of an Eye" is featured in the series itself: at the end of episode 18 and in the episode 24, when Margaret is humming its tune to herself in the flower field.

In the insert song "nowhere", there is a frequently repeated background refrain "Yanmaani" (ヤンマーニ *Yanmāni*). It doesn't have any particular meaning but since the song usually plays when Madlax is fighting, "Yanmaani" has become something of a joke to Japanese fans, claiming that it apparently gives her superpowers.

Media
Anime series
Originally, *Madlax* was broadcast in Japan by TV Tokyo from 5 April to 27 September 2004, from 1:30 to 2:00 a.m. every Tuesday (formally, Monday night). Shortly before the series finished airing, it has been licensed in North America and Europe by ADV Films, which has previously acquired distribution rights for *Noir* and has long had plans to license its successor, as well. The official English dub has been released in the United States under the trademark *MADLAX* on a total of seven DVDs from 12 April 2005 to 28 March 2006. A complete collection was released by ADV on 17 July 2007. *Madlax* has become the first series on which ADV Films' director and producer David Williams tested the technology of distributing promotional materials via P2P network BitTorrent. As of September 1, 2009, all of the titles from ADV's catalog, including Madlax, were transferred to AEsir Holdings, with distribution from Section23 Films.

The North-American DVD release contains extras available in English only, such the controversial self-parody *Conversations with SSS* and *Sock Puppet Theater*, an Easter egg live action about Madlax going after Chris Patton, Badgis' voice actor and an annoying womanizer.

Since 7 February 2006, *Madlax* airs on Anime Network (which is, like ADV Films, a subsidiary of A.D. Vision). On 4 April, shortly after the last DVD volume has been released, the consequent broadcast was put on halt and until 27

June, only the first 8 episodes were repeated. Since then, the series has been relaunched multiple times.

Madman Entertainment, who previously licensed *Noir* in its region, has acquired rights for distribution of *Madlax* in Australia and New Zealand and released it on seven DVD volumes between 20 July 2005 and 26 July 2006. A complete collection was released on 4 April 2007.

Soundtrack

The cover of the first *Madlax* soundtrack album

The series' original soundtrack was released on two albums on 21 July and 22 September 2004 by Victor Entertainment. Two singles, *Hitomi no Kakera* and *Inside Your Heart*, were published in the same year by FictionJunction Yuuka, each containing an opening/ending theme and one insert song, as well as their respective karaoke versions.

Artbook

MADLAX the Bible (ISBN 4-89425-375-5) is a 95-page artbook that was published in Japan on 21 May 2005 by Hobby Japan. Aside from illustrations and artworks for the series, it contains interviews with its authors and seiyū, as well as diverse additional information about the show in Japanese. The artbook has never been published outside of Japan. Since the word "Bible" is derived from Ancient Greek: "τὰ βιβλία τὰ ἅγια", meaning "holy books", it is likely that the artbook's title is a reference to the Holy Books that play an important role in the series' plot.

Merchandise

A resin model kit known as "Madlax with Guns" has been produced, featuring a figurine of Madlax dual wielding her signature SIG P210s. A polystone figurine entitled simply "Madlax", was launched in August 2007. In Japan, a T-shirt with *Madlax* logo has been added to the limited edition of the first DVD volume, and the "first press" of the OST albums came with logotype mousepads.

Reception

Madlax was often accused of being secondary and reusing *Noir*'s stylistic solutions, such as the story premise, the two heroines' appearance, and the musical style. Nevertheless, some sources praised the story for being more monolithic and consequent than its predecessor, owing to all its episodes and subplots being tightly intertwined and held together by the primary plot.

The majority of reviewers perceived the early episodes of *Madlax* as boring and too slow-paced, but some of the same critics later remarked that the prolonged exposition is crucial to the unusual finale of the series, which fully establishes the series' own identity and sets it apart from other works. According to them, after the initial volume, the story gets better and better with every new episode, though some have been dissatisfied with its "pseudo-existentialistic" ending. Erica Friedman, the president of Yuricon, highly praised Kuroda's script, naming it "the best writing that Bee Train has done". Professional reviewers welcomed the increased number of sympathetic characters, especially the distinguishable male ones (Friday, Carrossea, Colonel Burton), as opposed to stormtrooper-like operatives of Soldats in *Noir*, but the female character designs were still said to be much more detailed (to the point of fanservice in case of Madlax) than the more generic male characters.

The high quality of the animation in *Madlax* was generally acknowledged. On the negative side, the episodes that involve computer use and hacking received criticism for their lack of realism. In terms of soundtrack, *Madlax* has not become as innovative as *Noir*, with critics suggesting its OST to be a blend of *Noir* and *.hack//Sign* styles. Nevertheless, the reviewers acknowledged its superiority over the majority of contemporary works. The English translation released by ADV Films was praised for preserving most of the series' original stylistic aspects and inviting veteran voice actors for the dub. Reviewers went as far as to suggest that several English voices (especially Mike Kleinhenz's) match the characters better than the Japanese ones. Others, however, criticized the dub, e.g. Carl Kimlinger of Anime News Network in his 2009 review of the series rated the performance as "wildly uneven, ranging from good... to plain amateurish", citing "delivery issues" as main problem of the dub.

The initial slow pacing, especially compared to the first episodes of *Noir*, became a main reason why the audience often dropped watching *Madlax* before it could present its later story turns which eventually resulted in the moderate success of the series. Among other suggested reasons behind the mediocre popularity of the show were: the market saturation, which resulted from other anime series attempting to repeat the success of *Noir* since 2001; the expectable disinterest against a "*Noir* remake", found among the fans of the first series; the over-the-top action scenes that some felt to be ridiculous; and its unconventional genre, which straddled *Madlax* uncomfortably between fans of mystical science fiction and those who prefer *Noir*'s strict realism.

Source (edited): "http://en.wikipedia.org/wiki/Madlax"

Neon Genesis Evangelion

The *Neon Genesis Evangelion* (新世紀エヴァンゲリオン *Shin Seiki Evangerion*) franchise is an umbrella of Japanese media properties generally owned by the anime studio Gainax. It has grossed over 150 billion yen since 1995. The central (and original) works of the franchise feature an apocalyptic mecha action story which revolves around the efforts by the paramilitary organization Nerv to fight hostile beings called Angels. Nerv's primary weapon against the Angels are giant humanoids called Evangelions which are piloted by select teenagers, one of whom, Shinji Ikari, is the primary protagonist. Other works deviate from this theme to varying degrees, focusing more on romantic interactions between the characters, side stories which did not appear in the original works, and/or reimaginings of the conflicts from the original works.

Development

The franchise's central works, both titled *Neon Genesis Evangelion*, are an anime and a manga serial, both of which follow the same storyline, although with numerous minor differences between them. The manga, written by Yoshiyuki Sadamoto, debuted in the February 1995 issue of *Shonen Ace* (published in December 1994) and is still running as of 2010. The manga was intended to raise interest for the anime (directed by Hideaki Anno with character designs by Sadamoto), which was in development at that point and was intended to be Gainax's next major anime release.

The anime consists of 26 television episodes which were first aired on the terrestrial TV Tokyo network from October 4, 1995 to March 27, 1996. It was later aired across Japan by the anime satellite television network, Animax. The series won the Animage Anime Grand Prix prize in 1995 and 1996.

Early on, Anno Hideaki who had promised the series would give "every episode...something for the fans to drool over" later began removing the fan service imagery in later episodes; in addition those later episodes that did contain fan service elements juxtaposed them with imagery of the character in some kind of emotional trauma.

The anime succeeded wildly beyond expectation and has spawned countless derivative works and imitators. The series established a number of distinctive features of future works in the franchise: a stock set of distinctive characters such as Shinji Ikari, Asuka Langley Soryu, Rei Ayanami, Toji Suzuhara, and others such as Misato Katsuragi (for a complete list, see here); a number of philosophical, psychological, and religious themes; and an idiosyncratic vocabulary of symbols and allusions drawing heavily on Christian and Kabbalistic symbolism, Buddhist beliefs, and the Japanese otaku subculture. Similarly, *Evangelion* properties consistently focus on a number of themes and dilemmas, as discussed by Anno:

Eva is a story that repeats. It is a story where the main character witnesses many horrors with his own eyes, but still tries to stand up again. It is a story of will; a story of moving forward, if only just a little. It is a story of fear, where someone who must face indefinite solitude fears reaching out to others, but still wants to try.

After the series

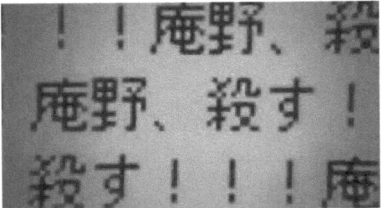

E-mail response to *Evangelion: Death and Rebirth*: "Anno, I'll kill you!!! Anno, I'll kill you!!! ..."; included in *The End of Evangelion*.

Graffiti spray painted on Gainax Headquarters front wall: "Tenchuu" (Divine retribution) "Ikari (Kanji meaning: *Angry*) rape-man"; image was included in *The End of Evangelion*.

Gainax launched a project to create a movie ending for the series in 1997. The company first released *Death and Rebirth*, consisting of a highly condensed character-based recap and re-edit of the TV series episodes 1-24 (*Death*) and the first half of the new ending (*Rebirth*, which was originally intended to be the full ending, but couldn't be finished due to budget and time constraints). The project to complete the final episodes was completed later in the year, and released as *The End of Evangelion*. *The End of Evangelion* is an alternate ending of the series and retells episodes 25 and 26. *The End of Evangelion* replaces the *Rebirth* portion of the first film *Death and Rebirth*. The two films were compiled as a single movie (the way they were originally intended to be), called *Revival of Evangelion* in 1998.

The two endings are similar in plot, but while in the film Shinji rejects Instrumentality, the television series ends after his decision is made but before it is clear which option he chose. In still frames in episodes 25 and 26, Unit 01 is depicted with wings and the corpses of Misato and Ritsuko are shown, hinting that these events had been planned. In the English-language Director's Cut version of episode 24, the preview of the next episode shows concept frames from the fight between Asuka and the mass-produced Evas, and the title of the next episode is presented as "Air", which is the title of the first chapter from *The End of Evangelion*, rather than showing scenes from the TV series ending as it does in the original cut. There was a sudden shift in tone around episode 16 of the series. This was partly due to scheduling restraints, which drastically reduced the number of frames that could be drawn for each episode, and partly due to the Sarin gas attack on the Tokyo subway on March 20, 1995, which occurred while the series was under production; Anno decided to remove elements of the series plot that he felt were too similar to the real-life attack. Anno stated before production that he did not know how the show would end, nor what would become of the characters. Reaction was decidedly mixed; reception of the latter quarter of the TV series had often been hostile to the point of death threats, and the movies were seen as being even more incomprehensible (such as the ending), bizarre and even disgusting.

Regardless, *Evangelion* is perennially popular, especially among otaku such as cosplayers or doujinshi artists.

Tax problems

In May 1998, Gainax was audited by the National Tax Agency at the urging of the Tokyo Regional Taxation Bureau: Gainax was suspected of committing tax evasion on the massive profits accruing from various *Evangelion* properties. Gainax had concealed 1.56 billion yen worth of income (thereby failing to pay 560 million yen due in corporate taxes) which it had earned between the release of *Evangelion* and July 1997. Gainax would pay companies closely related to it various large fees, ostensibly to pay for animation expenses, but then immediately withdraw 90% of the sums from the other company's accounts as cash and store it in safe deposit boxes (leaving 10% as a reward for the other company's assistance).

Eventually Takeshi Sawamura and tax accountant Yoshikatsu Iwasaki were arrested on 13 July 1999 for concealing income of 1.5 billion yen failing to pay corporate taxes of 580 million yen. Yasuhiro Takeda defends Sawamura's actions as being a reaction to Gainax's perpetually precarious finances and the shaky accounting procedures internally: "Sawamura understood our financial situation better than anyone, so when *Evangelion* took off and the money really started rolling in, he saw it as possibly our one and only opportunity to set something aside for the future. I guess he was vulnerable to temptation at that point, because no one knew how long the *Evangelion* goose would keep laying golden eggs. I don't think he purposely set out with the goal of evading taxes. It was more that our level of accounting knowledge wasn't up to the task of dealing with revenues on such a large scale."

Rebuild of Evangelion series

On September 9, 2006, Gainax confirmed a new animated film series called *Rebuild of Evangelion*, consisting of four movies to be released in 2007 and 2008 originally. However, only the first film was released in 2007, and the second in 2009. The first three movies will be an alternate retelling of the TV series (including new scenes, settings, backgrounds, characters), and the fourth movie will be a completely new conclusion to the story. The first of the new movies was released in Japan on September 1, 2007 under the name *Evangelion: 1.0 You Are (Not) Alone*. The second, *Evangelion: 2.0 You Can (Not) Advance* debuted in theaters on June 27, 2009.

Media

The franchise has spread beyond the anime into a number of different media.

Anime

Manga

A number of manga series based on the anime have been released. *Neon Genesis Evangelion*, by series character designer Yoshiyuki Sadamoto, has been serialized since February 1995, eight months previous to the official premiere of the series. *Evangelion* was originally conceived as an anime series, and the early publication of the manga appears to be a way of promoting the anime even before its actual release. Two other manga based on non-canonical video games have been created: *Neon Genesis Evangelion: Angelic Days*, by Fumino Hayashi, *Shinji Ikari Raising Project* by Takahashi Osamu and *Gakuen Datenroku* by Min Min. *Evangelion* has also inspired various doujinshi, like *RE-TAKE*. Even famous mangaka have contributed their own NGE manga: "Birth of Evangelion" was drawn by Yun Kōga, the mangaka who designed *Earthian* and *Loveless*.

Video games

Several video games have been released around the franchise for Windows, Mac OS, and several home game systems, including the Sega Saturn, Nintendo 64, Nintendo DS, PlayStation, and PlayStation 2. Many of the games are RPGs and dating simulators, while others are more combat-oriented.

Merchandise

Asides from the many releases and forms of the TV series and movies, merchandise for *Evangelion* appears in many media; one catalog of only officially licensed merchandise as of 1997 fills a book of 144 pages. The book is described as covering:

"...cards, posters, toys, models (fifty different figurines of Rei alone—plug suit Reis; school uniform [standard and Episode 26] Reis; swimsuit Reis; not to forget the inevitable hospital gurney Rei and summer-fireworks-festival-yukata Rei), videos, CD-ROMs, games, books, manga, "official" fan comics (doujinshi) collections, T-shirts, bags, caps, ties (Kaji's), gloves (Misato's), wearable plug suits (Rei's; wouldn't Asuka's have been more appropriate?), keychains, pins, watches, bookmarks, stationery, pens, pencils, rubber stamps, a Prog Knife-shaped, knife, binders, wallets, floppy disks, mice, lighters, mugs, coasters, a Spear of Longinus-shaped fork, SEELE "Sound Only" speakers, washtubs and soap, towels, umbrellas, fans, postcards, laminated cards, playing cards, phone cards... None of this, by the way, covers the rare Evangelion items—they get their own, 13-page section.

As of 2007, NGE merchandise is estimated at over 6,000 distinct items. Action figures of the Evas, the Angels, and the pilots have been created. Asuka and

Rei in particular are popular subjects for garage kits and models. There have been two Pinky:St figure sets based on the show. Overall sales of the merchandise are tremendous; *Evangelion* music and OSTs sold more than 6.3 million CDs as of 1999.

Some of the merchandise is tenuously connected to the series, such as an Evangelion humidifiers, Doritos, buckets, bentos, chopsticks, operating system utilities, calculators, calendars, Spandex biking shorts, and wetsuits; the merchandise is sometimes very expensive, such as $624 sparkling wine or "$900 laser engraved Rei (EVANGELION) crystal cube" (limited edition of 10,000 for 98,000¥). Perennially popular are the NGE-themed pachinko machines.

A great deal of the merchandise is otaku-oriented (such as headphones, cosplay-accurate Mari & Gendo glasses or Misato's sunglasses, iPhone batterypacks, or dakimakura body pillows) and has a much lighter tone than the series, something for which Anno has expressed considerable discontent, although he has not been involved in production for any of the merchandise. Two dolls featuring Pullip by Junplaning were released in February and March 2008. The Rei Ayanami Pullip was released in February 2008, while the Asuka Langley Soryu Pullip was released in March 2008. Animate's Animate Costume Museum (ACOS) store sells cosplay outfits for Kaworu and Mari cosplayers.

In 2010, Lawson opened a temporary Evangelion-only store in the Hakone region (site in the anime of Tokyo-3); due to excessive popularity & demand, it was shut down within days.

Amusement park
On 22 July 2010, Fuji-Q Highland opened a 1,460m section devoted to *Evangelion*, featuring a lifesize entry plug & statue of Mari Makinami & a ~3-meter titanium Lance of Longinus, NERV hallways with character cutouts that lead to a hangar room with the 1:1 bust of Eva Unit-01, SEELE monoliths, appropriate cosplay, Eva-themed hotel rooms, and food products. A similar bust of Eva Unit-02 from a scene in *Rebuild of Evangelion 2.0* was announced in 2011 and has been installed.

Development of a live-action movie version of *Neon Genesis Evangelion* was announced in May 2003 by the Houston-based anime distributor ADV Films, who held worldwide rights to the series outside of Asia and Australia, and Universal Studios would be the American distributor. The film was to be be made by ADV, Gainax, and Weta Workshop Ltd.. Its release is currently projected to occur at any time ranging from as early as 2010 to as late as 2015. In December 2005, *Fortune* magazine reported in an article about ADV Films that it had raised "about half of the $100 million to $120 million" needed to produce the film. It is not completely clear if this money was raised by ADV alone or if part of that amount was contributed by Gainax.

The project has since become considered to be in "development hell", as a director has yet to become available or announced officially. In a panel discussion at Tekkoshocon on April 2, 2006 featuring Matt Greenfield and wife Tiffany Grant, many aspects of the project were revealed. Greenfield recalled that Weta approached ADV about a live-action *Eva* movie after completing work on *The Lord of the Rings* film trilogy, but work was delayed by *King Kong* and *The Chronicles of Narnia*. It was revealed that three described "A-list" directors and several celebrities had approached the project, rather than the other way around, and the slug script was written by a writer of several other well-known science fiction movies (though this is subject to be rewritten and tailored to the director's vision). Greenfield also reiterated his belief that they did not want to make the movie for profit, but because they wanted to do it and have it done right (as with the *Lord of the Rings* trilogy), and promised effort toward a trilogy of *Evangelion* films (as opposed to trying to condense the story into one film and lose vast amounts of material), similar again to the *Lord of the Rings* trilogy.

Beyond these official announcements and some concept art produced by Weta Workshop, little or no more information about the film(s) has been made available. At Anime Expo 2008, ADV founders Matt Greenfield and John Ledford, in response to a question over the progress of the live-action film, revealed they had hired the producer for *Appleseed Ex Machina*, John Woo, and pitched the idea to other producers such as Jerry Bruckheimer and Steven Spielberg. They went on to say that interest in the project had been boosted by the success of the 2007 film *Transformers*.

At Ohayocon 2009, ADV director Matt Greenfield announced that several U.S. studios are competing for final rights to the project, meaning that actual production would soon begin. Matt Greenfield predicted that an official announcement, including naming the studio, the director, and perhaps casting information, would be made within the next 9 months. During the opening ceremonies when ADV head Matt Greenfield was introduced, someone in the crowd shouted a question about whether or not fans would ever see the long-promised live-action *Neon Genesis Evangelion* movie. "Soon, and I'm not kidding" was Mr. Greenfield's response. He clarified a bit later that evening during an *Evangelion* panel, saying that the closer he gets to sealing the deal, the less he can say anything about it.

The current status of the film is unknown following the sudden collapse and asset sale of A.D. Vision on September 1, 2009; producer Joseph Chou said in February 2010 that the project was still active, and delays owed more to the general deterioration of the US anime market than to ADV's internal issues. John Ledford, a co-founder of ADV Films is still attached to the film. During a panel at the June 2011 Supanova Pop Culture Expo, Greenfield said that while he now had only minimal involvement, the project was still alive at a studio and Chou still involved, and it was searching for a director.

Cast

No cast has yet been announced for the film, as several parties have stated that one of the goals of the production is to cast children of ages appropriate to their roles and then cast adults who will be able to work well with them.

One point worth noting is that in the earliest days of disclosure, Tiffany Grant stated through interviews and self-published articles, that the film would feature a cast "mostly of European descent," as well as mentioning ADV Films toying with the idea of giving the English dub actors cameos in the film. Not long after Grant's statements, concept art produced by Weta Workshop was released featuring character slug names such as "Kate Rose" (in lieu of Asuka Langley), "Ray Ayanami" (Rei Ayanami), and "Susan Whitnall" (assumed by some to be Misato Katsuragi). The art was later changed to reflect the original, Japanese names, but caused a great deal of controversy among NGE fans.

Legacy

The Keroro Gunso (Sgt. Frog) anime features many aspects of the Evangelion series, when Saburo first appears in the Hinata's House it is shown his A.T. field is appearing through the door. Later he descends to their underground base, much like Kaworu Nagisa (the final angel in the series, Tabris), with the same music, Handel's Messiah, playing in the background. Episode 48 is almost seen as a tribute or parody to the series when Keron March Energy gains a human like form that resembles Rei Ayanami and threatens to destroy the planet with the March Impact (a parody of the series' plot device "Third Impact", being as March is the third month).

British Post-hardcore band Fightstar's album *Grand Unification* is a concept album based upon the anime franchise. Grindcore band Discordance Axis is also referenced it in some of the song titles of their album The Inalienable Dreamless.

The long-running *Super Robot Wars* video game franchise features *Evangelion* characters in *Super Robot Wars F*, *Super Robot Wars Alpha*, *3rd Super Robot Wars Alpha*, *Super Robot Wars MX*, and *Super Robot Wars L*. In the video game *KOF: Maximum Impact 2*, the character Leona Heidern has alternate costumes based on Asuka and Rei's plug suits.

Source (edited): "http://en.wikipedia.org/wiki/Neon_Genesis_Evangelion"

Neon Genesis Evangelion (anime)

Neon Genesis Evangelion (新世紀エヴァンゲリオン *Shin Seiki Evangerion, lit. New Century Evangelion*), commonly referred to as ***Evangelion***, is a commercially and critically successful Japanese anime series that began airing in October 1995. The series was highly influential, and launched the *Neon Genesis Evangelion* franchise. It won several major animation awards. The anime was created by Gainax, written and directed by Hideaki Anno, and co-produced by TV Tokyo and Nihon Ad Systems (NAS).

Evangelion is an apocalyptic mecha action series which revolves around the efforts by the paramilitary organization Nerv to fight monstrous beings called Angels, primarily using giant mecha called Evangelions which are piloted by select teenagers, one of whom is the primary protagonist.

Events in the series refer to Judeo-Christian symbols from the Book of Genesis and Biblical apocrypha among others. Later episodes deconstruct the themes and motifs of the mecha genre and shift focus to psychoanalysis of the main characters, who display various emotional problems and mental illnesses; the nature of existence and reality are questioned in a way that lets *Evangelion* be characterized as "postmodern fantasy". Hideaki Anno, the director of the anime series, suffered from clinical depression prior to creating the series, and the psychological aspects of the show are based on the director's own experiences with overcoming this illness. The anime is an early example of the genre/concept "sekai-kei", anime/manga/light novels which mirror their protagonists' lives with the end of the world.

Plot

Setting

The story of *Evangelion* primarily begins in 2000 with the "Second Impact", a global cataclysm which almost completely destroyed Antarctica and led to the deaths of half the human population of Earth. The Impact is believed by the public at large and even most of Nerv to have been the impact of a meteorite landing in Antarctica, causing devastating tsunamis and a change in the Earth's axial tilt (leading to global climate change) and subsequent geopolitical unrest, nuclear war (such as the nuking of Tokyo), and general economic distress. Later, Second Impact is revealed to be the result of contact with and experimentation on the first of what are collectively dubbed the Angels: Adam. The experiments were sponsored by the mysterious organization Seele, and carried out by the research organization Gehirn.

In 2010, Gehirn had accomplished a number of its scientific and engineering goals and corporately changed into the paramilitary organization Nerv which is headquartered in Tokyo-3, a militarized civilian city located on one of the last dry sections of Japan; Nerv's central mission is to locate the remaining Angels predicted by Seele, and to destroy them. However, Nerv has its own secret agenda, as directed by its Machiavellian commander Gendo Ikari: the Human Instrumentality Project, which, according to Gendo in episode 25, is the task of uniting all human minds into one global spiritual entity. Associated with Nerv is the Marduk Institute, which has the task of selecting the pilots for the Evas, the most capable being children conceived after the Second Impact (14 year olds). The institute consists of Commander Ikari, and Nerv's chief scientist Ritsuko Akagi; supporting the two are 108 companies which are all revealed to be ghost companies.

Story

As the first episode opens in 2015, Tokyo-3 is being attacked by the third Angel. Conventional weapons prove ineffective, largely due to its projected force field called an AT Field. Nerv takes command of the battles, and is able to intercept and defeat the Angels using the Evangelions (Evas), biomechanical mecha previously developed in secret by Gehirn inside the underground Geofront; the Geofront is located underneath Tokyo-3.

Not knowing why his father summoned him, Shinji Ikari, a 14 year old boy arrives to Tokyo-3 just as the Third Angel attacks the city. Shinji reluctantly agrees to join Nerv to pilot Evangelion Unit 01, and begins living with Captain Misato Katsuragi. He and Rei Ayanami battle the successive advances of the Angels together and are later joined by Asuka Langley Soryu, the pilot of Unit 02.

Each Eva has its own designated pilot (Unit 00–Rei, Unit 01–Shinji, Unit 02–Asuka, and subsequently Unit 03–Toji Suzuhara), and operates by synchronizing the pilot's soul and the human soul inside the Eva via the enigmatic liquid substance known as LCL. (In the context of *Evangelion*, a "soul" refers to an individual's conscious existence, mental structure and identity, rather than a more conventional "supernatural" entity.) Surrounded by LCL, the pilot's nervous system, mind and body join with the Eva's controls, allowing the Eva to be controlled by the pilot's thoughts and actions. The higher a pilot's synchronization ratio, the better the pilot can control the Eva and fight more adeptly.

While Ritsuko mentions at the series' beginning that the Evas do have some biological components to them, the extent of this is not immediately apparent. Unit 01 is connected to Yui Ikari, Gendo's wife and Shinji's mother, since it absorbed her body and soul in a failed experiment, as shown in episodes 16 and 20. Rei herself is suspected to be a partial clone of Yui, and is known to harbor the soul of Lilith, the second Angel.

The Eva Unit 02 landing on the missile destroyer USS *Ramage*

It is finally revealed, towards the end of the series, that the Evas are not really "robots" but are actually cloned Angels (Units 00, 02, 03, and 04 are made from Adam, and 01 is made from Lilith) onto which mechanical components are incorporated as a means of restraint and control. This control is not perfect, as various units are shown over the course of the series driving into "berserker" mode, in which they can act of their own will, independent of any artificial power input.

Along with the battles against the Angels, the central characters struggle to overcome their personal issues and personality conflicts, which factor heavily into the events of the series and its eventual conclusion. Throughout the series, many of the main characters constantly have to cope with several social and emotional problems: characters are unwillingly forced to confront socially complex and challenging situations; unresolved sexual tensions grow between numerous characters; injuries, deaths, and defeats cause blows to their psyches; and previously steady relationships begin to falter.

Over the final months of 2015, the characters begin to learn of the true plan of Nerv and Seele, the Human Instrumentality Project. Its purpose is to force the completion of human evolution, and thereby save it from destroying itself. To do so, they plan to break down the AT fields that separate individual humans, and in doing so, reducing all humans to LCL, which is revealed to be the "primordial soup", the fundamental composite of human beings. All LCL would then be united into a supreme being, the next stage of humanity, ending all conflict, loneliness and pain brought about by individual existence. At the end of the series, Seele and Nerv come into direct conflict over the implementation of Instrumentality.

In the last two episodes (the second set in 2016), Gendo and Rei initiate the Human Instrumentality Project, forcing several characters (especially Shinji) to face their doubts and fears and examine their self-worth, with sequences that "suggest animated schizophrenia" This ending was made up of flashbacks, sketchy artwork, and flashing text "over a montage of bleak visuals, that include black and white photos of desolate urban motifs such as a riderless bicycle or vacant park benches interspersed with graphic stills of the devastated Nerv headquarters in which Shinji's colleagues are seen as bloodstained bodies", and a brief interlude depicting an "alternate" *Evangelion* universe with the same characters but apparently in the high school comedy genre, eventually seems to depict Shinji concluding that life could be worth living and that he did not need to pilot an Eva to justify his existence; he is then surrounded by most of the cast, clapping and congratulating him. The introduction implies that this same process took place for everyone.

Characters

The cast of *Neon Genesis Evangelion* as depicted on the Japanese "Genesis" (volume) 14 LD and VHS cover.

" It's strange that 'Evangelion' has become such a hit - all the characters are so sick! "

—Hideaki Anno

The characters of *Evangelion* are continuously struggling with their interpersonal relationships, their inner demons, and traumatic events in their pasts, creating a complex pattern of relationships.

Anno described the hero, Shinji Ikari, as a boy who "shrinks from human contact", and has "convinced himself that he is a completely unnecessary person, so much so that he cannot even commit suicide." He describes Shinji and Misato Katsuragi as "extremely afraid of being hurt" and "unsuitable — lacking the positive attitude — for what people call heroes of an adventure." When compared to the stereotypical hero, Shinji is characterized more by lack of energy and emotion than by any sort of heroism or bravery. Rei Ayanami and Asuka Langley Soryu, the other major protagonists, have similar flaws and difficulty relating to other people.

According to Anno, *Evangelion* was an attempt to make all perspectives into one, creating characters that represent different things to different viewers to make it impossible for everyone to arrive at a single theory. To some viewers, the characters are psychological representations, while to others, they are philosophical, religious, historical, and even themselves. It seems the main goal was to present characters who reflected the deep depression and eventual recovery that Anno experienced before beginning work on *Evangelion*; the characters all reflect at least a little of Anno.

However the deeply pessimistic nature of the series as well as the rarely seen huge array of problems in all the characters has drawn curiosity on why there is no real happiness in the setting's world. Assistant Director Kazuya Tsurumaki said of the series, "But when all is said and done, Hideaki Anno's comments on 'Evangelion' + 'Evangelion' are that it is a message aimed at anime fans including himself, and of course, me too. If a person who can already live and communicate normally watches it, they won't learn anything."

The character designs by Yoshiyuki Sadamoto have also contributed to the popularity of *Evangelion*. Sadamoto's attractive designs of the three main female leads, Asuka, Rei and Misato, led to extremely high sales of merchandise (especially of Rei, the "Premium Girl"), and they have been immortalized in the dōjinshi community, garage kit models, and in subsequent anime (such as *Burst Angel*).

Origin and production

With the failure of the Royal Space Force: The Wings of Honnêamise sequel project, Anno, who had been slated from the beginning to direct *Aoki Uru*, was freed up. Legendarily, he would soon agree to a collaboration between King Records and Gainax while drinking with Toshimichi Ōtsuki, a representative at King; with King Records guaranteeing a time slot for "something, anything", Anno set about actually making the anime. Unsurprisingly, elements of *Aoki Uru* were incorporated into the nascent *Evangelion*:

"One of the key themes in *Aoki Uru* had been "not running away." In the story, the main character is faced with the daunting task of saving the heroine … He ran away from something in the past, so he decides that this time he will stand his ground. The same theme was carried over into *Evangelion*, but I think it was something more than just transposing one show's theme onto another …"

The original early plot line for *Evangelion* remained relatively stable through development, although later episodes appear to have changed dramatically from the fluid and uncertain early conceptions; for example, originally there were 28 Angels and not 17, and the climax would deal with the defeat of the final 12 Angels and not with the operation of the Human Instrumentality Project. As well, Kaworu Nagisa's initial design was a schoolboy who could switch to an "Angel form", accompanied by a pet cat.

Production was by no means placid. Sadamoto's authorship of the manga (*Neon Genesis Evangelion*) caused problems as multiple publishers felt "that he was too passé to be bankable"; the stylized mecha design that *Evangelion* would later be praised for was initially deprecated by some of the possible sponsors of a mecha anime (toy companies) as being too difficult to manufacture (possibly on purpose), and that models of the Evangelions "would never sell." Eventually, Sega agreed to license all toy and video game sales.

Reception

In general, the animation and dub, as well as the character design, have often been praised.

The radically different and experimental style of the final two episodes confused or alienated many fans and spawned debate and analysis, both scholarly and informal, and accusations of meaninglessness; even mainstream publications like the *Mainichi Times* would remark that "When Episode 25 first aired the following week, nearly all viewers felt betrayed...when commentator Eiji Ōtsuka sent a letter to the *Yomiuri Shimbun*, complaining about the end of the *Evangelion* series, the debate went nationwide." (It is worth noting that the ending received such coverage in part because *Evangelion* had attracted viewers not typically interested in such fare; the TV series was extremely popular.) After the end of the series, Anno 'broke down' and delayed the upcoming films.

The series enjoyed incredible popularity among its fan base. In 1995, the series won first place in the reader-polled "Best Loved Series" category of the Anime Grand Prix, a reader-polled award series published in *Animage* magazine. The series was once again awarded this prize in 1996, receiving 2,853 votes, compared to the second place show (which was unmentioned) with only 903 votes. *The End of Evangelion* would win first place in 1997, allowing *Neon Genesis Evangelion* to be the first anime franchise to win three consecutive first place awards. This feat would not be duplicated again for several years, until *Code Geass* won the 2006, 2007, and 2008 awards. "*A Cruel Angel's Thesis*" won the Song category in 1995 & 1996; "The Beginning and the End, or "Knockin' on Heaven's

Door"" won the 1996 Episode category; and Rei Ayanami won in the Female Character category in 1995 and 1996 (followed by Shinji Ikari winning in the Male Character category in 1996 and 1997), contributing to Megumi Hayashibara's 1995-1997 wins in the Seiyuu category (and until 2001 for other series). In 1998, EX.org's readers voted it the #1 US release and in 1999, the #2 show of all time.

In response to the backlash by fans against the nature of the series finale, Anno made several controversial comments in the months following the series conclusion, and preceding the release of *The End of Evangelion*. Anno commented in various interviews after the conclusion of the series that "anime fans need to have more self-respect" and to "come back to reality"; in a *Newtype* interview on 10 May, after the announcement on 26 April of a new movie and re-edited versions of the TV series, he also stated that "computer networking is graffiti on toilet walls." These statements were even more controversial.

Re-releases

After the series ended, Anno was not completely satisfied due to issues of time, financial troubles, and network censorship. Thus, when the series was released on VHS and Laserdisc, each episode was remastered and cuts were reincorporated into episodes 21-26, with the first four being drastically enhanced and the final two being completely remade as the double-feature *Death and Rebirth*. However, again, due to time and budget constraints, the remastering and reanimating of episodes 21-24 was put on hold in favor of the movie. However, the *Rebirth* animation wasn't finished and it was decided to later release the second half of *Death and Rebirth* as a stand alone release. *Death* included some of the scenes that were already completed for the remastered episodes 21-24. It was then decided that *Evangelion: Rebirth II* should also include the previous animation and was then renamed *The End of Evangelion*.

After that, the tapes "Genesis 0:11 and 0:12" were released and contained the redone episodes 21-24 and "Genesis 0:13 and 0:14" contained both endings, 0:13 containing both the TV and film versions of episode 25 and 0:14 containing the TV and film versions of episode 26. In 1998, the *Evangelion* films were released in their original intended form, without the extra scenes in the recap movie (*Death(true)²*) and with the full new ending.

In 2000, the "Second Impact Box" was released in 3 parts, containing the 26 uncut, remastered episodes and the 2 movies (also including *Rebirth*).

In 2003, the nine-volume "Renewal of Evangelion" DVDs were released, with the series' sound and picture remastered for HD and 5.1 technology (for example, new background sounds were recorded). The first eight volumes covered the original 26 episodes (with two versions of episodes 21-24: the uncut version and a reconstruction of the edited version). The ninth volume, containing two discs, named *Evangelion: The Movie*, contained *Death(true)²* and *End of Evangelion*. The Renewal release formed the basis for the western "Platinum Edition" (which didn't include the movies, as the movies were licensed by Manga Entertainment, while the series was licensed by A.D. Vision). The "Platinum Edition" features slightly different English subtitles than the original VHS and DVD releases. The original dub of episodes 25 and 26 were replaced with only the 'Director's Cut' dubs of these episodes.

In 2007 Evangelion: 1.0 was released as the first film of the Rebuild of Evangelion's tetralogy.

Inspiration

Evangelion is filled with allusions to biological, military, religious, and psychological concepts, as well as numerous references or homages to older anime series (for example, the basic plot is seen in earlier anime like *Space Battleship Yamato*) – a tendency which inspired the nickname for the series, the "remixed anime". Anno's use of Freudian jargon and psychoanalytical theory as well as his allusions to religion and biology are often idiosyncratically used and redefined to carry his message. This tendency of Anno's has been criticized as "Total plagiarism!" and "just more mindgames from the animation crew". However, Anno has defended himself by denying the possibility of really original work without borrowing in anime: "There is no longer room for absolute originality in the field of anime, especially given that our generation was brought up on mass-produced anime. All stories and techniques inevitably bring with them a sense of *déjà vu*. The only avenue of expression left open to us is to produce a collage-like effect based on a sampling of existing works." "The people who make anime and the people who watch it always want the same things. The creators have been making the same story for about 10 years; the viewers seem to be satisfied and there's no sense of urgency. There's no future in that."

Regardless, Anno seems to have hoped to reinvigorate the medium of anime – seen as lifeless and moribund in the early 1990s – and restore originality: to create a new anime. This desire is also the reason Anno cited for creating the *Rebuild of Evangelion* movies:

"Many different desires are motivating us to create the new "Evangelion" film … The desire to fight the continuing trend of stagnation in anime.

The desire to support the strength of heart that exists in the world…

Many times we wondered, "It's a title that's more than 10 years old. Why now?"

"Eva is too old", we felt.

However, over the past 12 years, there has been no anime newer than Eva.

The interpretation of the symbols and concepts varies from individual to individual, and it is not clear how many are intentional or meaningful, nor which were merely design elements or coincidences. Anno himself said, "It might be fun if someone with free time could research them." A number of these symbols were noted on the English DVD commentary for *Death and Rebirth* and *End of Evangelion*.

Many of the characters share their

names with Japanese warships from World War II (such as the *Sōryū*, *Akagi*, and *Katsuragi*; though the ship names and character names are written with different kanji, they share the same pronunciations.) Other characters' names refer to other works of fiction, such as the two characters named after the protagonists of Ryu Murakami's *Ai to Genso no Fascism* ("Fascism in Love and Fantasy"; the two main characters are named Aida Kensuke and Suzuhara Toji; Anno later directed a Murakami adaptation, *Love & Pop*).

Psychoanalysis

Evangelion has long been taken as a deeply personal expression of Hideaki Anno's personal struggles. From the start, *Evangelion* invokes many psychological themes. Phrases used in episodes, their titles, and the names of the background music frequently derive from Sigmund Freud's works, in addition to perhaps some Lacanian influences in general. Examples include "Thanatos", "Oral stage", "Separation Anxiety", and "Mother Is the First Other" (the mother as the first object of a child's love is the basis of the Oedipus complex). The scenery and buildings in Tokyo-3 often seem laden with psychological import, even in the first episode.

The connection between the Evas and their pilots, as well as the ultimate goal of the Human Instrumentality Project, bear a strong resemblance to Freud's theories on internal conflict and interpersonal communication.

The hedgehog's dilemma is a concept described by philosopher Arthur Schopenhauer and later adopted by Freud. It is the subtitle of episode 4 and is mentioned in that episode by Misato Katsuragi as descriptive of her relationship with Shinji.

Many of the characters have deep psychological traumas in relation to their parents. Shinji's introversion and social anxiety stem from the death of his mother at an early age and his abandonment by his father. Asuka was the target of her mother's insanity, and discovered her mother's body after she hanged herself; her tough, bullying personality is a means of distracting herself from her pain, and she has made piloting Unit 02 her only source of pride and satisfaction. Misato's father neglected her when she was a child; after he was killed in the Second Impact, she stopped talking for a couple of years. In episode 25, Misato states that she was both attracted to and afraid of Ryoji Kaji because he reminded her of her father. Ritsuko saw her mother having an affair with Gendo Ikari; after her mother's suicide she felt both attraction and hate towards Gendo. Indeed, the last two episodes are "stripped of the high-tech gadgetry and the colorful visuals that characterize the earlier episodes in the series, these last two episodes take place largely in muted tones... a form of interrogation proceeds to be carried out as he [Shinji] asks himself – or is asked by an unseen voice – probing psychological questions." The questions elicit unexpected answers, particularly the ones dealing with Shinji's motivation for piloting the Eva – he feels worthless and afraid of others (especially his father) if he is not piloting the Eva. Asuka and Rei are also depicted in deep introspection and consideration of their psyches. Asuka comes to the realization that her entire being is caught up in being a competent Eva pilot and that without it, she has no personal identity: "I'm the junk... I'm worthless. Nobody needs a pilot who can't control her own Eva." Rei, who throughout the series has displayed minimal emotion, reveals that she does have one impulse; it is *Thanatos*, an inclination to death: "I am Happy. Because I want to die, I want to despair, I want to return to nothing." In episode 25 Shinji and Asuka both show that they in fact suffered similar pasts and found different ways of dealing with it. This is further established in Shinji when he claims he has no life without Eva and this is disproven by the world shown in episode 26 followed by the famous "Congratulations" scene.

Besides the references to Freudian Psychoanalysis there are also some minor references to the theories behind Gestalt Therapy, a form of psychotherapy influenced by both psychoanalytic ideas as well as philosophical notions of a holistic self, personal responsibilities and the consciousness. In episode 15 there is a reference to Gestalt's theory of change, the constant shifting between 'homeostasis' and 'transistasis' on which Fritz Perls wrote in his work 'The Gestalt Approach'. Furthermore episode 19 is entitled 'Introjection', a psychoanalytical term used by many Gestalt Therapists to indicate a neurotic mechanism used for the mental processing of the things humans experience. Introjection is closely related to three other neurotic forms of mental processing; namely projection, confluention and retroflection.

Religion

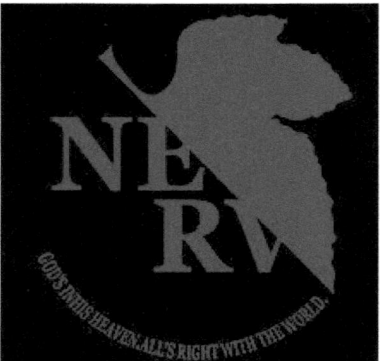

Nerv's logo featuring half a fig leaf; "God's in his Heaven, all's right with the world" is a quote from a song from Robert Browning's *Pippa Passes*.

The destruction of the Second Angel caused an explosion which was cross-shaped: one example of Christian icons being used in *Evangelion*.

The most prominent symbolism takes its inspiration from Judeo-Christian sources and frequently uses iconography and themes from Judaism, Christianity, Gnosticism, and Kabbalism, in the series's examination of religious ideas and themes.

Assistant director Kazuya Tsurumaki said that they originally used Christian symbolism only to give the project a unique edge against other giant robot shows, and that it had no particular meaning, and that it was not meant to be controversial (like it was). Anno has said that Eva is susceptible to multiple interpretations. Hiroki Sato, head of Gainax's PR department, has made similar statements, as has Toshio Okada.

References, with multiple equally plausible interpretations which exist, include:

- The Christian cross is often shown, frequently represented by energy beams shooting up skyward.
- The Angels are a reference to the angels of God from the Old Testament (in Japanese, the word used is the same one used for apostle (or messenger), as in the New Testament). They are named after angels from Biblical angelology, including Sachiel, Shamshel, and Arael. The first Angel is named Adam, just as the biblical Adam is the first man created by God. The second Angel is named Lilith, a reference to the Jewish folklore in which Lilith is the first wife of Adam. Lilith is shown crucified and impaled with a spear named the "Lance of Longinus", the same lance used to pierce the side of Jesus during his crucifixion, according to the Gospel of Nicodemus. Eve or Eva comes from Adam's rib; similarly, most of the Evas come from the Angel first identified as Adam.
- The Magi supercomputers are named Melchior, Balthasar and Caspar after the names traditionally given for the Magi who were mentioned in the Gospel of Matthew as having visited Jesus in Bethlehem. (often called "the three wise men", though the number of visitors is not recorded in the Gospel)
- The Tree of Sephiroth (Tree of Life) is mentioned, as well as shown in the opening title sequence and on the ceiling of Gendo's office, with Hebrew inscriptions on it (the terms written there are mostly Kabbalic). It also appears in *The End of Evangelion* during Seele's version of Instrumentality.
- The Marduk Institute is a front organization for Nerv, tasked with finding the teenagers suitable for piloting Evangelion units. Marduk was the name of the chief Babylonian deity and patron god of the city of Babylon.

Human Instrumentality Project

Neon Genesis Evangelion and particularly the Human Instrumentality Project show a strong influence from Arthur C. Clarke's novel *Childhood's End*, an influence Anno acknowledged. Similarities between the works, such as the larger themes and the declining birth rate after the Second Impact, were gleaned from this work.

Evangelion shows influences from the science fiction author Dr. Paul Linebarger, better known by his pseudonym, Cordwainer Smith. Linebarger was raised in China, became the godson of the nationalistic leader Sun Yat-sen, and during World War II, worked in psychological warfare on behalf of the U.S. Army, including propaganda efforts by the U.S. against the Japanese. Linebarger's work included strong influences from both East Asian culture and Christianity. His science fiction novels revolve around his own concept of the Instrumentality of Mankind, an all-powerful central government of humanity. Like Seele, the Instrumentality of Mankind see themselves "to be shapers of the true destiny of mankind." Although Anno insisted that *Hokan* (補完, complementation, completion) be translated as "Instrumentality" in English, perhaps as a way to pay homage to Linebarger, the two authors' conceptions of "instrumentality" are extremely different.

Other fiction allusions Philip K. Dick's *The Divine Invasion*, and "*The Prisoner, Thunderbirds, Ultra Seven, UFO, The Andromeda Strain*, even *The Hitcher*."

Existential themes of individuality, consciousness, freedom, choice, and responsibility are heavily relied upon throughout the entire series, particularly through the philosophies of Jean-Paul Sartre and Søren Kierkegaard. Episode 16's title, "The Sickness Unto Death, And..." (死に至る病、そして *Shi ni itaru yamai, soshite*) is a reference to Kierkegaard's book, The Sickness Unto Death. The Human Instrumentality Project may be inspired by the philosophy developed by Georg Wilhelm Friedrich Hegel. The title of Episode 4, "The Hedgehog's Dilemma", is a reference to the Hedgehog's dilemma, Arthur Schopenhauer's analogy about the challenges of human intimacy.

Legacy

From the period from 1984 to the release of *Evangelion*, most highly acclaimed anime had a style somehow distanced from the usual styles of anime. For example, Hayao Miyazaki's *My Neighbor Totoro* (1988), and *Kiki's Delivery Service* (1989) were both low-key works, while *Akira* (1988) was influenced by American comic books. Acclaimed director Mamoru Oshii had said that, in the words of Hiroki Azuma, nobody wanted to watch "simple anime-like works" anymore. *Evangelion*, however, shows the reversal of this trend. It fully embraced the style of mecha anime, and in particular shows a large influence from Yoshiyuki Tomino's *Space Runaway Ideon*, which Anno recommends; particularly, there are scenes in *The End of Evangelion* which are clear homages to the last movie for the Ideon series.

As much as *Evangelion* has been impacted by other works like *Devilman*, the series itself has become a staple in Japanese fiction. The nature of the show made it a landmark work in the more psychological and sophisticated vein of anime that would be picked up by later works such as *Revolutionary Girl Utena* (1997) that, like *Evangelion*, center on an ambiguous world-changing event to come. *Serial Experiments Lain* is a later anime which dealt with many of the same themes as *Evangelion*, and so is often thought to be influenced by *Neon*

Genesis Evangelion, although the writer did not see any of *Evangelion* until he had finished the fourth episode of *Lain*, and attributes the utility pole visual motif to independent invention and the screen captions to his borrowing from Jean-Luc Godard and Anno from Kon Ichikawa. The show *His and Her Circumstances* (1999), which was also directed by Hideaki Anno, shares techniques (the experimental 'ripping-apart' of the animation and use of real photographs) and portrayed psychological conflicts in much the same way (although the various cinematic devices can be traced back to works other than Eva, for instance the works of Osamu Tezuka.).

Evangelion dramatically changed the design of giant robots in animated works. Previously, mecha or giant robot shows took their "mechanical suit" designs from *Mobile Suit Gundam*, *Mazinger*, and other similar shows from the 70s and 80s. *Evangelion* changed this with its fast and sleek Evas, making a noticeable contrast to the comparatively bulky and cumbersome looking Patlabors and Mobile Suits of the past. Indeed, the style set and created by *Evangelion* has become more common since its release, yet series like *The King of Braves GaoGaiGar* have continued to use the classic "mecha" style. *RahXephon*, a show with designs inspired by 1970s mecha shows, was compared to *Evangelion* by many English language reviewers. *Evangelion* is generally viewed to be a part of the soft science fiction genre, by avoiding the technical hard S.F. approach of *Gundam* and other popular mecha anime in favor of psychological struggle and metaphysical symbolism. Some anime have been made in direct opposition to NGE; Tomino Yoshiyuki publicly stated that with *Brain Powerd* he intended to "outdo *Evangelion*". Shows or works involving similar mixtures of religion and mecha are often compared to NGE, such as *Xenogears* or *Gasaraki* or *El Shaddai: Ascension of the Metatron*.

The UK band Fightstar's debut album, *Grand Unification*, is purported to have been heavily influenced by *Neon Genesis Evangelion*.

Source (edited): "http://en.wikipedia.org/wiki/Neon_Genesis_Evangelion_(anime)"

Taxi Driver

Taxi Driver is a 1976 American drama film directed by Martin Scorsese and written by Paul Schrader. The film is set in New York City, soon after the Vietnam War. The film stars Robert De Niro and features Jodie Foster, Harvey Keitel, and Cybill Shepherd. The film was nominated for four Academy Awards, including Best Picture, and won the Palme d'Or at the 1976 Cannes Film Festival. The American Film Institute ranked *Taxi Driver* as the 52nd greatest American film ever made on their AFI's 100 Years…100 Movies (10th Anniversary Edition) list.

Plot

Travis Bickle (Robert De Niro) is a lonely and depressed young man and former Marine living in Manhattan. He becomes a night time taxi driver in order to cope with his chronic insomnia, working 12-hour shifts nearly every night, carrying passengers around all five boroughs of New York City. His restless days, meanwhile, are spent in seedy porn theaters. He keeps a diary, excerpts from which are occasionally narrated via voice-over during the film. Bickle is an honorably discharged Marine, and it is implied that he is a Vietnam veteran; he keeps a charred Viet Cong flag in his squalid apartment and has a large scar on his back.

Bickle develops a romantic attachment to Betsy (Cybill Shepherd), a campaign volunteer for New York Senator Charles Palantine (Leonard Harris). Palantine is running for President on a platform of dramatic social change. After watching her from his taxi through the windows of Palantine's campaign office, Bickle enters the office asking to volunteer as a pretext to talk with Betsy. Bickle convinces her to join him for coffee and pie, and she later agrees to let him take her to a movie. She says he reminds her of a line in Kris Kristofferson's song "The Pilgrim, Chapter 33": "He's a prophet and a pusher, partly truth, partly fiction–a walking contradiction." On their date, Bickle takes her to see *Language of Love*, a Swedish sex education film. Offended, she leaves the movie theater and takes a taxi home alone. The next day he tries to reconcile with Betsy, phoning her and sending her flowers, to no avail.

Bickle's thoughts begin to turn violent. The only person in whom he vaguely confides his new views and desires is fellow taxi driver "Wizard" (Peter Boyle), who tells Travis that he's seen all kinds in his time driving cabs, and he believes Travis will be fine. Disgusted by the petty street crime (especially prostitution) that he witnesses while driving through the city, he now finds a focus for his frustration and begins a program of intense physical training. He buys four guns from an illegal dealer, "Easy Andy" (Steven Prince). He then constructs a sleeve gun to attach on his right arm and practices concealing and drawing his weapons. He develops an interest in Senator Palantine's public appearances. One night, Bickle enters a run-down grocery just moments before a man attempts to rob the store. Bickle shoots the man in the neck. The grocery owner (Victor Argo) encourages Bickle to flee after he expresses worry for shooting the man with an unlicensed gun. As Bickle leaves, the store owner repeatedly clubs the near-dead man with a steel pole.

On another night, Iris (Jodie Foster), a 12-year-old child prostitute, enters Bickle's cab, attempting to escape her pimp, "Sport" (Harvey Keitel). When Bickle fails to drive away, Sport drags Iris from the cab and throws Bickle a crumpled twenty-dollar bill. Bickle later meets Iris in the street and pays her for her time, not to have sex, but to try and persuade her to quit prostitution. They meet again the next day for breakfast, and Bickle becomes obsessed with helping Iris leave Sport and return to her parents' home.

Bickle sends Iris several hundred dollars attached to a letter telling her he will soon be dead. After shaving his head into a Mohawk haircut, he attends a public rally where he attempts to assassinate Senator Palantine. Secret Service agents notice him approaching and Bickle flees. He returns to his apartment, then drives to the East Village, where he and Sport get into a confrontation in which the two insult each other. Bickle shoots Sport in the gut, then storms into the brothel and kills the bouncer. After the wounded Sport shoots Bickle in the neck, slightly wounding him, Bickle shoots him dead, as well as Iris' mafioso customer. Bickle is shot several times. Kneeling on the floor of Iris' room, he attempts several times to fire a bullet into his own head, but all his weapons are out of ammunition, so he resigns himself to resting on a sofa until police arrive. When they do arrive, he places his index finger against his temple like a gun and pretends to shoot himself in the head several times.

The film's dénouement reveals Bickle recuperating. He has received a handwritten letter from Iris' parents who thank him for saving their daughter, and the media hail him as a hero. Bickle returns to his job, and encounters Betsy as a fare. She discusses his newfound fame, but he denies being a hero. He drops her off without charging her. As he drives away, he glances anxiously at an unseen object in his taxi's rearview mirror.

Cast
- Robert De Niro as Travis Bickle
- Jodie Foster as Iris "Easy" Steensma
- Harvey Keitel as Matthew "Sport" Higgins
- Cybill Shepherd as Betsy
- Albert Brooks as Tom
- Leonard Harris as Senator Charles Palantine
- Peter Boyle as "Wizard"
- Harry Northup as Doughboy
- Martin Scorsese as a passenger in Travis' taxi
- Victor Argo as a grocery store owner
- Steven Prince as "Easy Andy"
- Joe Spinell as Travis' personnel officer at the taxi depot

Production

According to Scorsese it was Brian De Palma who introduced him to Schrader. In *Scorsese on Scorsese*, edited by David Thompson and Ian Christie, the director talks about how much of the film arose from his feeling that movies are like dreams, or like taking dope and that he tried to induce the feeling of being almost awake. He calls Travis an "avenging angel" floating through the streets of New York City, which was meant to represent all cities. Scorsese calls attention to improvisation in *Taxi Driver*'s many scenes, such as in the scene between De Niro and Cybill Shepherd in the coffee-shop. The director also cites Hitchcock's *The Wrong Man* and Jack Hazan's *A Bigger Splash* as inspiration for his camerawork in the movie.

In *Scorsese on Scorsese* the director mentions the religious symbology in the story comparing Bickle to a saint who wants to clean up both life and his mind. Bickle attempts suicide at the end of the movie as a way to mimic the Samurai's "death with honour" principle.

Shot during a New York summer heat wave and garbage strike, *Taxi Driver* came into conflict with the MPAA for its violence (Scorsese desaturated the color in the final shoot-out and got an R). To achieve the atmospheric scenes in Bickle's cab, the sound men would get in the trunk and Scorsese and his cinematographer, Michael Chapman, would squish themselves on the floor of the back seat and use available light to shoot.

In writing the script, Paul Schrader was inspired by the diaries of Arthur Bremer (who shot presidential candidate George Wallace in 1972) and Dostoevsky's *Notes from Underground*. However, the writer also used himself as an inspiration. Prior to writing the screenplay Schrader was in a lonely and alienated position, much like Bickle. Following a divorce and a break-up with a live-in girlfriend, he spent a few weeks living in his car. He wrote the script in under a month while staying in his former girlfriend's apartment while she was away.

Schrader decided to make Bickle a Vietnam vet because the national trauma of the war seemed to blend perfectly with Bickle's paranoid psychosis making his experiences after the war more intense and threatening. Thus, Bickle chooses to drive his taxi anywhere in the city as a way to feed his hate.

While preparing for his role as Bickle, De Niro was filming Bernardo Bertolucci's *1900* in Italy. According to Boyle, he would "finish shooting on a Friday in Rome...get on a plane...[and] fly to New York." De Niro obtained a cab driver's license, and when on break would pick up a cab and drive around New York for a couple of weeks, before returning to Rome to resume filming *1900*. De Niro apparently lost 35 pounds and listened repeatedly to a taped reading of the diaries of Arthur Bremer. When he had time off from shooting *1900*, De Niro visited an army base in Northern Italy and tape recorded soldiers from the Midwestern United States, whose accents he thought might be appropriate for Travis's character.

When Bickle determines to assassinate Senator Palantine, he cuts his hair into a Mohawk. This detail was suggested by actor Victor Magnotta, a friend of Scorsese's who had a small role as a Secret Service agent and who had served in Vietnam. Scorsese later noted, "Magnotta had talked about certain types of soldiers going into the jungle. They cut their hair in a certain way; looked like a Mohawk... and you knew that was a special situation, a commando kind of situation, and people gave them wide berths ... we thought it was a good idea."

Jodie Foster was far from being the first choice to play Iris. Scorsese considered other actresses to play that role, including Melanie Griffith, Linda Blair, Bo Derek and Carrie Fisher. A newcomer, Mariel Hemingway, auditioned for the role of Iris, but turned it down due to pressure from her family. After the other actresses turned down the role, Foster - an experienced child actor - was chosen by Scorsese.

In the original draft Schrader had written the role of Sport (Harvey Keitel) as a black man. There were also additions of other negative black roles. Scorsese believed that this would give the film an overly racist subtext so they were changed to white roles, although the film implies that Travis himself is a racist. Among other things, cab drivers in the film refer to black people with various racial aspersions, the black neighborhood of Harlem is referred to as Mau Mau land, and Travis exchanges hostile eye contact with several black characters. Schrader's original screenplay also set the action in Los Angeles; it was moved to New York City because taxis were much more prevalent there than in L.A. during the 1970s.

The music by Bernard Herrmann was his final score before his death on December 24, 1975, and the film is dedicated to his memory. Robert Barnett of MusicWeb International has said that it contrasts deep, sleazy noises representing the "scum" that Travis sees all over the city with the saxophone, a musical counterpart of Travis, creating a mellifluously disenchanted troubadour. Barnett also observes that the opposing noises in the soundtrack — gritty little harp figures — are as hard as shards of steel as well as a jazz drum-kit placing the drama in the city – indicative of loneliness while surrounded by people. Deep brass and woodwind are also evident. Barnett heard in the drumbeat a wild-eyed martial air charting the pressure on Bickle, who is increasingly oppressed by the corruption around him, and that the harp, drum and saxophone play extremely significant roles in all this music.

The soundtrack for the film, re-released in 1998 on CD, includes an expanded version of the score as well as the re-recorded tracks from the original 1976 LP. It also features album notes by director Martin Scorsese, as well as full documentation for the tracks linking them in great detail to individual takes.

Track 12, "Diary of a Taxi Driver", features Herrmann's music with Robert De Niro's voiceover taken direct from the soundtrack.

Also featured in the film is Jackson Browne's "Late for the Sky", appearing in a scene where couples are dancing on the program *American Bandstand* to the song as Travis watches on his small TV.

Track listing

Some of the tracks feature relatively long titles, representative of the fact that similar reprises are heard in many scenes.

1. Main Title
2. Thank God for the Rain
3. Cleaning the Cab
4. I Still Can't Sleep/They Cannot Touch Her (Betsy's Theme)
5. Phone Call/I Realise how much She is Like the Others/A Strange Customer/Watching Palantine on TV/You're Gonna Die in Hell/Betsy's Theme/Hitting the Girl
6. The .44 Magnum is a Monster
7. Getting into Shape/Listen you Screwheads/Gun Play/Dear Father & Mother/The Card/Soap Opera
8. Sport and Iris
9. The $20 Bill/Target Practice
10. Assassination Attempt/After the Carnage
11. A Reluctant Hero/Betsy/End Credits
12. Diary of a Taxi Driver
13. God's Lonely Man
14. Theme from *Taxi Driver*
15. I Work the Whole City
16. Betsy in a White Dress
17. The Days do not End
18. Theme from *Taxi Driver* (reprise)

Controversies

The climactic shoot-out was intensely graphic. To attain an "R" rating, Scorsese had the colors desaturated, making the brightly colored blood less prominent. In later interviews, Scorsese commented that he was actually pleased by the color change and he considered it an improvement over the originally filmed scene, which has been lost. However, in the special edition DVD, Michael Chapman, the film's cinematographer, regrets the decision and the fact that no print with the unmuted colors exists any more, as the originals had long since deteriorated.

Some critics expressed concern over 13-year-old Jodie Foster's presence during the climactic shoot-out. However, Foster stated that she was present during the setup and staging of the special effects used during the scene; the entire process was explained and demonstrated for her, step by step. Rather than being upset or traumatized, Foster said, she was fascinated and entertained by the behind-the-scenes preparation that went into the scene. In addition, before being given the part, Foster was subjected to psychological testing to ensure that she would not be emotionally scarred by her role, in accordance with California Labor Board requirements.

John Hinckley, Jr.

The film gained further notoriety when John Hinckley, Jr. claimed that it was his obsession with Foster's role that made him attempt to assassinate Ronald Reagan in 1981.

Taxi Driver formed part of the delusional fantasy of John Hinckley, Jr. which triggered his attempted assassination of President Ronald Reagan in 1981, an act for which he was found not guilty by reason of insanity. Hinckley stated that his actions were an attempt to impress actress Jodie Foster, on whom Hinckley was fixated, by mimicking Travis's mohawked appearance at the Palantine rally. His attorney concluded his defense by playing the movie for the jury.

Interpretations of the ending

Roger Ebert has written of the film's ending:

"There has been much discussion about the ending, in which we see newspaper clippings about Travis's 'heroism' of saving Iris, and then Betsy gets into his cab and seems to give him admiration instead of her earlier disgust. Is this a fantasy scene? Did Travis survive the shoot-out? Are we experiencing his dying thoughts? Can the sequence be accepted as literally true? ... I am not sure there can be an answer to these questions. The end sequence plays like music, not drama: It completes the story on an emotional, not a literal, level. We end not on carnage but on redemption, which is the goal of so many of Scorsese's characters."

James Berardinelli, in his review of the film, argues against the dream or fantasy interpretation, stating:

"Scorsese and writer Paul Schrader append the perfect conclusion to *Taxi Driver*. Steeped in irony, the five-minute epilogue underscores the vagaries of fate. The media builds Bickle into a hero, when, had he been a little quicker drawing his gun against Senator Palantine, he would have been reviled as an assassin. As the film closes, the misanthrope has been embraced as the model citizen—someone who takes on pimps, drug dealers, and mobsters to save one little girl."

On the Laserdisc audio commentary, Scorsese acknowledged several critics' interpretation on the film's ending being Bickle's dying dream. However, he admitted that the last scene of Bickle glancing at an unseen object implies that he might fall into rage and recklessness in the future, and he is like "a ticking time bomb." Writer Paul Schrader confirms this in his commentary on the 30th anniversary DVD, stating that Travis "is not cured by the movie's end," and that, "he's not going to be a hero next time."

Reception

Taxi Driver was a financial success earning $28,262,574 in the United States. Roger Ebert instantly praised it as one of the greatest films he'd ever seen, claiming:

"Taxi Driver" is a hell, from the opening shot of a cab emerging from stygian clouds of steam to the climactic killing scene in which the camera finally looks straight down. Scorsese wanted to look away from Travis's rejection; we almost want to look away from his life. But he's there, all right, and he's suffering.

It was also nominated for four Academy Awards, including Best Picture, Best Actor (De Niro), and received the Palme d'Or, at the 1976 Cannes Film Festival. It has been selected for preservation in the United States National Film Registry. The film was chosen by *Time* as one of the 100 best films of all time.

As of 2010, Rotten Tomatoes reported that 98% of critics gave positive reviews.

The July/August 2009 issue of *Film Comment* polled several critics on the best films to win the Palme d'Or at the Cannes Film Festival. *Taxi Driver* placed first above films such as *Il Gattopardo*, *Viridiana*, *Blowup*, *The Conversation*, *Apocalypse Now*, *La Dolce Vita* and *Pulp Fiction*.

In the American Film Institute's top 50 movie villains of all time, Bickle was named the 30th greatest film villain. *Empire* also ranked him 18th in their "The 100 Greatest Movie Characters" poll.

Legacy

Taxi Driver, *American Gigolo*, *Light Sleeper*, and *The Walker* make up a series referred to variously as the "Man in a Room" or "Night Worker" movies. Screenwriter Paul Schrader (who directed the other three films) has stated that he considers the central characters of the four films to be one character, who has changed as he has aged.

Taxi Driver influenced the Charles Winkler film *You Talkin' to Me?*

Taxi Driver is referenced in the song "Red Angel Dragnet" on The Clash's 1982 record *Combat Rock*.

Home video releases

The first collector's edition (DVD), released was in 1999 packaged as a single disc edition release. It contained special features such as behind-the-scenes and several trailers including one, for *Taxi Driver*.

In 2006, a 30th anniversary 2-disc collector's edition was released. The first disc contains the movie itself, two commentaries (one by writer Paul Schrader and the other by Professor Robert Kolker), and trailers. This edition also retains some of the special features from the earlier release on the second disc, as well as some newly-produced documentary material.

A Blu-ray of the film was released on April 5, 2011, in time to commemorate the film's 35th anniversary. It includes the special features from the previous 2-disc collector's edition, plus an audio commentary released in 1991 by director Martin Scorsese for The Criterion Collection, previously released on Laserdisc.

As part of the Blu-ray production, Sony gave the film a full 4K digital restoration, which included scanning and cleaning the original negative (removing emulsion dirt and scratches). Colors were matched to director-approved prints under guidance from Scorsese and director of photography Michael Chapman. An all new lossless DTS-HD Master Audio 5.1 soundtrack was also made from the original stereo recordings by Scorsese's personal sound team. The restored print premiered in February 2011 at the Berlin Film Festival, and to promote the Blu-ray, Sony also had the print screened at AMC Theaters nationwide on March 19 and 22.

Sequel

In late January 2005 a sequel was announced by Robert De Niro and Martin Scorsese. At a 25th anniversary screening of *Raging Bull*, De Niro talked about the story of an older Travis Bickle being in development. Also in 2000, De Niro mentioned interest in bringing back the character in conversation with Actors Studio host James Lipton.

At the Berlinale 2010, De Niro, Scorsese, and Lars von Trier announced plans to work on a remake of *Taxi Driver*. The film will be produced in a similar manner to von Trier's *The Five Obstructions*.

American Film Institute recognition

American Film Institute recognition

- AFI's 100 Years... 100 Movies - #47
- AFI's 100 Years... 100 Thrills - #22
- AFI's 100 Years... 100 Heroes and Villains:
  - Travis Bickle, Villain #30
- AFI's 100 Years... 100 Movies (10th Anniversary Edition) - #52
- AFI's 100 Years... 100 Movie Quotes - #10

- for the line "You talkin' to me?"

Awards

Wins

- BAFTA Award for Best Actress in a Supporting Role (Jodie Foster)
- BAFTA Award for Best Newcomer (Jodie Foster)
- BAFTA Anthony Asquith Award for Film Music (Bernard Herrmann)
- Cannes Film Festival – Palme d'Or
- New York Film Critics Circle Award for Best Actor (Robert De Niro)

Nominations

- Academy Award for Best Picture
- Academy Award for Best Actor (Robert De Niro)
- Academy Award for Best Supporting Actress (Jodie Foster)
- Academy Award for Original Music Score (Bernard Herrmann)
- BAFTA Award for Best Film
- BAFTA Award for Direction (Martin Scorsese)
- BAFTA Award for Best Editing (Marcia Lucas, Tom Rolf, Melvin Shapiro)
- Golden Globe Award for Best Actor - Motion Picture Drama (Robert De Niro)
- Golden Globe Award for Best Screenplay - Motion Picture (Paul Schrader)
- DGA Award for Outstanding Directorial Achievement in Motion Pictures (Martin Scorsese)
- WGA Award for Best Drama Written Directly for the Screen (Paul Schrader)
- Grammy Award for Best Original Score Written for a Motion Picture (Bernard Herrmann)

Source (edited): "http://en.wikipedia.org/wiki/Taxi_Driver"

Themes in Blade Runner

Despite the initial appearance of an action film, *Blade Runner* operates on an unusually rich number of dramatic levels. As with much of the cyberpunk genre, it owes a large debt to film noir, containing and exploring such conventions as the femme fatale, a Chandleresque first-person narration in the Theatrical Version, and the questionable moral outlook of the hero — extended here to include even the humanity of the hero, as well as the usual dark and shadowy cinematography.

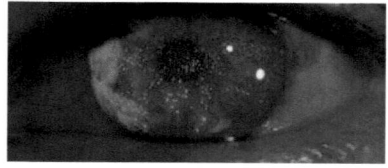

Eye reflecting the "Hades" landscape.

It is one of the most literate science fiction films, both thematically — enfolding the moral philosophy and philosophy of mind implications of the increasing human mastery of genetic engineering, within the context of classical Greek drama and its notions of hubris — and linguistically, drawing on the poetry of William Blake and the Bible. This is a theme subtly reiterated by the chess game between J.F. Sebastian and Tyrell based on the famous Immortal Game of 1851 symbolizing the struggle against mortality imposed by God. The *Blade Runner* FAQ offers further interpretation of the chess game, saying that it "represents the struggle of the replicants against the humans: the humans consider the replicants pawns, to be removed one by one. The individual replicants (pawns) are attempting to become immortal (a queen). At another level, the game between Tyrell and Sebastian represents Batty stalking Tyrell. Tyrell makes a fatal mistake in the chess game, and another fatal mistake trying to reason with Batty."

Blade Runner depicts a future whose fictional distance from present reality has grown sharply smaller as 2019 approaches. The film delves into the future implications of technology on the environment and society by reaching into the past using literature, religious symbolism, classical dramatic themes and film noir. This tension between past, present and future is apparent in the retrofitted future of *Blade Runner*, which is high-tech and gleaming in places but elsewhere decayed and old.

A high level of paranoia is present throughout the film with the visual manifestation of corporate power, omnipresent police, probing lights; and in the power over the individual represented particularly by genetic programming of the replicants. Control over the environment is seen on a large scale but also with how animals are created as mere commodities. This oppressive backdrop clarifies why many people are going to the off-world colonies, which clearly parallels the migration to the Americas. The popular 1980s prediction of the United States being economically surpassed by Japan is reflected in the domination of Japanese culture and corporations in the advertising of LA 2019. The film also makes extensive use of eyes and manipulated images to call into question reality and our ability to perceive it.

This provides an atmosphere of uncertainty for *Blade Runner's* central theme of examining humanity. In order to discover replicants an empathy test is used with a number of questions focused on empathy; making it the essential indicator of someone's "humanity". The replicants are juxtaposed with human characters who are unempathetic, and while the replicants show passion and concern for one another, the mass of humanity on the streets is cold and impersonal. The film goes so far as to put in doubt the nature of Deckard and forces the audience to reevaluate what it means to be human.

Paranoia

Paranoia pervades *Blade Runner* just as the rain falls on Los Angeles 2019. Every major theme adds to the paranoia of the film and envelops the audience in suspicion and uncertainty.

At the beginning of the film, the replicant Leon is being interviewed by the Blade Runner Holden, who is working undercover at the Tyrell Corporation's employment office to screen for escaped replicants using the Voight-Kampff test, highlighting the widespread paranoia of replicant infiltration.

Advertising blimps float over the dark sprawl of 2019 Los Angeles; their searchlights penetrating into every dark corner, as seen when Deckard enters the Bradbury building. This gives the impression that the population is always being watched. Even Deckard seems to be watched by Gaff. The way Gaff interacts with Deckard implies that Gaff is Deckard's "handler" and Gaff also seems to know things about Deckard that Deckard doesn't even know. For example, the origami unicorn presumably left by Gaff, leads the audience to believe Gaff knows the truth of Deckard's (lack of) humanity.

An additional level to the paranoia is the lifetime time-limit imposed on each replicant, and that the limit, while conceived and implemented by the Tyrell Corporation, is now intrinsic to their being. It is ironic to note that one of the most violent of the replicants, Roy, is the only one to execute his genetic programming to his endpoint, as all the rest perish through violent interactions with humans. The callousness and implied cruelty of the design imposed on the replicants is the palpable driving force of the paranoia.

Technicism

Technicism is the concept that all problems, all needs, and all reality will eventually be controlled using technological means, methods, and devices. It is a notion that dominates the dystopian Los Angeles of *Blade Runner* as it seems to blindly accept technological improvements. Many of the themes in the film reflect on this idea further. Humans appear to be fleeing *from* the Earth (to the Off-World Colonies) while replicants (machines) are fleeing *to* Earth.

Other futuristic novels have examined this idea, such as Burgess' *A Clockwork Orange*, Orwell's *1984*, and Huxley's *Brave New World*. Some critics of *Blade Runner* state that the technology of the film dominates the characters, and that the depth of characters is second to the depth of technology. Whether by design or not, it is quite apropos for this film as it reflects on a consequence of technicism — the pursuit of ignoble ends, technology for its own sake, devoid of any personal, ethical or moral consideration.

The first draft of the entire human genome was decoded on June 26, 2000, by the Human Genome Project, followed by a steadily-increasing number of other organisms across the microscopic to macroscopic spectrum. The short step from theory to practice in using genetic knowledge was taken quickly: genetically modified organisms have become a present reality.

The embryonic techniques of somatic cell nuclear transfer from a specific genotype via cloning, as well as some of the problems pre-figured in *Blade Runner*, were demonstrated by the cloning of Dolly the sheep in 1996. Since 2001, political efforts have been mounting in many countries to ban human cloning, impelled by a sense of its abhorrence and imminence, while rumors abound that the first human clones may already have been produced, the most famous example being a claim by the extraterrestrial worshipping Raelians, a religious group who have offered no proof to support their extraordinary claims. In all of these developments, a clear tension between commercial and non-commercial interests is apparent, as scientific and business motivations conflict with ethical and religious concerns about the appropriateness of human intervention in the deepest fabric of nature. In many ways *Blade Runner* serves as a cautionary tale in the tradition of Mary Shelley's novel *Frankenstein*.

Eyes and memories

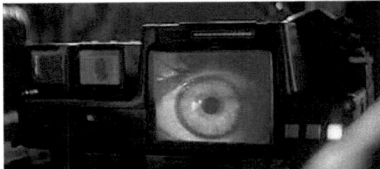

A Voight-Kampff machine reading the minute emotional responses to a test.

Eye symbolism appears repeatedly in *Blade Runner* and provides insight into themes and characters therein. The film opens with an extreme closeup of an eye which fills the screen reflecting the hellish landscape seen below. When reflecting one of the Tyrell Corp. pyramids it evokes the all-seeing Eye of Providence.

In Roy's quest to "meet his maker" he seeks out Chew, a genetic designer of eyes, who created the eyes of the Nexus-6. When told this, Roy quips, "Chew, if only you could see what I've seen with your eyes", ironic in that Roy's eyes *are* Chew's eyes since he created them, but it also emphasizes the importance of personal experience in the formation of self. Roy and Leon then intimidate Chew with disembodied eyes and he tells them about J.F. Sebastian.

It is symbolic that the man who designed replicant eyes shows the replicants the way to Tyrell. Eyes are widely regarded as "windows to the soul", eye contact being a facet of body language that unconsciously demonstrates intent and emotion and this meme is used to great effect in *Blade Runner*. The Voight-Kampff test that determines if you are human measures the emotions, specifically empathy through various biological responses such as fluctuation of the pupil and involuntary dilation of the iris (as pointed out by Dr. Tyrell). Furthermore, Tyrell's trifocal glasses are a strong indicator of his reliance on technology for his power and his myopic vision. Later he is killed by Roy who forces his thumbs into Tyrell's eyes.

The glow which is notable in replicant eyes in some scenes creates a sense of artificiality. According to Ridley Scott, "that kickback you saw from the replicants' retinas was a bit of a design flaw. I was also trying to say that the eye is really the most important organ in the human body. It's like a two-way mirror; the eye doesn't only see a lot, the eye gives away a lot. A glowing human retina seemed one way of stating that". He considers the glow to be a stylistic device only, but Brion James, Leon's actor, suggests that pollution was the "cause" for the glow.

The relationship between sight and memories is referenced several times in *Blade Runner*. Rachael's visual recollection of her memories, Leon's "precious photos", Roy's discussion with Chew and soliloquy at the end, "I've seen things you people wouldn't believe". However, just as prevalent is the concept that what the eyes see and the resulting memories are not to be trusted. This is a notion emphasized by Rachael's fabricated memories, Deckard's need to confirm a replicant based on more than appearance, and even the printout of Leon's photograph not matching the reality of the Esper visual.

Also in the Director's Cut, when at the Tyrell corporation the owl's eyes flicker with a red tint. This was derived from *Do Androids Dream of Electric Sheep?*, in which real animals are rare, and owls were the rarest of all, since they were the first animals to start dying of the pollution which forced the humans to the Off-World colonies. The red tint indicates that the owl is a replicant of Tyrell's creation.

Religious and philosophical symbolism

There is a subtext of Christian allegory in *Blade Runner*, particularly in regard to the Roy Batty character. Given the replicants' superhuman abilities, their identity as created beings (by Tyrell) and "fall from the heavens" (off-world) makes them analogous to fallen angels. In this context, Roy Batty shares similarities with Lucifer as he prefers to "reign in hell" (Earth) rather than "serve in heaven". This connection is also apparent when Roy deliberately misquotes William Blake, "Fiery the angels fell..." (Blake wrote "Fiery the angels rose..." in *America, A Prophecy*). Nearing the end of his life, Roy creates a stigmata by driving a nail into his hand, and becomes a Christ-like figure by sacrificing himself for Deckard. Upon his death a dove appears to symbolise Roy's soul ascending into the heavens.

Zhora's gun shot wounds are both on her shoulder blades. The end result makes her look like an angel whose wings have been cut off. Zhora makes use of a serpent that "once corrupted man" in her performance.

A Nietzschean interpretation has also been argued for the film on several occasions. This is especially true for the Batty character, arguably a biased prototype for Nietzsche's übermensch -- not only due to his intrinsic characteristics, but also because of the outlook and demeanor he displays in many significant moments of the film. For instance:

- *A modern audience might admire Batty's will to flee the confinements of slavery and perhaps sympathize with his existential struggle to live. Initially, however, his desire to live is subsumed by his desire for power to extend his life. Why? In Heidegger's view, because death inevitably limits the number of choices we have, freedom is earned by properly concentrating on death. Thoughts of mortality give us a motive for taking life seriously. Batty's status as a slave identifies him as an object, but his will to power casts him as an agent and subject in the Nietzschean sense. His physical and psychological courage to rebel is developed as an ethical principle in which he revolts against a social order that has conspired against him at the genetic, cultural, and political levels. In Heidegger's view, Batty's willingness to defy social conformity allows for him to authentically pursue the meaning of his existence beyond his programming as a soldier. Confronting his makers becomes part of his quest, but killing them marks his failure to transcend his own nature.*

Economic inequality, corporatism

The dark and dirty urban sprawl Deckard explores in searching for the replicants is contrasted with Dr. Eldon Tyrell's offices and by the bright skyscrapers in the distance. People are migrating to off-world colonies in outer space to escape poverty and contamination. Corporations dominate this world, much as their buildings and pervasive advertising dominate both the city and the surrounding landscape, strongly implying that corporatism is widespread.

Environment and globalization

The climate of the city of Los Angeles, in A.D. 2019, is very different from today's. It is strongly implied that industrial pollution has adversely affected planet Earth's environment, i.e. global warming and global dimming. Real animals are rare in the Blade Runner world. In Philip K. Dick's 1968 novel, *Do Androids Dream of Electric Sheep?*, animal extinction and human depopulation of the planet were consequent to the radioactive fallout of a nuclear war; Owls were the first species to become extinct. This ties in with Deckard's comment about Dr. Tyrell's artificial owl: "It must be expensive." *(cf. post-apocalyptic science fiction)*

Given the many Asian peoples populating Los Angeles in A.D. 2019, and the cityspeak dialect policeman Gaff speaks to the Blade Runner, Rick Deckard, clearly indicates that much cultural mixing has happened. Globalization also is reflected in the name of the Shimago-Domínguez Corporation, whose slogan proclaims: "Helping America into the New World". This indicates that a mass migration is occurring, as there is a status quo that people want to escape.

The cultural and religious mixing can also be verified at the scene where Deckard chases Zhora. At the streets, we can see people dressed traditionally as Jews, hare krishnas, as well as young boys dressed as punks.

Death and immortality are prominent concepts throughout the movie. Some examples are:

- Replicants are programmed to have short lives (4 years) and therefore seek a way to avoid death.
- Deckard realizes replicants are acting like humans as they get close to death.
- J.F. Sebastian was aging fast like the replicants.
- The chess game between Tyrell, Sebastian, and Batty is the famous

Immortal Game.
- Batty saves Deckard's life not only out of compassion, but also so that he would live on in Deckard's memories.
- Roy's final monologue in which he says, "All those moments will be lost in time, like tears in rain. Time to die." Also, shortly after in the same sequence, the statement from Gaff, "It's too bad she won't live, but then again, who does?"

Gaff's Origami unicorn from the Director's Cut, perhaps indicating that Deckard's unicorn daydream was an implant and that Deckard is a replicant.

There is a sequence added in the Director's Cut version (that was not in the original theatrical release) where Deckard dreams about a unicorn, and at the end of film finds an origami unicorn that Gaff leaves in Deckard's apartment, possibly suggesting to the viewer (and to Deckard) that Gaff knows about Deckard's dream in the same manner that Deckard knows about Rachael's implanted memories.

Even without considering the unicorn dream scene inserted in the director's cut, there is other evidence which allows for the possibility of Deckard being a replicant, but do not eliminate the possiblity of Deckard being human.
- the fact that Deckard's flat is full of photographs, none of them recent or in color. Replicants have a taste for photographs, because it provides a tie to a non-existent past.
- the scene in which Rachael asks Deckard whether or not he has passed the Voight-Kampff test himself, and receives no answer.
- the fact that Gaff, who had shown no sympathy for Deckard throughout the film, tells him "You've done a man's job, sir!" after Roy expires, lets Rachael live and does not intervene when she and Deckard leave his apartment.

Relevant opinions from those involved:
Philip K. Dick
- Philip K. Dick wrote the character Deckard as a human.
- Hampton Fancher (original screenwriter) has said that he wrote the character Deckard as a human, but wanted the film to suggest the possibility that he may be a replicant. When asked, "Is Deckard a replicant?", Fancher replied, "No. It wasn't like I had a tricky idea about Deckard that way." During a discussion panel with Ridley Scott to discuss *Blade Runner: The Final Cut*, Fancher again stated that he believes Deckard is human (saying that "[Ridley Scott's] idea is too complex"), but also repeated that he prefers the film to remain ambiguous: "I like asking the question and I like it to be asked but I think it's nonsense to answer it. That's not interesting to me."
- Ridley Scott stated in an interview in 2002 that he considers Deckard a replicant.
- Harrison Ford considers Deckard to be human. "That was the main area of contention between Ridley and myself at the time," Ford told interviewer Jonathan Ross during a BBC1 *Hollywood Greats* segment. "I thought the audience *deserved* one human being on screen that they could establish an emotional relationship with. I *thought* I had won Ridley's agreement to that, but in fact I think he had a little reservation about that. I think he really wanted to have it both ways." (However, in an interview in Wired magazine in 2007, Ridley again states that he believes Deckard is a replicant, and says that Harrison Ford may have given up the idea of Deckard being human.)

Source (edited): "http://en.wikipedia.org/wiki/Themes_in_Blade_Runner"

Welcome to the N.H.K.

Welcome to the N.H.K. (N・H・Kにようこそ! *N.H.K. ni Yōkoso!*) is a Japanese novel written by Tatsuhiko Takimoto, with a cover illustration by Yoshitoshi ABe, and was published by Kadokawa Shoten in Japan on January 28, 2002. The novel was first published in English by Tokyopop on October 9, 2007. The story centers around a twenty-two-year-old *hikikomori* who gets aid from a strange girl who seems to know a lot about him, despite never meeting him before. A common theme throughout the story deals with the hardships of life and how people must deal with them in their own way.

Welcome to the N.H.K. was adapted into a manga series, also written by Takimoto, with art by Kendi Oiwa. The manga was serialized between June 2004 and June 2007 in Kadokawa Shoten's manga magazine *Shōnen Ace*. The manga's forty chapters have been collected into eight bound volumes released in Japan and overseas. The English edition of the manga is published by Tokyopop, and the first volume was released in October 2006. The novel was also adapted into a twenty-four-episode anime television series by Gonzo which aired in Japan between July and December 2006. ADV Films announced at Anime Central that they acquired the English rights to the anime, and they released DVD volume one in October 2007 with volume two released in December 2007. In 2008, the anime became one of over thirty ADV titles acquired by Funimation Entertainment.

In Japan, "NHK" refers to the public broadcaster Nippon Hōsō Kyōkai, but within the series, the main character believes it stands for *Nihon Hikikomori Kyōkai* (日本引きこもり協会, "The Japanese Hikikomori Association"), which is a reference to the protagonist's claim of a subversive conspiracy led by NHK (the real-life broadcaster) to create *hikikomori*. While it mainly deals with the reclusive phenomenon of *hikikomori*, the plot also explores many other Japanese subcultures—for example: *otaku*, *lolicon*, and internet suicide. Despite the show's name, *Welcome to the N.H.K.* was not broadcast on the NHK television channels, but it was syndicated throughout Japan, from July 9, 2006 to December 23, 2006, with Chiba TV (July 9 - December 17, 2006, every Sunday) as a flagship station. It aired mostly on Japanese Association of Independent Television Stations stations, and Hiroshima Home TV (July 16 - December 23, 2006, every Saturday), a local All-Nippon News Network station in Hiroshima.

Plot

Story

Welcome to the N.H.K. revolves around the lives of several young-adults all living in or around the city of Tokyo. Many different lifestyles are shown though most of the time the story focuses on the concepts of being a *hikikomori*, anime otaku, and having most of the characters experience intense feelings of depression and loneliness.

The main protagonist is Tatsuhiro Satō, a university dropout entering his fourth year of unemployment. He leads a reclusive life as a *hikikomori*, ultimately coming to the conclusion that this happened due to some sort of conspiracy. One day just when his life seems entirely unchanging, he meets Misaki Nakahara, a mysterious girl who claims to be able to cure Tatsuhiro of his *hikikomori* ways. She presents him with a contract basically outlining that once a day they would meet in the evening in a local park where Misaki would lecture to Tatsuhiro in an effort to rid him of his lifestyle. During these outings, many subjects are discussed, though they almost always pertain in some way to psychology or psychoanalysis. One of their first meetings in fact deals with interpreting Tatsuhiro's recent dreams. Both Tatsuhiro and Misaki, however, have a tendency of over-doing things, such as hiding the truth, especially from each other and themselves. Despite Misaki's offer and pressing attempts at salvation, it is Tatsuhiro's neighbor and high school friend, Kaoru Yamazaki, who Tatsuhiro often turns to in moments of need and support. Also, despite his own idiosyncrasies, Yamazaki is one of the more stable characters in the story.

The plots within the novel, manga and anime are each rather different from one another, and many themes and personalities differ between each. The novel also regularly mentions drug use by the main character, and later, his friend, Yamazaki. This element of the story is downplayed in the manga (drugs Satō uses are referred to as "legal psychedelics purchased off the internet"), and left out of the story altogether in the anime (with the exception of Hitomi). This is likely due to several reasons, including a more public-friendly rating, as well as ultimately being unneeded for the progression of the plot. Lolita themes present within the novel and manga have also been downplayed within the anime, where most of the women the characters lust after are of mature age, although brief hints still remain.

N.H.K.

The *Nihon Hikikomori Kyokai (N.H.K.)* (日本ひきこもり協会) of Satō's imagination is supposedly a sinister conspiracy which aims to turn people into *hikikomori* and NEETs. No clear reason why they would do this is offered, although Satō considers the potential of an "army" of displaced individuals. It is also mentioned twice that *hikikomori* are needed in society for the purpose of giving people someone to look down upon, making themselves feel superior. The N.H.K. could possibly play the role of creating Hikikomori to give people someone to look down upon. The majority of the N.H.K.'s work is done through the media, via broadcasting anime and other material that is likely to turn the viewer into an otaku. Throughout the series, many shots of advertising hoardings or movie posters incidentally displayed in other locations bear N.H.K. references.

Satō on occasion also believes that the N.H.K. takes a more active role via the use of agents, although of course these agents only appear in dream sequences or flashbacks. Three types of N.H.K. agents are seen: the first are classic Men in Black who appear to have the ability to disguise themselves as anyone else they wish. They occupy key roles in a target's life, ensuring that they fail to develop. The second are cute, or more precisely moé girls who directly break the hearts of targets or who, via celebrity status, induce targets to have impossible or unrealistic expectations of relationships, destroying their ability to develop them in the real world (Satō never considers how, or even if, the N.H.K. would target women). Satō at one point fears that Misaki may be an agent of this type. The final type of agents are bizarre, Goblin-like creatures who are grey all over but for a letter (usually "N", "H" or "K") written in yellow on their belly. These creatures appear to be the masterminds of the entire N.H.K. conspiracy, but more likely than not they are Satō's mental image of the spreading mindset or circumstances he associates with the N.H.K. In the novel, it is hinted that Tatsuhiro may not actually believe the conspiracy to exist but instead needed an imaginary enemy to vent his frustrations on and to help motivate him into overcoming his hikikomori ways.

The real-life public broadcaster NHK, which is the source of the acronym that is parodied by the series, really does provide a support website for real-life *hikikomori*. In the manga and novel, a concrete link between the public broadcaster NHK and Satō's Nihon Hikikomori Kyokai is implied; in the anime, although the conspiracy is still named NHK, no such correspondence is drawn and it appears that the NHK does not even exist as a broadcaster in the anime's version of Japan (in the anime, Misaki has never heard of the acronym when Satō says it to her). This may have been because the anime was broadcast on TV channels operated by other Japanese broadcasting companies, thus implying that it related to the real TV company could have been interpreted as slander against a competitor.

Puru Puru Pururin

Puru Puru Pururin (プルプルプルリン) is a fictitious magical girl anime of which Kaoru Yamazaki is a fan, featured only in the anime version. It is never explicitly stated, but strongly suggested, that Satō believes this series to be controlled by the N.H.K.; in fact, it is after seeing an episode of the series which inspires him to think up the N.H.K. as a concept. The series has a real web-site, which further suggests this. For example, although it appears to be a children's style of series, the schedule on the website suggests that it is shown almost daily in the small hours of the morning, when children would not be awake, but *hikikomori* frequently are. Although the website lists the names of several real-world broadcast channels which supposedly carry the show, none of them are operated by the real-world NHK, again suggesting that in the anime's version of Japan, the N.H.K. is not a broadcasting company and is a conspiracy spanning all media. The listed broadcast times and channels are in fact the times at which the *Welcome to the N.H.K.* anime aired.

Only brief excerpts of *Puru Puru Pururin* are ever seen, and it is not possible to guess what powers the main character, Pururin, would have. It appears that Pururin is a good, heroic character and is assisted by a number of animated household objects, including a vacuum cleaner upon which she flies; her trademark is to randomly append the word *Purin* to the end of sentences, similarly to the title character in *Di Gi Charat*. The theme song first heard in the first episode is sung by Rumi Shishido. This theme appears in ringtone version throughout the series.

Characters

Tatsuhiro Satō (佐藤 達広 *Satō Tatsuhiro*)

Voiced by: Yutaka Koizumi (Japanese), Chris Patton (English)

The story's protagonist is a 22-year-old hikikomori and NEET of nearly four years. He is highly unstable, easily manipulated, obsessive, and often blames the N.H.K. conspiracy, a fabrication of his mind, for his shortcomings. He lives in a rented apartment, but depends on his parents' allowance to live. Within the novel and manga, he engages in fairly hard drug use, which is the cause of his delusional visions, although this does not occur within the anime. Near the beginning of the series he finds out one of his few high school friends, Kaoru Yamazaki, has been living next door to him for quite some time. Yamazaki's influence inadvertently makes Sato become an otaku. Sato also decides to help Yamazaki on the creation of a gal game by writing the script. However, the reason for accepting the writing task was initially to get a girl he met, Misaki Nakahara, off his back. Misaki wants Sato to participate in her project, a therapy of sorts. Although he was extremely reluctant at first, he eventually agrees to take part in Misaki's project, albeit not taking it seriously at first. As they spend more time together he quickly falls in love with her, but is afraid to show it since he knows so little about her despite the fact she knows so much about him. His paranoia drives him to tail Misaki one day to find out where she lives. The result of the expedition reveals that Misaki lives on a nearby hill which gives her a perfect view of Sato's apartment as well as the park where they meet for their sessions. Again driven by paranoia, he tries to save himself from potential betrayal by claiming he doesn't want to see her ever again. Shortly thereafter, Sato accidentally becomes involved in a suicide party but ends up being the closest one to go through with it. Yamazaki and Misaki talk him out of it, and he resumes Misaki's project, but his feelings for her have become platonic rather than amorous. Near the end of the series, Sato's true feelings for her are revealed when Misaki makes up another contract that will bind them together as a couple forever. Despite how he feels, he rejects the contract thinking that he has to protect her from his own condition, and believing she deserves someone much better than he is even if it would mean that he reverts back to being a hikikomori. Later, Sato finds a suicide note from Misaki, but because of an earlier conversation he knows where she will be. Sato eventually finds Misaki and confesses the truth that he needs and loves her in an attempt to prevent her from going through with the suicide. In the end, they decide to continue their relationship while Misaki finishes her high school equivalency, and they go to college together. In the closing scene Sato signs a new contract proposal from Misaki that binds their actual lives together.

Misaki Nakahara (中原 岬 *Nakahara Misaki*)

Voiced by: Yui Makino (Japanese), Stephanie Wittels (English)

A mysterious girl who claims to be a volunteer from a "charity project" to help *hikikomori* like Tatsuhiro. She has the tendency to lie and hides facts such as the fact that she dropped out of high school, but she does not mean any harm. She tells Tatsuhiro whatever it takes to make him pay attention to her. She seems to have a deep attachment to Tatsuhiro, and often shows symptoms suggesting she has a borderline personality disorder such as histrionic personality disorder. She makes a contract with Tatsuhiro in order to believe that she is needed by somebody and therefore not an unwanted person who only makes others around her unhappy. Although not the case in the manga, it is explained within the anime that her biological father died when she was very young and her mother died by falling off the cape in her hometown. After her mother's death, she was forced to live with her abusive stepfather who constantly beat her. Due to this experience, when Tatsuhiro is about to hit her following the events at the island, she flinches by instinct. She loves Sato and tries to make it seem like he needs her more but in reality she is even more lonely than he is to the point where she attempts to commit suicide after Sato refuses her feelings in a second contract she makes. She is seen at the end of the anime getting help from Sato to finish her high school degree, so that she and Sato can go and finish college in order to start their life (relationship) officially together. Misaki's personality greatly differs between the manga and the novel and anime; in the manga she appears more sarcastic and doesn't hesitate to reprimand Tatsuhiro, even showing a more manipulative, controlling side, while in the novel and anime, she has an introverted personality and is portrayed to be more innocent.

Kaoru Yamazaki (山崎 薫 *Yamazaki Kaoru*)

Voiced by: Daisuke Sakaguchi (Japanese), Greg Ayres (English)

Tatsuhiro's former kouhai (Junior) in high school, who is an otaku. Tatsuhiro once stood up for him when he was still in middle school being beat up by some bullies, since then, he respects Tatsuhiro greatly and decided to join the literature club with him when he went into high school. Although appearing to be very mellow, he has a tendency to lash out at those who anger him. He seems to be disappointed with the current state of Tatsuhiro. He is currently Tatsuhiro's neighbor and a college student aspiring to be a game creator. He made Tatsuhiro join his dōjin soft eroge project, and was also responsible for turning Tatsuhiro into an otaku. His family owns a sizable farm in Hokkaidō. Later, he is forced to return to the farm due to his father's sickness; at that point, realizing he has no hope of continuing any aspect of his life in Tokyo, he drives away his crush, Nanako. In the end of the story, he is living happily at his parents' farm and also dating a girl who looks exactly like Nanako whom he hopes to marry in the future. In the manga counterpart tends to be more openly absorbed with lolicon

and introduced Sato to illicit drugs as well as other schemes.

Hitomi Kashiwa (柏 瞳 *Kashiwa Hitomi*)

Voiced by: Sanae Kobayashi (Japanese), Luci Christian (English)

Tatsuhiro's senpai in high school (she is never given a name), now a public servant. Due to stress, Hitomi develops a dependence on drugs. Hitomi met Tatsuhiro when she persuaded him to join the Literature Club, though most of the time they only ever played card games. She has always been fascinated by the concept of conspiracy theories and is one of the reasons Tatsuhiro suspects the conspiracy against himself by the N.H.K. Also, it is noted in both the anime and novel that she had sex with Tatsuhiro during the last day of school before she graduated because Tatsuhiro kept her company in literature club for her last two years of high school. She attempts a suicide through an internet suicide pact called the Offline Meeting Notice (an offline meeting is a slightly slang term for a meeting of people who have met on the Internet, not really having much to do as a pun for "shutting one's life off like a computer"). However, she changes her mind after her boyfriend proposes to her. She gets married and has a healthy kid, though on New Year's Eve, before her marriage she asks Tatsuhiro if he wants to have an illicit affair with her and have sex in a love hotel they were standing in front of, but Tatsuhiro reminds her that since she's happy she should have a good life.

Megumi Kobayashi (小林 恵 *Kobayashi Megumi*)

Voiced by: Risa Hayamizu (Japanese), Monica Rial (English)

Tatsuhiro's classmate in high school, was the class representative back then. They meet frequently in manga, but none of them realizes the existence of each other until later. After her father died, she had to work in order to support herself and her brother, who is also a hikikomori, though ended up entangled in a shady pyramid scheme. During school, she had a very uptight personality which Tatsuhiro

commented about himself to her face. After high school, she retains much of this personality, though has also become somewhat manipulative in order to survive. She develops a lack of empathy to others and isn't beyond exploiting anyone, including friends to meet ends.

Media

Novel

Welcome to the N.H.K. began as a single novel written by Tatsuhiko Takimoto, with the cover drawn by Yoshitoshi ABe of *Serial Experiments Lain* fame. The novel was first published on January 28, 2002 in Japan by Kadokawa Shoten, and the bunko edition was published in 2005. According to Takimoto, the idea of the story came one night as a result of a writer's block. He phoned Yūya Satō, a friend of his who is also a novelist, and said: "Tomorrow there is a conference in Kadokawa Shoten, but I can't think of a story, please think of something." With that, the two stayed in a family restaurant late at night until they came up with *Welcome to the N.H.K.*

Manga

Cover to first English-release manga volume.

The manga series is illustrated by manga author Kendi Oiwa. It was serialized in Kadokawa Shoten's manga magazine *Shōnen Ace* between June 24, 2004 and June 2007. The manga's forty chapters have been collected into eight bound volumes released in Japan. Tokyopop licensed the manga for release in English, and the first volume was published on October 10, 2006. The manga version diverges from the original version later in the story.

In November 2005, the limited edition of the fourth Japanese volume was published with a Misaki figurine which caused sales of the manga to skyrocket, and was once ranked third at Japan's Amazon website in terms of sales. The limited edition of the sixth volume, released in November 2006 in Japan, included the hard copy of the bishōjo game from the manga, *True World: Shinjitsu no Sekai*. The game was authored by Tatsuhiko Takimoto, the characters designed by Kendi Oiwa and produced by Circus (famous for *D.C. : Da Capo*). The limited edition of the eight volume included a diploma signifying graduation from being a *hikikomori*.

Anime

A twenty-four-episode anime adaptation produced by Gonzo and directed by Yusuke Yamamoto aired in Japan between July 9, 2006 and December 17, 2006. The series was coordinated by Satoru Nishizono, featured character design by Takahiko Yoshida, and the music was headed by Masao Fukuda. ADV Films released the first DVD of the English edition in October 2007. In 2008 the English license was transferred to Funimation. Siren Visual has licensed the series for release in Australia and New Zealand.

The anime has four pieces of theme music; two opening themes and two ending themes. The first opening theme, "Puzzle" (パズル *Pazuru*) was written by Rieko Ito, composed by Kitagawa Katsutoshi, and performed by Round Table featuring Nino. The second opening theme is a remix of the first entitled "Puzzle -extra hot mix-" (パズル -extra hot mix -) which was produced by the same people as with the first opening theme. The first ending theme used for episodes one through twelve, "Odoru Akachan Ningen" (踊る赤ちゃん人間, lit. "Dancing Baby Humans"), was written by Kenji Otsuki, composed by Fumihiko Kitsutaka, and featured vocals by Otsuki and Kitsutaka. The second ending theme used for episodes thirteen through twenty-four, "Modokashii Sekai no Ue de" (もどかしい世界の上で, lit. "On Top of a Frustrating World"), was written and composed by Yugo Sasakura, arranged by Masanori Shimada, and performed by Yui Makino.

Reception

A. E. Sparrow of IGN gave the light novel a nine out of ten while comparing it to *Catcher in the Rye*, saying "there's enough Holden Caulfield, or even Tyler Durden, in Satou and the events that surround him to make this story a solid read for anyone interested in books that examine the human condition."

The manga version of *Welcome to the N.H.K.* was also positively reviewed. Writing for Anime News Network, Carlo Santos rated the Tokyopop releases of the third manga volume with a B grade for story, an A- for art, and an A- overall. Speaking on the volume's art, Santos noted "it's endlessly entertaining to watch the parade of shocked, disturbed and stressed-out faces as Satou confronts each of society's ills," as well as highlighting the "detailed backgrounds" and "clean, rectangular layouts and frequent speedlines." Concerning the writing, "the dialogue is full of vigor and wit, with a straightforward tone that conveys mad outbursts, tearful breakdowns, and everything in between." And with regards to the adaptation, Santos praised the volume by writing "out of Tokyopop's many, many translations, this series stands among one of their best, if not the best." Santos was more couched in his approval for the fourth volume, giving it a C+ for story, an A- for art, and a B grade overall. While criticizing that "the plot has taken a vacation," he wrote that "those who are into NHK for the highly developed character drama, however, will find these chapters to be some of the most memorable yet," and concluded "it may not be the best or most entertaining volume of NHK, but it does serve its purpose, which is to deepen the story and make the characters even more dysfunctional and twisted than they already are."

The anime series was generally well-received by critics. In his review for *Animation World Magazine*, James Brusuelas wrote "*Welcome to the NHK* is a true anime gem," describing it as "a delicately human tale." He went on to praise the series, saying "This is more than just anime. This is film." Concluding his review, he remarked "I cannot recommend this series enough. It is perhaps the best anime I saw during 2008." Source (edited): "http://en.wikipedia.org/wiki/Welcome_to_the_N.H.K."

Wolf's Rain

Wolf's Rain (ウルフズレイン *Urufuzu Rein*) is an anime series created by writer and story editor Keiko Nobumoto and produced by Bones Studio. The series was directed by Tensai Okamura and featured character designs by Toshihiro Kawamoto with a soundtrack produced and arranged by Yoko Kanno. It focuses on the journey of four lone wolves who cross paths while following the scent of the Lunar Flowers. They form a pack and decide to seek out the Flower Maiden in order to open the way to Paradise. Along the way, they must avoid a fanatical wolf hunter and the nobles who wish to use the Flower Maiden to create their own Paradise. The wolves have an advantage in the form of a curious ability to take on a human guise, but this power brings its own complications when it gives rise to entanglements in human society.

Wolf's Rain spans twenty-six television episodes and four original video animation (OVA) episodes, with each episode running approximately twenty-four minutes. The series was originally broadcast in Japan on Fuji TV and the anime CS television network, Animax. The complete thirty episode series is licensed for Region 1 release by Bandai Entertainment, in Region 2 (Europe) by Beez Entertainment and in Region 4 by Madman Entertainment. The series was adapted into a short two-volume manga series written by Keiko Nobumoto and illustrated by Toshitsugu Iida. The manga, which was released while the series was airing, is a retelling of the story rather than a straight adaptation. It was originally serialized in *Magazine Z* and has been released in North America by Viz Media.

The anime series was well received in Japan, being the third ranked anime series in its time slot while airing on Fuji TV. The Bandai Entertainment English language release sold well in North America. It helped Bandai gain the 2004 Anime Company of the Year award from industry news company ICv2 in the ICv2 Retailers Guide to Anime/Manga. The manga adaptation was selected as one of their top ten anime products of 2005 and sold well in North America. Reviewers of the series gave it high marks for characterization, visual presentation, and its soundtrack, while disparaging the existence of four recapitulation episodes in the middle of the series. The manga adaptation also sold well in North America and received good reviews, though reviewers felt its short length resulted in a rushed plot and neglected supporting characters.

Plot

According to an old legend, when the end of the world comes, Paradise will appear; however, only wolves will know how to find it. Although wolves are believed to have been hunted to extinction nearly two hundred years ago, they still exist, surviving by taking human form. Freeze City is a northern human city in a world where the majority of people live in poverty and hardship.

Kiba, an injured lone white wolf, goes to Freeze City following the scent of the Lunar Flower, which is the key to opening Paradise. There he encounters Tsume, Hige, and Toboe, three other wolves who were drawn to Freeze City by the scent of the Lunar Flower and are now living in the city. The wolves encounter Quent Yaiden, a former Sheriff of Kyrios who is obsessed with hunting down wolves, and his dog Blue. Cheza, the Flower Maiden who is destined to lead the wolves to Paradise, is being studied at a laboratory under the care of Cher Degré. She is awakened by the smell of wolf's blood. As Kiba and Hige approach the lab to find her, she is stolen away by Lord Darcia the Third, whose people created Cheza.

With the Flower Maiden gone, the wolves have no reason to stay in the city. Despite some initial misgivings and suspicions, they decide to stay together and follow Kiba in his search for the Flower Maiden and Paradise. As they pursue Cheza, the wolves travel through various cities and the remnants of former habitations. Cher joins the city's army to try to recover Cheza, while Cher's ex-husband Hubb Lebowski searches desperately for Cher, and Quent continues his relentless pursuit of the wolves. When Blue eventually encounters Cheza, it awakens her wolf blood from dormancy and causes her to leave Quent and take on her own human illusion. She joins Kiba's pack and travels with them for a while, developing a relationship with Hige. After she becomes separated from the pack, she travels with Cher, while Hubb finds himself traveling with Quent, who is now searching for Blue as well as the wolves.

The wolves and the humans come together in Jaguara's city, where the captured Cheza is being held. In attempting to rescue the abducted Cheza, Kiba, Tsume, and Toboe are captured. Tsume and Toboe are thrown into a dungeon with Hubb while Jaguara attempts to use Kiba's blood to force Paradise to open. Blue and Cher also make their way into the Keep, as does Quent. Darcia interrupts the ceremony as Kiba and the other wolves break free and rush to free the Flower Maiden. Darcia battles Jagara along with Kiba, and finally slays her as the keep begins to collapse. The wolves and the humans barely escape with their lives, and Quent is gravely wounded saving Blue from an oncoming vehicle after escaping from Jaguara's city.

The wolves, now accompanied by Cheza, Cher, Hubb, and Quent, continue trying to make their way to Paradise, pursued by the now insane Darcia. A combination of environmental factors and Darcia's hostility cause most of the characters to die, leaving only Kiba, Cheza, and Darcia alive at the place where Paradise can be opened. Darcia is killed when he attempts to enter Paradise, and Cheza's body disintegrates into seeds. Fatally wounded, Kiba concludes that his quest has failed, but as he lays dying, rain begins to fall and Cheza's seeds grow into thousands of lunar flowers. Kiba is then plunged into the waters depths as he dies, the blood red moon turning back to its normal color.

At the series' close, Toboe, Tsume, Hige, and Kiba are in a modern city. They appear to be human (Reincarnated); Tsume is riding a motorbike and Toboe is holding a small kitten (some speculate that this may be Blue). Hige is eating a hotdog while walking down the street. Kiba, walking down a busy sidewalk, begins running faster and faster. Near by a lunar flower in a puddle (Cheza) waits, waiting for wolves to search for paradise once again.

Changes in manga adaptation

The two-volume manga adaptation includes some of the core events of the anime series with few changes, but as a whole the manga veers greatly from its anime inspiration. Many events from the anime do not occur in the manga, and some of the events from the anime that are presented in the manga are completely different in terms of dialogue, chronological sequence, and final outcomes. In particular, the second volume tells an almost completely different story, with Darcia recruiting Blue to help him open the door to Paradise with her blood. The wolves must go to Darcia's keep, rather than Jaguara's, in order to free Cheza, with Kiba missing but appearing at the end to make the final rescue effort. At the end of the manga, the four wolves and Cheza are sitting on a rock as the clouds break and sunlight streams through for the first time. The world rejoices the end of the Ice Age and rumors that Paradise has been found abound.

In the manga most of the characters are similar in appearance and personality to their anime counterparts, but some characters seen in the anime do not appear in the manga, including the Nobles Lord Orkham and Lady Jaguara.

Characters

- **Kiba** (キバ *lit. "Fang"*) is an Arctic Wolf dedicated to finding the Lunar Flower and opening the way to Paradise. Kiba primarily acts on his instincts, which sometimes lead him to act rashly. Full of wolf pride, Kiba initially expresses disgust at wolves who use human disguises, but eventually realizes that it is necessary to survive. *Voiced by:* Mamoru Miyano (Japanese), Johnny Yong Bosch (English)
- **Tsume** (ツメ *lit. "Claw"*) is a Grey Wolf with a scar across his chest. Rough and self-reliant, Tsume is portrayed as a strong fighter who keeps his true feelings to himself. He joins the others out of boredom and does not initially believe in Paradise. Though he frequently quarrels with Kiba over their journey, he eventually comes to believe as strongly as Kiba. *Voiced by:* Kenta Miyake (Japanese), Crispin Freeman (English)
- **Hige** (ヒゲ *lit. "Whisker"*) is a Mexican Wolf with a carefree attitude, who seems quite comfortable living in human societies. After meeting Kiba, he goes along with the idea of searching for Paradise without much argument, though he doesn't show the same passion as Kiba. Hige wears a collar around his neck, but he doesn't remember how he got it. He also has the strongest sense of smell in the group. *Voiced by:* Akio Suyama (Japanese), Joshua Seth (English)
- **Toboe** (トオボエ *Tōboe*, lit. "Howling") is a Red Wolf and the youngest of the group. He is considered the pup or the runt by the others in the early part of the series. He was raised by an old woman who found him as a very small pup outside the city, and still wears the bracelets she gave him. Due to his raising, Toboe is friendly and protective towards most humans. Toboe has the strongest sense of hearing in the pack. *Voiced by:* Hiroki Shimowada (Japanese), Mona Marshall (English)
- **Cheza** (チェザ) is also called the "Flower Maiden." The wolves need Cheza to find and open the gateway to Paradise. She was created via alchemy from a Lunar Flower. Originally asleep and under study in a lab in Freeze City, Cheza is eventually able to join the wolves, whom she loves. She often refers to herself in the third person, usually adapting to the words 'This One'. The spilling of a wolf's blood makes Cheza scream, and she has the ability to heal and put wolves into a restful sleep through her song and touch. *Voiced by:* Arisa Ogasawara (Japanese), Sherry Lynn (English)

Media

Anime

The *Wolf's Rain* anime series was produced by BONES and directed by Tensai Okamura. Keiko Nobumoto was the writer and story editor, while Toshihiro Kawamoto created the character designs. The series premiered in Japan on Fuji TV on January 6, 2003 and ran for a full season of twenty-six episodes, with the final episode airing on July 29, 2003. A four episode original video animation (OVA) was later created and released to DVD to provide a fuller conclusion to the story than the original television run did, and to make up for the four recapitulation episodes that originally broadcast in the middle of the series. The first two OVA episodes were released on January 23, 2004, with the final two released a month later on February 25, 2004. Animax also aired the series on its respective networks worldwide, including East Asia, Southeast Asia, South Asia, Latin America, and other regions.

Except for the four recap episodes, the entire *Wolf's Rain* anime series aired in the United States as part of Cartoon Network's Adult Swim lineup in 2004. It was broadcast on Europe's digital specialty station Rapture TV from November 14, 2005 to July 6, 2006. It also aired in the UK on Anime Central starting November 4, 2007, with only the first 26 episodes airing.

Wolf's Rain is licensed for Region 1 DVD release by Bandai Entertainment. The entire series, including the four OVAs, were released in seven individual volumes that contained four episodes, except for the first two volumes, which had five episodes. With the first volume, Bandai offered a stand-alone version and a limited edition version, which included an art box, Kiba plushie, and the first CD soundtrack. Bandai also released the thirty episodes in a complete series box set and in a two part "Anime Legends" collection.

In Region 2 (Europe) the series is licensed by Beez Entertainment, which also released the entire series, including the OVAs, in seven individual volumes. In Region 4, Madman Entertainment owns the series license and released all twenty-six episodes and four OVA episodes in the form of a complete series box set.

CDs

All of the music for the *Wolf's Rain* soundtrack was composed and arranged by Yoko Kanno. The vocal songs are performed by various artists, including Maaya Sakamoto, Raj Ramayya, Ilaria Graziano, Steve Conte, and Joyce, and they were recorded around the world, including Japan, Poland, Brazil, the United States, and Italy to offer a diverse range of music and give the soundtrack an international flavor. Two CD soundtracks, produced by Yoko Kanno, Toshiaki Ota, and Shiro Sasaki, were released in Japan by Victor Entertainment.

Wolf's Rain Original Soundtrack,

Volume 1 was released March 29, 2003. It contains twenty-one tracks, including the opening and closing themes throughout most of the main series "Stray" and "Gravity" and many of the background sounds used during key points in the main series. The soundtrack was released in the United States by Bandai Entertainment on May 11, 2004 under the title of *Wolf's Rain Original Soundtrack*.

Wolf's Rain Original Soundtrack, Volume 2 was released on January 21, 2004. It contains an additional 23 tracks, including the closing theme for the final episode of the main series "Tell Me What The Rain Knows", sung by Maaya Sakamoto and with lyrics by Chris Mosdell. It also includes background music from the final episode not included in the broadcast version, and music from the four OVA episodes. The second CD has not been licensed for release outside of Japan.

Manga

The two volume manga series was originally serialized in *Magazine Z*, a monthly seinen magazine, with the first chapter premiering in April 2003. The manga, which was written by Nobumoto and illustrated by Toshitsugu Iida, is an almost complete retelling of the anime story. Each chapter of the manga series is called a "grope" which is a reference to a Japanese phrase for arriving somewhere after enduring hardships.

The two volumes were released in North America by VIZ Media as individual volumes in 2004 and 2005. An exclusive edition of the first volume was released on November 5, 2004 in Borders and Waldenbooks stores that included a collectible box to hold both volumes and a 3D lenticular card. The Viz English release is adapted by David Ury, who also acted as translator and Egan Loo. The series has also been released in German by Heyne, in Italian by Shin Vision, and in Polish by Japonica Polonica Fantastica.

Reception

In Japan, *Wolf's Rain* ranked third among anime series airing in the same time slot behind Air Master and Dear Boys. The series was considered "a big hit in 2004" for the North American market, selling well in mass markets as well as in on-line markets and at independent retailers. ICv2 notes that it has "a strong appeal to the growing teen and older anime audience." The series was selected as one of the top ten anime properties of 2005 for the ICv2 Retailers Guide to Anime/Manga. Its release was also a central reason Bandai Entertainment earned the ICv2 Anime Company of the Year award for 2004.

Tasha Robinson of *SciFi Weekly* praised the series for its unusual focus on non-human characters and the interesting dynamic of wolves behaving like wolves as they interact with the human characters and environments in the series. Carlo Santos of Anime News Network praised the visuals of the series, noting that they "showcase Studio BONES at their most imaginative, with beautiful backgrounds that depict settings from high-tech mysticism to urban decay to open wilderness. The character designs are equally striking: in their human form, the wolves wear contemporary outfits, making them the most accessible of all characters." Both Santos and Chris Beveridge of Mania.com noted that the Region 1 DVD volume containing the four recapitulation episodes should be left unbought and skipped as a waste of money; however, they praised Bandai's release of the episodes for putting the episodes on a single volume, unlike in the Japanese release where they were spread over two DVDs requiring them to be bought to get the new episodes on the same volumes. Other critics have complained that while the show had an original and innovative storyline with beautiful visuals and appealing characters, the episodes themselves were poorly paced, undeveloped, and plagued with plot holes.

In *The Anime Encyclopedia*, Jonathan Clements and Helen McCarthy criticized the production delays and the haituses that led to the creation of the four recap episodes, stating that "if the makers had spent less time recounting the story so far, they might have had more than enough space to finish the entire run within the requisite 26 episodes." They praised the series soundtrack, feeling it supported "the atmosphere and character development", and felt the "moody, dark, and understated" art was attractive.

Yoko Kanno's soundtrack for the series has also been hailed for its beauty and the way it adds to the series' emotional impact. The instrumental tracks were found to mirror the show's tone perfectly, evoking feelings of sorrow and loss. According to one reviewer, the soundtrack "...shows [Kanno's] skills as both composer and pianist..." and is "...a treat to hear." Kanno's work in the series was nominated for an Annie Award in the "Music in an Animated Television Production" category in 2006.

The Wolf's Rain manga adaptation has also enjoyed success in the North American market, with the second volume being the ninth best selling graphic novel on the Nielsen BookScan list for February 13, 2007. It was considered a "major manga hit" among manga series adapted from an anime series. Anime News Network's Liann Cooper praised its artwork, but also felt its short length and rushed story line made it hard to connect to the characters. He also felt the supporting characters, Cher, Hubb and Quent, were only included "just to have them included". Carlos Santos, also of Anime News Network praised the "snappy pacing" while also considering it the primary downfall of the series. In reviewing the series for *Manga: The Complete Guide*, Rebecca Brown felt the series was a "transparent grab for cash" and criticized its extreme brievity and the art, which she felt was "barely adequate and at times not even that."

Source (edited): "http://en.wikipedia.org/wiki/Wolf%27s_Rain"

Acts of Literature

Acts of Literature is a philosophical and literary book based on essays by Jacques Derrida. This book is the first collection of Derrida's essays on Western-culture literary texts. Derek Attridge edited the book in close association with Derrida himself. Among the discussed authors there are Jean-Jacques Rousseau, Stéphane Mallarmé, James Joyce, William Shakespeare, and Franz Kafka.

A part highly cited by scholars is the chapter dedicated to James Joyce: *'Ulysses' Gramophone: Hear Say Yes In Joyce.* (pp. 253-309).

Editions

- 1st edition published by Routledge, November 20, 1991. 472 pages. ISBN 0-415-90057-3. ISBN 978-0-415-90057-7
- Google books page:

Source (edited): "http://en.wikipedia.org/wiki/Acts_of_Literature"

Archive Fever

Mal d'Archive: Une Impression Freudienne is a French language book of philosophy by Jacques Derrida first published in 1995 by Éditions Galilée. An English translation, *Archive Fever: A Freudian Impression* by Eric Prenowitz, was published in 1996.

Archive Fever discusses the nature and function of the archive, particularly in Freudian terms and in light of the death drive. The book also contains discussions of Judaism and Jewish identity and of electronic technology such as e-mail.

Source (edited): "http://en.wikipedia.org/wiki/Archive_Fever"

Echographies of Television

Echographies of Television: Filmed Interviews (French: *Échographies de la télévision. Entretiens filmés*) is a book by Jacques Derrida and Bernard Stiegler. It was originally published in France in 1996, by Éditions Galilée. The English translation by Jennifer Bajorek was published by Polity Press in 2002.

Echographies of Television discusses a number of subjects, but the overall theme concerns the impact of technological acceleration, and in particular the social, political and philosophical significance of the development of digital media.

Contents

The book consists of three parts.
- **Artifactualities**. This section is by Derrida, and consists of excerpts from an interview with Derrida published in the French journal *Passages* in 1993.
- **Echographies of Television**. This section forms the bulk of the volume and consists of Stiegler conducting an extended interview with Derrida. The interview was filmed by Jean-Christophe Rosé under the auspices of the Institut National de l'Audiovisuel, on December 22, 1993. The interview was originally intended for broadcast on television, but this never took place.
- **The Discrete Image**. The third section consists of an article by Stiegler, which was first published in *Art/Photographie numérique. L'image réinventée* (Aix-en-Provence: Cyprès, 1995).

Artifactualities

In "Artifactualities," Derrida begins by stating that "to think one's time" means, more than ever, thinking how this "time" is artificially produced, an artifact. He argues that "actuality" is always a matter of "artifactuality," involving selection, editing, performativity, and thus amounting to a "fictional fashioning." Derrida therefore argues that we must develop a "critical culture" concerning this production of actuality, but he immediately appends three cautions to this statement:

- the need to recall that despite the "internationalisation" of communication, ethnocentrism still predominates in the form of the "national"
- advances in the domain of "live" broadcast and recording give the illusion of an actuality which is not produced
- the artifactuality of actuality must not be used as an alibi, by concluding that therefore nothing ever happens and there is nothing but simulacrum and delusion.

What is least acceptable in the media today, he argues, is to take one's time, or to waste time, and hence what is perhaps most required is to effect a change in the *rhythm* of the media.

Derrida then asks what it means to be concerned with the present, or to do so as a philosopher. It may be a matter, he notes, of in fact being *untimely*, of *not* confusing the present with actuality. One must, on the one hand, take one's time, hold back, defer, while, on the other hand, one must rush into things headlong, urgently—one must be both hyperactual and anachronistic. Derrida has never thought there to be an opposition between urgency and *différance*. If *différance* involves a relation to alterity which is a form of deferral, it is nevertheless also, and for this reason, a relation to "what comes," to the unexpected, to the event as such, and therefore to the urgent. We cannot oppose the event, which is the very possibility of a future—we only oppose those particular events which bring things which are not good. The performativity of the event exceeds all anticipation or programming, and hence contains an irreducible element of messianism, linking it to justice (here distinguished from law), as well as to revolution.

Between the most general logics and the most unpredictable singularities comes "rhythm." If, for example, we could know in advance that the Communist regimes of Eastern Europe were doomed to failure, the pace and rhythm at which this occurred could only be understood retrospectively, taking into account causalities which had been previously overlooked, such as the way in which the fall of the Berlin Wall was immediately inscribed in a global telecommunications network.

Politics must retain a sense of the unanticipated, of the arrival of the absolutely unexpected, the absolute *arrivant*. A politics which loses all reference to a principle of unconditional hospitality is a politics, Derrida argues, that loses its reference to justice. This may mean, for example, that it is necessary to distinguish a politics of immigration from a politics of the right to asylum, because the former presumes the equivalence of the political and the national (immigration policy is a matter for the nation-state), while the latter does not (since, for example, motives for immigration, such as unemployment, may fail to conform to immigration requirements, but nevertheless are a kind of dysfunction of the nation, if not indeed the indirect result on poor countries of decisions made by wealthy countries). On this basis, Derrida provides a critique of the way in which borders are conceived by Jean-Marie Le Pen and the French National Front.

It remains necessary, Derrida argues, to take up the battle fought by Enlightenment philosophy against the "return of the worst." As a struggle against return, it is a matter of a "law of the spectral," of spectres, ghosts, and phantoms. It is a matter of understanding that what comes back is on the one hand what must be fought against, and on the other hand irreducible, originary, and necessary. Thus when we are striving to remember the worst (for example, the complicity of the French state for the treatment of Jews during World War II), we are striving to recall the victims, but this means also to call them *back*, not just for the sake of a present, but for an *ongoing* struggle, and thus for a future.

All this is a question of spirit and of inheritance. There is more than one spirit, and thus when we speak of spirit, we *choose* one spirit over another, affirm one injunction or interpretation over another, and thus take up a responsibility. To inherit is to reaffirm an injunction, but to take it up as an assignation to be deciphered. In so doing, we are what we inherit. We must decide, and we can only decide, on the basis of what we inherit, but these decisions are also the transformation of what we inherit, and therefore always also involve invention.

Derrida concludes by stating that he does not believe in the return of Communism in the form of the party, yet he does believe in the return of critiques which are Marxist in inspiration and spirit. This new International without party, which does not accept the imposition of a new world order, must be more, Derrida argues, than a matter of being able to take the time to read Marx slowly and carefully, now that "Marx is dead." In this sense, it is a question of more than simply the elaboration of critiques.

Echographies of Television

Right of Inspection

In "Echographies of Television," Stiegler begins by noting that Derrida, in agreeing to record their interview, asked for a "right of inspection." He asks Derrida why he did so, and what this would mean in the era of television and "teletechnologies." Derrida responds that if he did so, he did not imagine such a right would be effective, and that it is difficult for intellectuals to adapt to the conditions of television, even if they must also not cut themselves off from a public sphere dominated by that medium. It may be a matter not of fighting today against teletechnologies but rather so that they are able to make more room for different norms, those of intellectuals, artists, scientists, etc. Today the "right to inspection" belongs, more than to anyone else, to those who show, edit, store, interpret and exploit images.

Stiegler points out that we learn from reading Derrida himself that writing is already a kind of teletechnology, and he therefore asks Derrida about the specificity of these more contemporary teletechnologies, especially television. Rather than immediately answering the question directly, Derrida first states that the answer *cannot* be a matter of opposing contemporary prostheses to some prior epoch of immediate or natural speech. If there *is* a specificity of modern teletechnology, then it has something to do with the directness of "live" recording and transmission, and the speed with which what is recorded can be made to travel the farthest distances. Nevertheless, however, we must also recognise that even the most "live" broadcasts are *produced*.

Artifactuality, Homohegemony

Stiegler asks Derrida about his term, "artifactuality," which indicates that the construction of "actuality" passes through the artifact or the artificial, that it involves a selection. Stiegler suggests that what is important about this is not so much that reality is "artificially" constructed on the basis of a selection, but rather what matters are the *criteria* of selection. He therefore asks Derrida if the problem today is that the selection criteria are overdetermined by the "commercial character of industry," and thus if when Derrida speaks of a "politics of memory," he is talking about regulating the effects of market pressure on the construction of actuality. Derrida responds by indicating that the concept of the market is complicated: the market cannot be opposed to state practice, insofar as, for example, public television channels, as soon as they are in competition with private channels, must themselves "conquer the market," becoming concerned with ratings, etc. To address Stiegler's question would mean, Derrida says, knowing what one means by the market in a world in which there is an increasingly "globalised" circulation of televisual commodities.

The Discrete Image

"The Discrete Image" is an essay by Stiegler about the significance of the invention of digital photography and digital cinema. He begins by stating that "the image in general" does not exist. The mental image (the image I see in my mind) cannot be separated from the image-object (a painting, photograph, etc.), and the latter is always inscribed in a technical history. Just as Derrida showed that there is no transcendental signified (no meaning) which can be shown to precede its inscription in a signifier, so too there is no "transcendental imagery" which precedes the image-object. If the mental image and the image-object cannot be opposed, however, they are nevertheless different, first of all because the image-object lasts while the mental image is ephemeral. But if there has never been an image-object without a mental image, even so, there has never been a mental image which is not, in some way, the *return* of an image-object.

Stiegler identifies three stages in the recent history of the image object:
- in the 19th century, the invention of the *analog image*, that is, photography
- in the 20th century, the *digital image*, that is, computer-generated imagery
- at the end of the 20th century, the *analogico-digital image*, that is, digital photography.

This third stage is part of a "systematic discretization of movement," a process of "grammatisation of the visible."

Great moments of technical innovation "suspend" a situation which previously appeared stable, and impose a new situation. Analogico-digital technology is one such moment, in which what is undergoing an intense evolution are the conditions by which we perceive and, therefore, the conditions by which we believe. This is because the digital photograph suspends a certain spontaneous belief which the analog photograph bore within itself: it calls into question what Roland Barthes called the "this was" of the photograph, its intentionality (in a phenomenological sense). Although it is possible to manipulate the analog photo, this is as it were an "accidental" possibility, whereas manipulation is the *essence* of the digital photo.

Nevertheless, the "accidental" possibility of manipulating the *analog* image is something which had already been increasingly undertaken by the mass media in recent years. The ability to do so derives from the fact that even the analog photo is a technical synthesis, and as such exposed to an irreducible potential for falsification. For this falsification to be effective, there must be an alteration of what was, but there must also be a *belief* on the part of the viewer in the "this was" of the photo. Today, however, with the analogico-digital photo, the conditions of this belief are diminished, leading to a general *doubt*, and one which affects, for example, democracy. This doubt must be doubled by another doubt, a positive, resolute doubt leading to new forms of "objective analysis" and "subjective synthesis," and therefore to a new kind of belief and of disbelief. The doubt and fear caused by the analogico-digital image is therefore *also* what would make possible this more *knowing* belief.

The destabilisation of knowledge caused by digitalisation may induce fear, but analog photography also caused people to be afraid: "in the first photographs, we saw phantoms." Analog photography is the result of a "contiguity of luminances," that is, light reflecting from an object strikes photosensitive film, which is then developed with the use of light, producing a photograph which I see when light reflects from the photograph onto my retina. There is a definite chain of light events, connecting the moment the camera records an image and the moment the developed photograph is seen. This is, in a way, a matter of the past touching me in the present, of something coming to touch me from out of the night of the past. With the digital photo, this chain is broken, or decomposed: there is a *treatment* involved in the production of the digital image, reducing the image to binary code to be manipulated and adjusted, which does not require this contiguity of luminances.

Digitalisation is a form of "discretisation": whereas the analog photo relies on the *continuity* of the chain of luminances, and the continuity of the way in which the spectrum is recorded, these two aspects become, in the digital photo, *discontinuous*. Reducing the image to binary code means breaking the spectrum down into discontinuous elements which can be treated in any way whatsoever. Yet the analogico-digital photo does retain *something* of the chain of light events which characterised the analog photo: insofar as it remains a *photo*. At the same time, however, there is no way for the viewer to *know* what aspects of the photo are actual records of a photographic event, and which parts have been altered, added, or subtracted, in a way completely disconnected from the photographic process.

Extending the analysis conducted by Walter Benjamin, Stiegler delineates three kinds of reproducibility which constitute three great epochs of memory:
- the reproducibility of the letter (first handwritten, then printed)
- the analog photographic and cinematographic reproducibility studied by Benjamin
- digital reproducibility.

The difference between the analog and the digital has traditionally been understood in terms of an opposition between the continuous and the discontinuous. The fact that the image has been understood as continuous in this sense is why it has been thought to resist semiological interpretation, which depends on the discreteness of the sign. But with the advent of the analogico-digital image, combining two kinds of reproducibility, it becomes clear that the image was always in a way discrete.

The production and realisation of images by an artist or filmmaker is a form of analysis, which treats images as discrete elements to be edited and assembled. The work of the spectator who puts this together in imagination as a "continuous" whole is a form of synthesis. That we experience the progression of images in film as a continuous movement is less the result of retinal persistence than it is of the spectator's *expectations*, which work to efface the editing. These expectations are always a question of the return of phantoms from the past: animation is always re-animation. Thus if the image is always discrete, it is so, as it were, discreetly, without drawing attention. But with digital technology it becomes possible not only to produce cinematic or televisual works in a new way, but to analyse and therefore interpret these in a new way—for example, to index images, camera movements, voices, etc.

In other words, digitisation "opens the possibility of new knowledges of the image." Discretising the continuous makes it possible to decompose the *this was*, and thus the spectator may come to have not only a synthetic but an analytic relation to the image. That this is possible is because the synthesis we make in our minds when we view an image happens according to conditions related to the technical synthesis effected by the recording apparatus. To view an image is to engage with that technical synthesis, and implies a kind of knowledge of the apparatus by the spectator that determines the conditions of the experience of spectatorship. So a change in the technical conditions of reproducibility will mean a mutation in the way in which a spectator synthesises an image. To each of the epochs of reproducibility corresponds three different kinds of *belief*. The fact that digitalisation makes very possible the representation of things which were never in front of a lens changes the conditions of belief, specifically the belief that photography is a matter of the return of the past in the present. As such, analogico-digital photography possesses a different spirit than previous photographic technology, because what the spectator *knows* about the image is that it has an uncertain relation to "reality": there is an irreducible non-knowledge inscribed in the spectator's knowledge.

Changes to the *analytic* capacities of the spectator inevitably produce changes in the way the spectator "intentionalises" imagery, that is, changes in spectatorial *synthesis*. This is similar to the way in which the alphabetisation of writing produced changes in the synthesis of language. It is the history and evolution of *writing* that made possible the critical and logical spirit which we attribute to language, and which we have until now *not* attributed to the apprehension of the image. Grammar claims to locate the rules of language, but as every language is always undergoing a process of becoming, and is never anything other than the sum of the "use" of that language by speakers, these grammatical rules can never be a matter of a "competence" which precedes those rules brought forth and invented in the course of linguistic *performance*. What this means for the analogico-digital image is that, as increasing analytical possibilities emerge from the technologies of the image, the descriptions and rules which emerge from these possibilities will at the same time mean the *transformation* of what is being described. The question is to know how to take advantage of these opportunities for transformation which will emerge from technological advances.

In other words, "the *evolution of the technical synthesis* implies the *evolution of the spectatorial synthesis*." As Derrida showed in relation to the sign, language is always already writing, a system of traces, composed of discrete elements. Stiegler proposes a similar hypothesis in relation to the image: "life (*anima* – on the side of the mental image) is always *already* cinema (animation – image-object)." Thus the evolution of *both* forms of synthesis, technical and spectatorial, occurs as one *composed* process, in what *Gilbert Simondon* calls a "transductive relation." The massive changes which will follow from digitisation are a chance to develop a "culture of reception." This is in contrast to the way in which Hollywood has taken up these changes: by *opposing* production and consumption, keeping analysis in the hands of the producers, and synthesis a matter for consumers. Changing this relation means creating a situation more like that of literature: one cannot read a work of literature without, in a sense, knowing how to write. A world in which the spectator will see the image analytically will also be a world in which "television" and "text" are no longer opposed.

Source (edited): "http://en.wikipedia.org/wiki/Echographies_of_Television"

Ethics, Institutions, and the Right to Philosophy

Ethics, institutions, and the right to philosophy, is a 2002 English book edited by Peter Pericles Trifonas which contains a lecture and a roundtable discussion by French philosopher *Jacques Derrida*, and a 50 pages essay by Trifonas himself. Derrida's lecture is ***The Right to Philosophy from the Cosmopolitical Point of View***.

Contents
The first chapter is the lecture *The Right to Philosophy from the Cosmopolitical Point of View*, held in 1991 by French philosopher *Jacques Derrida* at UNESCO. The second chapter of the book is a roundtable discussion in which Derrida responded to other philosopher's questions about the lecture of first chapter; participants at the roundtable were Hazard Adams, Ernst Behler, Hendrick Birus, Wolfgang Iser, Murray Krieger, J. Hillis Miller, K. Ludwig Pfeiffer, Bill Readings, Ching-hsien Wang, and Pauline Yu; the roundtable was held in 1994 and published by journal *Sourface*. The third and final chapter is an essay on Derrida by Trifonas. Derrida's lecture takes 18 pages,

the roundtable discussion 38 pages, and Trifonas' essay 50 pages.

Source (edited): "http://en.wikipedia.org/wiki/Ethics,_Institutions,_and_the_Right_to_Philosophy"

Glas (book)

Glas is a text by Jacques Derrida published in 1974. It combines a reading of Hegel's philosophical works and of Jean Genet's autobiographical writing. "One of Derrida's more inscrutable books," its form and content invite a reflection on the nature of literary genre and of writing.

Structure and content

Columns

Following the structure of Jean Genet's *Ce qui est resté d'un Rembrandt déchiré en petits carrés bien réguliers, et foutu aux chiottes* ["What Remains of a Rembrandt Torn Into Four Equal Pieces and Flushed Down the Toilet"], the text is written in two columns in different type sizes. The left column is about Hegel, the right column is about Genet. Each column weaves its way around quotations of all kinds, both from the works discussed and from dictionaries—Derrida's "side notes", described as "marginalia, supplementary comments, lengthy quotations, and dictionary definitions." Sometimes words are cut in half by a quotation which may last several pages. A Dutch commentator, recalling Derrida's observation that he wrote with two hands, the one commenting on the other, noted that the two-column format aims to open a space for what the individual texts excluded, in a auto-deconstructive mode.

Allan Megill described the text as a "literary-philosophical collage." Typography is an important part of the text's presentation and argument; the English translation was designed by Richard Eckersley, noted for his renderings of deconstructionist texts. Gregor Dotzauer, writing for *Der Tagesspiegel*, argues that the two columns are explicitly phallic symbols, opposing each other in a power struggle that neither can win. Gayatri Chakravorty Spivak, in a 1977 article published in *Diacritics*, sees a different image in the two columns, that of two legs: "As the father's phallus works in the mother's hymen, between two legs, so Glas works at origins, between two columns, between Hegel and Genet."

But as Spivak points out (since nothing in Derrida is a singular carrier of meaning), the two columns also overflow with signification—they are also architectural elements: "capital, pyramid, pillar, belfry and so on." In between those columns Derrida attempts to place his own signature. Hegel certainly is a Father to the author, and Derrida notes that his own father had died during the process of his writing *Glas*. Derrida's signature, the D, is found in many places: "The debris of d-words is scattered all over the pages. Derrida describes (*décrit*), writes d (dé-écrit), and cries d (*dé-crit*)." Spivak notes, "I can read Glas as a fiction of Derrida's proper name turning into a thing, of an autobiographical autotherapy or interminable self-analysis against the self-duping of self-sovereignty, crypting the signature so that it becomes impossible to spell it out."

Autobiography and the signature

The specific literary genre problematized in *Glas* is autobiography, and its inquiry traces the very concept of the signature, which in autobiography marks the identity of the author with the narrator of the text. Following Plato, Derrida sees the relation between author and text as one of filiation, but unlike Plato's idea of filiation, which involves only the father and the child, for Derrida author alternates between the father and the mother of the text. In this relationship, the author's signature becomes the guarantor of the text's truth, "it becomes its surrogate parent," according to Jane Marie Todd. The Genet column discusses his autobiographical writings, where one of the issues is Genet's very name—it is not that of his father, but of his mother, who abandoned him shortly after birth. According to Todd, "in the mother who abandons her bastard child, leaving only her name, Derrida finds a figure for the author/text/signature relationship."

Critical response

Glas is described as experimental and obscure. Literary theorist Geoffrey Hartman considered the text's playfulness "exhilarating to many within the discipline [of literary criticism]", acknowledging that to others it "may prove a disadvantage". Morris Dickstein, writing for *The New York Sun*, called it "a dizzying commentary on the work of Hegel and Genet".

According to Jane Marie Todd, *Glas* is a study of literary genre, and its seeming defiance of genre "allows this curious and challenging text [to offer] a direct contribution to literary theory: in both form and subject matter, it details a new way of viewing genre definitions." Derrida himself described the text as "a sort of a wake," in reference to James Joyce's *Finnegan's Wake*; Alan Roughley argues,

It is clear that his reading of Joyce's text haunts the way in which Derrida has constructed his exploration of Hegel and Genet by positioning separate and discrete textual columns next to each other so that it is necessary to read intertextually and follow the ways in which the textual play operates across and between the margins or borders of the page(s) and space(s) separating the columns.

John Sturrock, reviewing the English translation of *Glas* for *The New York Times*, commented that "as a piece of writing it has no known genre". In his estimation reading the book is "a scandalously random experience" given the problem of how to read the two printed columns—consecutively or alternately from section to section. Though it is an "exuberantly clever, punning text", it "asks too much of one's patience and intelligence; our defense against a text declaring itself to be unreadable may be to call its author's bluff and simply leave it unread." Sturrock praises the English translation (by Richard Rand and John P. Leavey Jr.), but notes that a text such as *Glas* by definition cannot be translated and "the notion that translation achieves a semantic identity from one language to another." Sturrock's review was severely criticized in two responses: one writer reprimanded Sturrock for a "dismissive account", another pointed out that what Sturrock refers to as a "random experience" (of the text's format) is in fact reminiscent of the "sacred texts of Judaism".

The English translation was praised by Ned Lukacher in *Modern Language Notes* as an "almost absolutely singular and exemplary achievement".

Influence

According to Denis Donoghue and Morris Dickstein, Geoffrey Hartman is heavily influenced by *Glas*. Luc Ferry and Alain Renaut referred to *Glas* as the "quintessence of the discourse of the 'sixties", though Ned Lukacher notes that this amounts to a "a glib dismissal of Derrida's masterpiece" by restricting its scope and enclosing it as a naive text whose erasure is willed by the writing subject, whereas Lukacher maintains that "Derrida never contests that there is always a subject that decides; his point is rather that the decision never took place on the grounds the subject thought it did and that the decision has effects that the subject cannot account for." According to Lukacher, "The publication of this translation and its brilliantly assembled apparatus will have a lasting and profound impact on philosophical and literary theory in English."

Italian painter Valerio Adami based three drawings on *Glas*, each called "Etude pour un dessin d'après *Glas*" (reprinted in his *Derriere le miroir*).

Editions

- Jacques Derrida, *Glas*, (Paris: Galilée, 1974)
- Jacques Derrida, *Glas*, trans. John P. Leavey, Jr. & Richard Rand (Lincoln & London: U of Nebraska P, 1986)
  - The English translation was accompanied by a companion volume, *Glassary*, by John P. Leavey (U of Nebraska P, 1986) with an introduction by Gregory L. Ulmer and a preface by Derrida

Source (edited): "http://en.wikipedia.org/wiki/Glas_(book)"

Limited Inc

Limited Inc is a book by Jacques Derrida, containing two essays and an interview.

In the first essay, "Signature Event Context," Derrida engages with J. L. Austin's theory of the illocutionary act outlined in his *How To Do Things With Words*. The second essay, "Limited Inc a b c...", is Derrida's response to John Searle's "Reply to Derrida: Reiterating the Differences," which criticizes Derrida's interpretation of Austin. The book concludes with a letter by Derrida, written in response to questions posed by Gerald Graff in 1988: "Afterword: Toward an Ethic of Discussion".

Searle's essay is not itself included: he denied Northwestern University Press permission to reprint it. A summary is included between the two Derrida essays, and Derrida quotes the essay extensively.

"Signature Event Context" was originally delivered at a Montreal conference entitled "Communication," organized by the Congrès international des Sociétés de philosophie de langue francais in August 1971. It was subsequently published in the Congrès' *Proceedings* and then collected in Derrida's *Marges de la philosophie* in 1972. It first appeared in English translation in the inaugural edition of the journal *Glyph* in 1977. Searle's "Reply to Derrida: Reiterating the Differences" was published in *Glyph's* second edition in 1977, along with Derrida's reply to Searle's reply: "Limited Inc a b c..."

Signature Event Context

The essay has three section headings, beginning with: "Writing & Telecommunication" on the third page, and then followed by "Parasites. Iter, of Writing: That It Perhaps Does Not Exist", and concluding with "Signatures".

Derrida highlights Austin's theory of illocutionary acts in the "Parasites..." section because he finds it in contradiction to the definition of communication he has formulated in "Writing & Telecommunication". There he considers all communication in terms traditionally reserved for writing. Derrida lists three traits of writing. First, it subsists without the subject who inscribed it. Second, the meaning of the text is never constrained by its context. "[T]he sign", Derrida explains, "possesses the characteristic of being readable even if the moment of its production is irrevocably lost and even if I do not know what its alleged author-scriptor intended to say at the moment he wrote it". Third, this possibility of rupture from its origin is provided by a text's elements (e.g. words) being separated by spacing. Derrida says that these traits "are valid not only for all orders of 'signs' and for languages in general but moreover, beyond semio-linguistic communication, for the entire field of what philosophy would call experience".

Source (edited): "http://en.wikipedia.org/wiki/Limited_Inc"

Of Grammatology

De la grammatologie is a book by French philosopher Jacques Derrida, first published in 1967 by Les Éditions de Minuit. *Of Grammatology*, the English translation by Gayatri Chakravorty Spivak, was first published in 1976 by Johns Hopkins University Press. A corrected edition of the translation was published in 1998.

Relevance

Of Grammatology is probably Derrida's most important work, and served to introduce his thought to a wide audience. It includes extensive discussion of the writings of Claude Lévi-Strauss, Ferdinand de Saussure, and Jean-Jacques Rousseau. Derrida also discusses the work of Étienne Condillac, Louis Hjelmslev, Edmund Husserl, Roman Jakobson, Gottfried Wilhelm Leibniz, André Leroi-Gourhan, and William Warburton. *Of Grammatology* introduced many of the concepts which Derrida would employ in later work, especially in relation to linguistics and writing.

It has been called a foundational text for deconstructive criticism.

Of Grammatology is one of three books which Derrida published in 1967, and which served to establish his reputation. The other two were *La voix et le phénomène* (Paris: Presses Universitaires de France, 1967), translated as *Speech and Phenomena* (Evanston: Northwestern University Press, 1973, trans. David B. Allison), and *L'écriture et la différence* (Paris: Seuil, 1967), translated as *Writing and Difference* (London & New York: Routledge, 1978, trans. Alan Bass).

Content

Derrida argues that throughout the Western philosophical tradition, writing has been considered as merely a derivative form of speech, and thus as a "fall" from the "full presence" of speech. In the course of the work he deconstructs this position as it appears in the work of several writers, showing the myriad aporias and ellipses to which this leads them. Derrida does not claim to be giving a critique of the work of these thinkers, because he does not believe it possible to escape from operating with such oppositions. Nevertheless, he calls for a new science of "grammatology" that would relate to such questions in a new way.

Source (edited): "http://en.wikipedia.org/wiki/Of_Grammatology"

Points...: Interviews, 1974-1994

Points...: Interviews, 1974-1994 is a 1995 book collecting interviews by French philosopher Jacques Derrida. It contains the translation of all the interview of the 1992 French collection *Points de suspension. Entretiens*, plus two additional interviews, *Honoris Causa* (on Cambridge granting him the onorary doctorate) and *The Work of Intellectuals and the Press*.

Source (edited): "http://en.wikipedia.org/wiki/Points...:_Interviews,_1974-1994"

Positions

Position is a book by French philosopher Jacques Derrida, published in 1972. It consist of a collection of interviews. Derrida talks about his earlier works and their relationships. He said that his 1962 essay, *Edmund Husserl's Origin of Geometry: An Introduction*, already contained many elements of his thought, that would be further elaborated later. He added: "that essay can be read as the other side (recto or verso, as you wish) of *Speech and Phenomena*."

On the relationship between is three foundational works of 1967, Derrida explained: "[*Speech and Phenomena*] is perhaps the essay which I like most. Doubtless I could have bound it as a long note to one or the other of the other two works. *Of Grammatology* refers to it and economizes its development. But in a classical philosophical architecture, *Speech...* would come first: in it is posed, at a point which appears juridically decisive for reasons that I cannot explain here, the question of the privilege of the voice and of phonetic writing in their relationship to the entire history of the West, such as this history can be represented by the history of metaphysics and metaphysics in its most modern, critical and vigilant form: Husserl's transcendental phenomenology."

Contents

1. «Implications. Entretien avec Henri René», pp. 9-24; 9-23 [cfr. b 1967(d)]
2. «Sémiologie et grammatologie. Entretien avec Julia Kristeva», pp. 25-50; 25-46 [cfr. b 1968(d)]
3. «Positions. Entretien avec Jean-Louis Houdebine Pee and diariah et Guy Scarpetta», pp. 51-133; 47-117 [cfr. b 1971(a)]
4. «Aver a=lxw=snoop doggie dog l'orecchio per la filosofia. Colloquio con Lucette Finas», pp. 119-135 (nella sola ed. it.) [cfr. b 1972(b)]

Source (edited): "http://en.wikipedia.org/wiki/Positions"

Right to Philosophy

Du droit à la philosophie (English: *On the Right to Philosophy* and also *From Law to Philosophy*) is a 1990 book by French philosopher Jacques Derrida. It collects all of Derrida's writings, from 1975 till 1990, on the issue of the teaching of philosophy, the academic institution and the politics of philosophy in school and in the university. This big book (660 pages in the original French edition) has been translated in English in two volumes: **Who's Afraid of Philosophy?: Right to Philosophy 1** (2002), and **Eyes of the University: Right to Philosophy 2** (2004).

Contents

Volume 1 contains the essay *Where a Teaching Body Begins and How It Ends*, (pp.67-91) first published separately in 1976 in France; and the 1977 essay *The Age of Hegel* (pp.117-157).

Source (edited): "http://en.wikipedia.org/wiki/Right_to_Philosophy"

Specters of Marx

Spectres de Marx: l'état de la dette, le travail du deuil et la nouvelle Internationale is a 1993 book by French philosopher Jacques Derrida first published by Éditions Galilée and translated into American English as ***Specters of Marx: The State of the Debt, the Work of Mourning & the New International***. It was first presented as a series of lectures during a conference, "Whither Marxism?", on the future of Marxism held at the University of California, Riverside in 1993.

Contents

The title *Spectres of Marx* is an allusion to Karl Marx and Friedrich Engels' statement at the beginning of the Communist Manifesto that a "spectre [is] haunting Europe." For Derrida, the spirit of Marx is even more relevant now since the fall of the Berlin Wall in 1989 and the demise of communism. With its death the spectre of communism begins to make visits on the earth. Derrida seeks to do the work of inheriting from Marx, that is, not communism, but of the philosophy of responsibility, and of Marx's spirit of radical critique. Derrida first notes that, in the wake of the fall of communism, many in the west had become triumphalist, as is evidenced in the formation of a Neo-con grouping and the displacement of the left in third way political formations. At the intellectual level, it is apparent in Francis Fukuyama's proclamation of the end of ideology. Derrida issued a timely reminder of the reasons for that spectre of Marx:

For it must be cried out, at a time when some have the audacity to neo-evangelise in the name of the ideal of a liberal democracy that has finally realised itself as the ideal of human history: never have violence, inequality, exclusion, famine, and thus economic oppression affected as many human beings in the history of the earth and of humanity. Instead of singing the advent of the ideal of liberal democracy and of the capitalist market in the euphoria of the end of history, instead of celebrating the 'end of ideologies' and the end of the great emancipatory discourses, let us never neglect this obvious macroscopic fact, made up of innumerable singular sites of suffering: no degree of progress allows one to ignore that never before, in absolute figures, have so many men, women and children been subjugated, starved or exterminated on the earth.

Derrida went on, in his talks on this topic, to list 10 plagues of the capital or global system. And then to an account of the claim the creation of a new grouping of activism, called the "New International".

Derrida's ten plagues are:

1. Employment has undergone a change of kind, e.g., underemployment and requires 'another concept'.
2. Deportation of immigrants. Reinforcement of territories in a world of supposed freedom of movement. As in, Fortress Europe and in the number of new Separation barriers being erected around the world, in effect multiplying the "fallen" Berlin Wall manifold.
3. Economic war. Both between countries and between international trade blocs: USA - Japan - Europe.
4. Contradictions of the free market. The undecidable conflicts between protectionism and free trade. The unstoppable flow of illegal drugs, arms, etc..
5. Foreign debt. In effect the basis for mass starvation and demoralisation for developing countries. Often the loans benefiting only a small elite, for luxury items, e.g., cars, air conditioning etc. but being paid back by poorer workers.
6. The arms trade. The inability to control to any meaningful extent trade within the biggest 'black market'
7. Spread of nuclear weapons. The restriction of nuclear capacity can no longer be maintained by leading states since it is only knowledge and cannot be contained.
8. Inter-ethnic wars. The phantom of mythic national identities fueling tension in semi-developed countries.
9. Phantom-states within organised crime. In particular the non-democratic power gained by drug cartels.
10. International law and its institutions. The hypocrisy of such statutes in the face of unilateral aggression on the part of the economically dominant states. International law is mainly exercised against the weaker nations.

On the New International Derrida has

this to say:
The 'New International' is an untimely link, without status ... without coordination, without party, without country, without national community, without co-citizenship, without common belonging to a class. The name of New International is given here to what calls to the friendship of an alliance without institution among those who ... continue to be inspired by at least one of the spirits of Marx or of Marxism. It is a call for them to ally themselves, in a new, concrete and real way, even if this alliance no longer takes the form of a party or a workers' international, in the critique of the state of international law, the concepts of State and nation, and so forth: in order to renew this critique, and especially to radicalise it.

Source (edited): "http://en.wikipedia.org/wiki/Specters_of_Marx"

Speech and Phenomena

Speech and Phenomena: And Other Essays on Husserl's Theory of Signs is a book by French philosopher Jacques Derrida. It was published in 1967 alongside Of Grammatology and Writing and Difference. *Speech and Phenomena* is Derrida's most well known work on the phenomenology of Edmund Husserl. The book puts forward a broad argument concerning Husserl's phenomenological project as a whole in relation to a key distinction in Husserl's theory of language in the *Logical Investigations* and how this distinction relates to his description of internal time consciousness. Derrida commented that *Speech and Phenomena* is the "essay I value the most" and it is widely considered one of his most important philosophical works. The book is an important articulation of Derrida's mature relationship to Husserl and develops key discussions of the terms deconstruction and différance.

Derrida's Work on Husserl

Speech and Phenomena is the culmination of a long period of study on the phenomenology of Edmund Husserl that Derrida began with his 1953/54 masters thesis *The Problem of Genesis in Husserl's Phenomenology*. This early thesis then formed the basis for his 1959 paper "'Genesis and Structure' and Phenomenology." Derrida also translated Husserl's "Origin of Geometry" from German into French and published his translation of this article with a book length introduction in 1962.

Structure

Speech and Phenomena consists of an introduction and seven chapters: (1) Sign and Signs, (2) The Reduction of Indication, (3) Meaning as Soliloquy, (4) Meaning and Representation, (5) Signs and the Blink of an Eye, (6) The Voice that Keeps Silence, (7) The Supplement of Origin.

1. Sign and Signs

Derrida identifies his theme in the first chapter as the twofold sense of the word sign for Husserl. Derrida notes that Husserl makes a conceptual distinction in the use of the word sign between expression and indication. For Husserl, Derrida argues, the expression and the indication are both signs but the latter is a sign without meaning or sense. Expression intends towards an ideal meaning and is "tied to the possibility of spoken language."

Commentary

For commentary on *Speech and Phenomena* see Leonard Lawlor's book *Derrida and Husserl* (2002) and Joshua Kates's book *Essential History* (2005).

Source (edited): "http://en.wikipedia.org/wiki/Speech_and_Phenomena"

The Rhetoric of Drugs

The Rhetoric of Drugs, *Rhétorique de la drogue* in the original French title, is a 1990 work by French philosopher Jacques Derrida. Derrida, interviewed, discusses the concept of "drug", and says that "Already one must conclude that the concept of drug is a non-scientific concept, that it is instituted on the basis of moral or political evaluations." In his philosophical-linguistic analysis, Derrida unmasks the socio-cultural mystifications made on the discourses on drugs.

Derrida also discusses the problem of drug use by athletes. Exploring its confines, he says: "and what about women athletes who get pregnant for the stimulating, hormonal effects and then have an abortion after their event?"

Derrida discusses how the link between the rhetoric of drugs and the Western ideology. He also says that "Adorno and Horkheimer correctly point out that drug culture has always been associated with the West's other, with Oriental ethics and religion", and adds: "The Enlightenment [...] is in itself a declaration of war on drugs."

Editions

This interview was made in 1989 and published more than one time as a journal article. It was included in the Derrida's 1992 book *Points de suspension. Entretiens*, as section XIV. The English edition of *Points de suspension. Entretiens*, titled *Points: Interviews 1974-1994* (1995), contained the interview at pp. 228–254, as the final part of the chapter *Autobiophotographies*.

- The Rhetoric of Drugs. an Interview Journal article by Jacques Derrida; Differences, Vol. 5, 1993
- *The Rhetoric of Drugs*, translated by Michael Israel. Published in *Points: Interviews 1974-1994* (1995)

Reactions

Neurobiologist and anti-drug activist Rita Levi Montalcini, which a few months earlier was the protagonist of an anti-drug TV ad campaign, was bothered by Derrida's work and commented: "Those [substances] that we call drugs are substances that are well identified both on the pharmacological-botanical level and on the behavioural level".

Source (edited): "http://en.wikipedia.org/wiki/The_Rhetoric_of_Drugs"

Writing and Difference

Writing and Difference is a 1967 book by French philosopher Jacques Derrida, collecting some of his ealy lectures and essay that established his international fame.

Contents

Structuralist Controversy

Included in the collection, his 1966 lecture at Johns Hopkins University, which changed the course of the conference leading it to be renamed *The Structuralist Controversy*, and caused Derrida to receive his first major attention outside of France. The lecture is titled *Structure, Sign, and Play in the Discourse of the Human Sciences*.

Debate with Michel Foucault

The collection contains the essay *Cogito and the History of Madness*, a critique of Michel Foucault. It was first given as a lecture on March 4th, 1963, at a conference at the *Collège philosophique*, which Foucault attended, and caused a rift between the two, likely prompting Foucault to write *The Order of Things* (1966) and *The Archaeology of Knowledge*.

Source (edited): "http://en.wikipedia.org/wiki/Writing_and_Difference"